Textual Politics

Textual Politics:
Discourse and Social Dynamics

Jay L. Lemke

Taylor & Francis
Publishers since 1798

UK Taylor & Francis Ltd, 4 John St., London WC1N 2ET
USA Taylor & Francis Inc., 1900 Frost Road, Suite 101, Bristol, PA 19007

First published 1995

A Catalogue Record for this book is available from the British Library

ISBN 0 7484 0215 2
ISBN 0 7484 0216 0 (pbk)

Library of Congress Cataloging-in-Publication Data are available on request

Typeset in 10/12pt Baskerville
by Graphicraft Typesetters Ltd., Hong Kong

Printed in Great Britain by Burgess Science Press, Basingstoke on paper which has a specified pH value on final paper manufacture of not less than 7.5 and is therefore 'acid free'.

Contents

Series Editor's Introduction

In *System and Structure* (1972), Anthony Wilden developed a model of human communication as symbolic and material exchange in ecosystemic contexts. Drawing from his work with Gregory Bateson and Jacques Lacan, Wilden made the case that the production and exchange of meanings is always socially 'mediated' by contextual 'levels of constraint'. For Wilden, the final, overarching constraint on human communication and social formation was the ecosystem itself. What was on the line, he argued, was nothing short of species survival. The alternatives he described ranged from the closed, homeostatic systems of oppressive societies, to dynamic 'open systems', where political agency was possible, where the limits and values needed for systems survival became the grounds for vigorous debate. In this model, Wilden stressed the need to understand the importance of 'logical types' at different 'levels' of communication in order to engage in political 'strategy and tactics'.

To this day, many of us believe that *System and Structure* is the major book of its generation: a critique of structuralism that actually leads somewhere, a visionary statement of the possibilities of a systems theory based on an ecological rather than technocratic world view. But the dialogue on Bateson, Wilden and colleagues (cf. Sluzki and Ransom, 1976) went strangely quiet in the 1980s. Then, however inadvertently, communications theory became a subset of cultural studies, which in turn shuffled uneasily between Marxist models of political economy and ideology critique, on the one hand, and poststructuralist models of writing and difference, on the other. For many, the emphasis on system, initially based on cybernetic systems theory, became unfashionable in the midst of textual models that stressed play and difference.

This work remains important in light of the persistent task facing educators and public intellectuals: how to sustain an affirmative politics of social justice in the midst of rapid economic change and political realignment. What is focal now is recognition of the new politics of difference, a politics where local, marginal constituencies speak and write for themselves, in their interests, and on their own behalf (Harvey, 1994). Part of the task, then, is to develop a political project that is both material and discursive, local yet generalisable, systemic without making Eurocentric, masculinist claims to essential and universal truths about human subjects.

Taking up this challenge, Jay Lemke's *Textual Politics* is a key step in the development of a political social semiotics. It is a powerful book and it is a political book. It ranges widely from explorations of key words to detailed text analysis, from philosophic essays on justice to debates on pedagogy and social policy. For those working in the fields of linguistics, pedagogy, cultural studies and semiotics, it offers many extraordinary juxtapositions of theories and ideas. For newcomers to these fields, it provides an accessible introduction to discourse analysis and relevant social theory. And for those working within Bateson and Wilden's legacy, it offers a reframing of ecological approaches to communications.

Talking about the political is not always easy, and it is proving increasingly difficult in applied fields like education and social policy. As Lemke's discussion of American educational policy here indicates, the more pressing and urgent issues of power and access for marginal groups become, the stronger the tendency to redefine issues of education and difference in technocratic, managerial terms. Where this occurs, researchers and policy-makers tend to see language and literacy in terms of neutral skills and competences, independent of wholescale questions about the social distribution of resources.

This should not be surprising. For those of us who grew up in the US in the 1950s the term 'ideology' had a strange red hue to it. It was taboo in our schooling and, by my recollection, it arose only in oblique references to the working of shadowy states. In 1960s public rhetoric, it was repatriated to mean, alternately, 'false consciousness' or generic systems of belief.

In such a context, Lemke's attempt to resituate functional linguistics and social semiotics within a political framework seems an act of necessity and bravery. In Chapter 1, Lemke describes his own social position and standpoint. Intellectually, Lemke moved down the path of M.A.K. Halliday's functional linguistics to inevitable encounters with Foucault and Bourdieu. In his view, ideology does not just concern false consciousness, but rather is tied directly to power. Its force is contingent on 'our vulnerability to pain and our need for the support of others'. Hence, any model of textual politics would need to explain how 'discursive ideological modes of power are modern alternatives to the use of material force and physical violence'.

To show the 'ideological functioning of discourses' at work in particular communities, Lemke turns to an array of texts, including fundamentalist commentaries on homosexuality and Reagan-era reports on education. He shows how such texts skilfully blend a range of disciplinary discourses to establish truth claims. At the same time, we begin to catch glimpses of the limitations of available semantic resources for discussing sex and gender, ethnicity and culture.

Each analysis focuses our attention on the politics of representation, on how semiotic codes stand in a necessary relationship with 'the political'. Meaning potential is realised relationally, and the political world consists of a set of contextual constraints on possible actions and possible meanings. Throughout, Lemke sheds new light on the workings of what sociolinguists and literary critics have called 'interpretive communities'. He views communities as 'material ecosystems', with complex social ecologies of cultural and social attitudes, beliefs and values. At the same time, Lemke wants to avoid a Eurocentric notion of community, to sidestep the supposition of homogeneity that has driven sociological theories from Dürkheim onwards. Lemke here is aiming for a model of discourse community as solidarity *in* difference: 'what makes a community is not homogeneity, but organised heterogeneity . . . the systematic articulation of differences'.

Where this is the case, communities are held together not by individuals, but rather by intercultural, heteroglossic repertoires of social practice. The notion of a social practice, Lemke points out, is itself an abstraction. But in a given instance of social practice, relations of meaning are material – that is, they are complex physical, chemical, biological and ecological relations. Lemke is not advocating a reductionist approach to social interaction. Quite the contrary, he is suggesting the relational and hybrid character of all interaction.

Approaches to critical pedagogy and literacy have suffered for want of a theory of meaning beyond naïve phonocentric models of student 'voice' and 'empowerment'. Foreshadowed in his earlier volume *Talking Science* (1990), Lemke's work suggests that classrooms can be reconceptualised as 'dynamic open ecosystems'. Accordingly, classrooms can be redefined as sites where students and teachers undertake matter/energy/symbolic exchanges as part of the work of producing discourse and cultural capital.

Textual Politics is a significant contribution to functional linguistics and semiotics. It is also a powerful text for contemporary education. Both Lemke and Wilden cite Bateson's (1972) definition of information as 'a difference that makes a difference'. Postmodern and postcolonial cultures increasingly have become places where we can see and hear, speak and write difference – differences in language and identity, differences in sexuality and gender, differences in colour and culture – often for the first time. But some differences 'matter' and others matter less. To figure out which count, for whom and in whose interests, requires nothing less than textual politics.

Allan Luke
Townsville, Australia
November 1994

References

Bateson, G. (1972) *Steps Towards an Ecology of Mind*, New York: Ballantine.
Harvey, D. (1993) 'Class relations, social justice and the politics of difference', in Keith M. and Pale, S. (Eds) *Place and the Politics of Identity*, London: Routledge, pp. 41–66.

Sluzki, C.E. and Ransom, D.C. (Eds) (1976) *Double Bind*, New York: Grune & Stratton.
Wilden, A. (1972) *System and Structure: Essays in Communication and Exchange*, London: Tavistock.

Chapter 1

Textual Politics:
An Introduction

This book is about meaning. It is about the meanings we make with words and with the symbolic values of every object and action. It is also about social relationships, from the temporary or enduring relationships among individuals to the more general and pervasive relationships between men and women, old and young, rich and poor, straight and gay, 'our kind' and 'their kind'. I believe that matters of meaning and matters of social relationship are so interdependent that we must understand both to understand either.

Texts record the meanings we make: in words, pictures and deeds. Politics chronicle our uses of power in shaping social relationships large and small.

When we think of power in the social world, we imagine the power to do things: the power to buy and sell, to command obedience, to reward and punish, to give or take, to do good to others or do them harm, physically or emotionally. In all of these, language can and often does play a critical role. We know that we do not need 'sticks and stones' to hurt others; words can cause pain that cuts just as deeply. The language we speak to ourselves decides whom we will help or hurt, and why. The language we speak to others can enlist their aid or provoke their enmity. The language others speak to us, from childhood, shapes the attitudes and beliefs that ground how we use all our powers of action.

The *textual*, in the broad sense of all the meanings we make, whether in words or by deeds, is deeply political. Our meanings shape and are shaped by our social relationships, both as individuals and as members of social groups. These social relationships bind us into communities, cultures and subcultures. The meanings we make define not only our selves, they also define our communities, our age-groups, our genders, and our era in history. Even more, they define the relationships between communities, age-groups, genders, social classes, cultures, and subcultures – all of which are quintessentially *political* relationships.

The *political*, in the broad sense of all the social relationships within and between communities and individuals that are shaped by our powers to help and to hurt, is in turn also profoundly textual. Power itself is both material and symbolic; its force over individuals arises from our vulnerability to pain and our need for the support of others, but its larger social effects are multiplied by our hopes and fears, our beliefs and expectations, our sensitivities and values. The power of actions and events is grounded both in their material effects on us and in their cultural meanings for us.

Most of this chapter is about a single concept which links the textual and the political: the concept of *ideology*. Ideology is a protean notion. It can mean what we wish it to mean; it can be fit into many theories, many texts, many politics. I want to enrich rather than narrow its meanings for us, to show many different ways in which this concept can help us understand the relations of meaning and power.

The central insight which the concept of ideology tries to sum up is simply this: there are some very common meanings we have learned to make, and take for granted as common sense, but which support the power of one social group to dominate another.

If common sense itself can be politically biased, can we still trust it as a guide? Can we continue to rely on it when we analyze social relationships and how they are shaped by power and meaning? And if we need to be cautious or skeptical even about what we take for granted as common sense, then how can we proceed and where can we safely begin?

Ideology and Us

From roughly the time of Descartes' *Meditations*, European intellectual traditions have sought to escape from the radical skepticism that ended the earlier age of religious faith. The principal strategy for this escape has been to find some basis of certainty other than faith in religious revelation: some common or uncommon sense way of proceeding toward understanding, some safe place from which to begin. This strategy produced a new faith in logic and logical inquiry, first in philosophy, then in mathematics, and finally in science. Each claimed to have discovered a trustworthy *method* of proceeding, a safe initial set of assumptions. These methods claimed to be universal: valid by logical necessity, in all times and all places, for all people and all purposes. They became our modern common sense.

Our modern common sense. But who is this *we*? Does it include people whose cultural background is non-European? people who have not been fundamentally influenced by the educational system and philosophical perspectives of the upper-middle class? people who are not male, masculine and heterosexual? people who are younger than the age at which this common sense starts to make sense? or older than the age at which it ceases to?

Whose strategy for life produced this common sense? Whose needs did the strategy address? Whose problems did it aim to solve? What did it replace? How did it displace the common sense that came before it? Did it become common sense for all of us, or only for some communities and categories of persons?

The modern European quest for a universally valid method of inquiry was a particular historical response to a particular historical need by a very small fraction of the population. One of the circumstances that shaped this enterprise was the need to best a specific political opponent: the theological worldview of a universalizing religion. It would not have made sense to the people of seventeenth and eighteenth-century Europe to construct purely local principles of truth, nor would the intellectual ideas that supported the rise of the new middle class have made much headway against those of the secular and clerical aristocracy if they had not also claimed universal validity.

The makers of our modern intellectual common sense were Europeans. They were mainly upper-middle class. They were mostly middle-aged (for their times). They were nearly all males. They shared common intellectual problems, they belonged to social groups and communities that shared common political problems, and they would hardly have seen the one as being very much separate from the other. They transformed the distinction between body and soul into one between body and mind. They transformed the universal truth of revelation into the universal truth of science. They transformed the superiority of the Christian religion over all others into the superiority of European culture over all others. They created and rationalized the radically unequal relations of labor and capital, the working class and the owning class. They preserved and found new rationalizations for the unequal relations between men and women, and between adults and children.

Their common sense, *our* common sense, was in large measure the product of their needs, their times, their point of view. This common sense has evolved from their day to ours, it has been elaborated into many more sophisticated and scientific forms, and all along the way it has been produced from the point of view of one particular segment of humanity. It is the product of a particular subgroup, a particular subculture. It is their product because they alone had, until very recently, the power to produce philosophy, science, logic, government, industry, education. Their common sense, our common sense, is part of *their* subculture. Their claim for its universal validity is also part of their subculture.

What about *our* cultures and subcultures? Will not whatever *I* write also be a product of *my* position in the system of social relationships that have shaped *my* attitudes and values, *my* beliefs and interests? Will not *your* responses to what I write also depend in part on *your* position in the social system? Yes, indeed they will – or so it seems to me from where I stand.

It also seems to me however, and, as we will see, to many other more or less *postmodern* writers on the subject, that this interdependence of the meanings we make and the social and political positions we occupy is a useful thing for humanity (and perhaps even for interests that transcend the merely human). We have become aware of this interdependence mainly because the relative power of non-European cultural traditions, of women, the elderly and the very young, gays and lesbians, subordinated social classes, and all the *Other* cultures, subcultures and communities in our world has increased significantly in the last few decades. Their growing power enables them to challenge more effectively the universal pretensions of modern European assumptions about logic, truth, science, mind, individuality, culture, gender, age, education, politics, literacy etc. Their challenges open up the intellectual space in which all of us can entertain a greater diversity of possible ways of making sense of life.

Perhaps this postmodern critique of the fundamental assumptions of a dominant subculture, our ruling ideology, will help us to redress further the imbalance of power between different cultures and different social groups in our world: between West and East, North and South, between men and women, younger and older, straighter and gayer, richer and poorer etc. Some even hope it can help us re-envision the relations between human interests and the larger interests of the ecosystems of which we are integral parts.

Ideology and Me

I am writing from a particular social position, making meanings that are shaped by the kinds of life experiences people in my position tend to have. Whatever I write is written from a viewpoint within the culture and subcultures to which I belong. I do not, no one can, write from an objective God's-eye view. No one sees *the* world as *it is*. We see the worlds our communities teach us how to see, and the worlds we make, always a bit uniquely, within and sometimes just a bit beyond what we've been taught.

It is not customary for authors to present themselves candidly as writing from a limited viewpoint, or to say in very specific terms where they are socially and culturally positioned. The *authority* of an author is reduced in the eyes of many readers if he or she 'intrudes' personally into what our modern common sense says should strive to be an impersonal, objective account of the ways things are, the way they would be seen by anybody. I do not believe, however, that the matters I am writing about *could* be seen the same way by everybody.

The traditional assumption is that only one view can be *the* right view, and so I should argue vehemently against all the others, to show that I must be right and they must be wrong, but I only believe that some views are more useful to some people for some purposes. I will try to show what I think my views are useful for, to whom, and why. I will also occasionally try to show what others' views are useful for, and sometimes I will conclude that these uses are not good for many of us, some of them perhaps not good for any of us.

For example, I do not believe that intellectual dialogue should be conducted as an adversarial process. I believe that the adversarial approach reinforces the notion that only one view can be the right one. Such a notion is most useful to those who wish to impose their views on others. I do not believe that imposing your views on others is a good thing to do in the interests of the community as a whole. I also believe that the adversarial approach reinforces a traditional view of the masculinity of the writer as a fighter who can best his opponent. This in turn serves to exclude many women, and men who find this view of masculinity distasteful, from influence in academic and intellectual communities. It reserves the power positions in these communities for aggressive males. This view of masculinity was perhaps once useful for the survival of earlier communities, but such atavistic views are now long overdue for critique and transformation (see Chapter 5).

Perhaps if I were more centrally a member of the power-wielding groups in our society, I would not be as critical of the common sense of their traditions. I would not resent the symbolic and material pressures to accept their point of view about gender, logic, science, truth and social relationships as natural, correct and inevitable.

So, where do I stand? From what standpoint do I observe, analyze and desire? I am in early middle-age, but my sympathies are mainly with those either younger or much older. I have always thought that most of the serious harm done in the world is done by those in later middle-age. My immediate family was of the American middle-middle class, which to the rest of the world is really the topmost fraction of the working class, white-collar office workers. Both my parents worked. My extended family included a fair number of genuinely upper-middle class small-business proprietors and one millionaire entrepreneur. Two of my grandparents were Central European immigrants, two were American-born of first-generation European immigrant parents. Their cultures were German, Danish, and East European Jewish. My family was an uncommon mix of Jews and Christians, none particularly religious. My personal religious beliefs are abstract and idiosyncratic, partly the product of what some might call firsthand spiritual experiences.

I was raised to be male and heterosexual and only became conscious of gender as an issue when I began a long relationship with a newly liberated woman in the 1970s. Feminist claims of oppression and arguments for equality seemed to me entirely justifiable, and I never felt threatened by them, but then I had never strongly identified with traditional masculinity. My viewpoint on gender issues has also been shaped by relationships with men. My personal experience of sexual orientation has never been as simple as being attracted only to men or only to women. I have never looked at the world solely from a straight or solely from a gay point of view. The identity I construct for myself remains that of a mostly masculinized male with a strong dislike for the excesses of traditional masculinity and for the limitations of exclusive categories of gender and sexuality.

These are the dimensions of social difference that matter to most of the people I know or read: age, social class, ethnic and religious background, national culture, gender and sexual orientation. In most of these respects, I fit the profile of our society's dominant caste closely enough to have been able to gain a fair understanding of how it sees itself. I was a scholarship student at a prestigious private university and acquired a good, Eurocentric liberal education and a doctorate in theoretical physics. I am a tenured full professor in a large urban university, and marginally upper-middle class. I have some small measure of power and respect in a few specialist academic communities.

I do not read the social world from dead center, however; my viewpoint is displaced from that of the sorts of people I would consider the true power-brokers. They would probably consider me somewhat alienated or just slightly perverse in my views. On the other hand, I cannot see the world at all from the viewpoint of women, of truly working-class people, of today's youngest or oldest Americans, or of any other culture, particularly a non-European one. I can only interpret what people who do see the world from these viewpoints tell me about how it looks to them, and try to find my own relationship to their realities.

Language, Discourse and Meaning

When we talk to one another, face-to-face or through various technological media from print to teleconferencing, we are engaged in *discourse*. Discourse is another protean concept. It can be used to mean something as specific as spoken language, or something as general as the social process of communication. It can refer to a general phenomenon, the fact that we communicate with language and other symbolic systems, or to particular kinds of things we say (e.g. the discourse of love, or the discourse of political science).

When I speak about *discourse* in general, I will usually mean the social activity of making meanings with language and other symbolic systems in some particular kind of situation or setting. I will also have in mind the participants in the discourse, whether they speak and write or only listen and read, and whether they are considered actually present in or only potentially relevant to the situation. As a writer, I address many sorts of potential readers, including other writers I have read. As a 'thinker', various viewpoints within me address other viewpoints that I may or may not identify with or even agree with, but that are also in a way parts of 'me'. In this sense all discourse, indeed all meaning-making, can be seen as social and communicative, whether or not it is addressed to a specific audience, and whether or not whomever it is addressed to is physically present, or even exists.

I will also speak about particular kinds of *discourses*, however, which are produced as the result of certain social habits that we have as a community. There are particular subjects some of us are in the habit of talking about in particular ways, often as part of particular sorts of social activity. Think of all the discourses we have as a community about, say, sexuality. There are biological, medical and psychoanalytic ways of talking about sexuality; there are religious, literary and pornographic discourses of sexuality; and there are the many discourses of sexuality between sexual partners as they engage in all the various kinds of sexual activity human ingenuity can construct, with all the diverse viewpoints about preferences and attitudes that exist in our community.

On each occasion when the particular meanings characteristic of these discourses are being made, a specific *text* is produced. Discourses, as social actions more or less governed by social habits, produce texts that will in some ways be alike in their meanings. They may be alike in the content of what they say about topics and subjects. They may be alike in their values, attitudes and stances toward their subjects and audiences. They may be alike in the sequence, structure and form of organization of what they say. These texts will always also be different as well, each will be in some ways unique. The notions of text and discourse are complementary. When we want to focus on the specifics of an event or occasion, we speak of the text; when we want to look at patterns, commonality, relationships that embrace different texts and occasions, we can speak of discourses.

Since discourse in general is an aspect of social action, of human activity, it never makes meaning just with language alone. We cannot speak pure linguistic words or sentences without also speaking with a recognizable personal voice-quality that does not affect the sense of which words we are saying, but which adds other, non-linguistic dimensions of potential meaning to the act of speaking. We do not, in fact, usually speak face-to-face without also making meanings with our movements, gestures, facial expressions and in a host of other symbolic ways that are fully integrated with language in our habits of communication.

Even more obviously, we cannot write without using a visual system of communication whose signs and symbols always allow us to make more than merely linguistic meaning. Our printed words must be printed in some typeface, with or without italics and bolding, underline or capitals, in large-point or small-point type, with or *sans serif.* They must be laid out on the page or the screen, creating new possibilities for displaying organization and highlighting particular verbal meanings. We can go far beyond the minimal integration of verbal and visual codes in writing; we can use colored and animated text, we can integrate writing with pictorial and graphic elements of many kinds. These conventions are quite normal in many sorts of communication.

Because we necessarily combine linguistic with other, especially visual and actional, resources when we speak and write, it is generally insufficient to analyze the total social meaning made, or read, merely in terms of the

7

semantics of language alone. Just as the meanings of words change in their verbal contexts, in the phrases and sentences that contain them, and the meanings of sentences change in the contexts of paragraphs and larger units of textual organization, so do all of these also change their meanings when they are juxtaposed with a picture or a graph, or when they are said by (or to) one person rather than another, or when they are said in one social situation rather than another.

Language does not operate in isolation. Meanings always get made in contexts where social expectations and non-linguistic symbols play a role. When I speak of the discourse that is being produced on a particular occasion, I am talking about a social process that always involves more than language. It is even useful, when speaking of the *text* produced on that occasion, to add to the verbal record of the discourse as much as we can of the visual and actional signs and symbols that contribute to its potential social meanings.

Speech is a material phenomenon as well as a social and cultural one. It does not just make meanings for us, it is part of the physical interaction of organisms in our community. It has physical effects, it has physical origins. As a process of the organism, it is not isolated from our gestures, our facial expressions, the rhythm of our movements, the darting of our glances, the whole 'dance' of material meaning-making (a dance that always assumes a partner, that always helps to create one).

One of the most important things we can say about language is that it has evolved, biologically and culturally, as part of patterns of motor activity that integrate the organism into its social and material environment. Language and speech are specialized components of this activity. They have evolved as part of a larger and older complex of (external and internal) communicative behavior which reaches back in evolution before humans. In human development this larger communicative complex is already functioning long before we can recognize language as such, and language always operates as an integral part of it.

Neither physically nor culturally is language an autonomous system of social practices. Neither in its material origins in the processes of brain, body and community, nor in its uses for the making of meanings does language stand on its own. This view of language is useful for reminding us that, fascinating as the work of pure, formal linguistics may be, we are not likely to understand the role of language in our culture or in our society if we divorce it from its material origins or from its integration into larger systems of resources for making meaning.

Gesture, drawing and writing are not so different from one another as we might think – not in their historical origins, in their relations during human development, or in the neurological and bodily processes that underlie them. Movement, gesture and speech likewise share important underlying unities. A theory of meaning cannot limit itself to the semantics of language viewed in isolation from more general forms of human activity. It must consider how and why every meaningful human action is meaningful to members of a community. A theory of meaning must be essentially social, historical, cultural and political, because the unit of meaning is a human action 'addressed' to real and potential others. It is an act-in-community, a material and social process that helps to constitute the community as a community.

Social Semiotics

The term *semiotics* is often used to refer to the general study of meaning-making (*semiosis*), including not just meanings we make with language, but meanings we make with every sort of object, event or action in so far as it is endowed with a significance, a symbolic value, in our community. How do meanings depend on contexts? On what sorts of context do they depend? How do new meanings get made? How is one meaning related to another? How do systems of meanings change? Semiotics is a discourse about meaning that is useful in considering such questions.

I use the term *social semiotics* as a reminder that all meanings are made within communities and that the analysis of meaning should not be separated from the social, historical, cultural and political dimensions of these communities. This approach is useful for studying meaning in a way that then enables us to see how the meanings we make function to sustain or challenge the relationships of power in our communities.

It may be helpful here to head off a possible confusion. Many people have been taught a social habit, a discourse, for speaking about meaning, which considers only the role of the individual organism, or the individual mind, in the process of making meanings. Later in this book, I will argue that mentalist discourses, by creating a separate mental realm and locating meanings there, are not useful for understanding the material and social aspects of meaning-making. Mentalist discourses depend on a common sense view of the separation of mind from body, and individual from society, which has ideological functions in our society. Particular aspects of these discourses deflect attention away from the social, cultural, historical and political dimensions of the meanings we make. They make it harder to critique the uses of language that support unjust power and privilege.

Instead of talking about meaning-making as something that is done by minds, I prefer to talk about it as a *social practice* in a community. It is a kind of *doing* that is done in ways that are characteristic of a community, and its occurrence is part of what binds the community together and helps to constitute it as a community. In this sense we can speak of a community, not as a collection of interacting individuals, but as a system of interdependent social practices: a system of doings, rather than a system of doers. These social meaning-making practices are *also* material processes that bind the community together as a physical ecosystem. In this kind of discourse about meaning we are led to examine the social functions and effects of the meanings we make: the politics of our texts.

Language, Ideology and Power

So accustomed are we to attaching meanings to individual minds, rather than seeing them as the product of social habits, that some of you are probably surprised (maybe disappointed, or even distressed) that, except for a lone mention of Descartes, I have been sketching a view of textual politics without explicitly connecting what I say to what has been said by others. This strategy has been deliberate, but temporary.

From here on, I will be making frequent citations to the writing of others. One of the most useful principles of social semiotics, and so of textual politics, is the principle of *intertextuality*. We are all constantly reading and listening to, writing and speaking, *this text* in the context of and against the background of *other* texts and other discourses. Discourses (i.e. *types* of discourse), particularly, are more characteristic of communities and subcommunities than of individuals. They provide us with a resource for making meaning that is equally as important as the grammar and lexicon of our language, though we use it in a rather different way. Each community and every subcommunity within it has its own *system of intertextuality*: its own set of important or valued texts, its own preferred discourses, and particularly its own habits of deciding which texts should be read in the context of which others, and why, and how.

When I cite others' texts, either for their specific statements, or as examples of a general discourse pattern on a subject, I am contributing to the system of intertextuality that binds *us* together into a subcommunity. These citations are social and political acts in this subcommunity. They may serve to refer you to helpful information, or to help clarify a point by placing it in the context of what you already know, but they also communicate value judgments about the usefulness of what these texts say, and they serve to multiply their influence in the community.

Not only do these social and political meanings attach to what I cite, but they attach as well to what I do *not* cite, especially for readers who might expect such a citation and wonder what I think about a particular text or discourse. *You* may be making these intertextual connections already, and if I do not acknowledge their plausibility, you may wonder if I disagree with them, or if I share the perspective that led to the connection in the first place.

According to the social conventions of the academic community in which I write, my own power and authority, my credibility, depends in part on my demonstrating that I can navigate the network of intertextual connections which are habitual in this community. When I introduce semiotics, I am expected to cite Saussure (1959) and/or Peirce (1955), and the specialist reader will take a cue from whether I cite only one or both. When I mention social semiotics for the first time, some readers will wonder if this is my own peculiar invention, or if there are others who write a similar discourse and use similar terms, and where they can read other texts of this discourse (e.g. Halliday 1978; Hodge and Kress 1988; Threadgold 1989; Threadgold and Kress 1988; Thibault 1991).

If I were a historian, or a philosopher, I would be expected to cite various studies of the history of ideas in talking about the origins of modern common sense, and when I speak the discourse of postmodernism and express skepticism towards claims of universal methods of valid inquiry, I am expected to acknowledge well-known texts that also put forward these arguments (e.g. Lyotard 1984; Jameson 1991).

In the course of this book I will be citing a very large number of texts, from a wide range of discourses about meaning and power. The citations and the list of references they refer to are an intertextual resource, but they are also visible traces of many political acts of meaning-making in a community.

There are, in fact, a few specific texts on the subject of language, ideology and power that I want to engage with as I close this introductory chapter. They are recent works, and they address many of the issues I am interested in in this book. They draw on many of the same discourses I will use, and in most cases I know their authors and we participate in some of the same subcommunities. It seems very likely that some of you will also have read one or more of these texts (Fairclough 1989; Gee 1990; Hodge and Kress 1988; Wertsch 1991) and that they may partly inform your reading of this book.

The discourses of these texts have much in common with one another and with my own ways of talking about meaning, power and ideology. We all read and use some of the same earlier texts on these subjects: Marx and Engels (1970) on ideology and politics, Bakhtin (1935, and Voloshinov 1929) on language and social relations, Foucault (especially 1966, 1969) on discourses in history. We all look at language as having social functions, and being shaped as a resource for meaning-making by these social functions. I will discuss the uses I make of the discourses of Bakhtin and Foucault (along with those of Halliday, Bernstein and Bourdieu) in the next chapter.

A principal issue in our ways of talking about meaning and power is the scope we give to the notion of ideology. James Gee (1990) and Bob Hodge and Gunther Kress (1988) take the broad view that *all* discourses are ideological. Norman Fairclough's (1989) view is narrower; his notion of ideology is that it is common sense assumptions which assist privileged interests to establish and maintain unequal power relations.

The broad view is useful when we want to examine the political dimensions of any utterance, any meaning we make. All meaning-making can be seen as having what I will call an *orientational* dimension (see Chapter 3). We orient our meanings toward prospective audiences and we orient them within a system of different viewpoints available in the community toward our topic. These orientations involve value preferences; they commit us to a political stance and a social point of view on our subject and toward our audiences. They are inescapable, and to the extent that our viewpoint is determined by our social position, and by our social and political interests in any conflict between social positions, orientational meaning situates us in the realm of textual politics.

Not all acts of meaning-making contribute equally to the maintenance of power relations or to social privilege for one group and social exploitation for another, however. Some acts of meaning-making, and some discourses, directly *contest* existing or dominant social relations, challenging their legitimacy and the discourses that rationalize them, or directly opposing them materially as well as symbolically. So it is also useful to have a narrower view of ideology, or more precisely of the *ideological functioning* of discourses. Some discourses contribute directly to the maintenance of social relations of power and privilege (e.g. overtly sexist, racist or homophobic discourses). Other discourses may do so sometimes, but usually just index the existing relations, weakly reinforcing them merely by remaining in general circulation and so readily available for their more directly ideological uses (e.g. discourses about cognitive abilities that can be used to rationalize ideological views about racial inferiority; or discourses about human development that can function in the same way for views about children or the elderly).

Some discourses may be the products of social institutions which embody inequitable social relations (e.g. scientific research laboratories), but the discourses themselves may be about matters so alien to human social relations (e.g. the interactions of electrons) that they do not function ideologically in themselves. They may of course be used as tools of power to further projects and agendas of some already dominant group, and they may have been created in part for this reason, but what they say about their subjects may not be specifically shaped by these wider social functions.

If we want to ask how a particular discourse functions ideologically, we need to look with both the broader and the narrower view of ideology. We need to see how the discourse is situated in the social and political relations of various communities and their interests *vis-à-vis* one another, and we need to ask specifically what it says about its subject that somehow works to the profit of a dominant social group. I will generally use the term ideological for the narrower sense, and terms like social, political or orientational for the more universal sense in which discourses participate in social relations of power and privilege.

Gee's (1990) specific view of ideological functioning is that discourses operate in communities to get some people more of the 'goods' they value than other people get. This interesting view sees discourses as 'identity kits' that people adopt, behaving according to the social habits of a discourse pattern (in action, not just in speech). Members of more powerful groups get equipped with kits that, for many reasons, bring them more of the 'goods'. This view generalizes a common observation about spoken and written *genres* (e.g. Kress 1982; Martin 1989), that power is often exercised by being able to use the right discourse 'form' (e.g. knowing how to write academic essays, draw up legal contracts, etc.).

Gee observes that people from some social groups more readily master these forms, and are prepared by their whole lives to feel comfortable with them, to operate with them more intuitively than others do. We will see that Bourdieu (1990b; see Chapter 2) offers a very sophisticated discourse about exactly how and why this happens.

Discourses do not just function ideologically as identity kits or to obtain 'goods'. They also function to legitimate, naturalize or disguise the inequities they sustain. They function to get us thinking along particular lines, the lines of a common sense, which are not as likely to lead to subversive conclusions as using some other discourses might.

Gee also provides a very insightful discussion of what he regards as some of the 'master myths' of our current ruling ideology, that is of our contemporary common sense, including discourses that transform much of human activity into just another commodity ('labor'), thus naturalizing its assimilation into an economics dominated by those in a position to buy *us*. The harm done through such discourses, however, is not simply that people can now be underpaid for their labor, ending up with less of the 'goods' of life (the rest of their share going to those whose 'capital' is correspondingly overvalued in this scheme of things). There is the broader harm that in order not to feel ourselves bought and degraded as human beings, we are encouraged to alienate ourselves from our own activities (in doing labor for others), from the very grounds of our being. These discourses encourage us to feel that it is not *us* that is being bought, and controlled by others, but something else, just our 'labor', when otherwise we might well imagine that what we do and how we live is the very essence of who and what we are. Finally there is the root harm, the physical violence done to those who too actively rebel against this order of things (strikers, whistleblowers, labor organizers), a violence which is justified and legitimated in law and 'common sense' by means of these same discourses (of ownership, property rights, contractual obligations).

Power, and so the ideological use of discourses which support power, is partly about the distribution of 'goods', but it is always also about positive harm, about physical pain and social dehumanization. Viewing harm only as the absence of a 'good', even of a 'necessity', would fail to direct our attention to the most painful realities of power, the most shameful aspects of human relationships (see discussion in Chapter 7).

Norman Fairclough's (1989) view of ideology is in many ways closer to my more restrictive sense of the ideological functioning of a discourse, but he adopts the viewpoint, often associated with the writing of Althusser (e.g. 1971), that discursive, ideological modes of power are modern alternatives to the use of material force and physical violence. The implied separation of words from deeds, of discourse from material action, of deceit from cruelty, fits too closely with the Cartesian separation of mind from body to escape my deep suspicion. Certainly it is true that people often regulate their own actions, using commonsensical and ideologically functional discourses, so as not to provoke the need for force to be used against them in the defense of unjust social relations. And it is very useful to see the institutions of education, mass communications and even academic scholarship as 'ideological apparatus': institutional machinery for promulgating such discourses. But, ideology alone could not sustain inequitable social relations for even one generation in the face of inevitable conflicts of interest in countless daily encounters, without the widespread application of force.

We underestimate, because it is unpleasant to do otherwise, the extent to which police brutality, child and elder abuse, marital violence, racial attacks, gay-bashing, and subtler but no less real ways of inflicting pain on people (humiliations, firings) actually function to maintain the dominance of rich over poor, middle-aged adults over children and the elderly, men over women, one race over others, straights over gays, bosses over workers, teachers over students. Ideology *supports* violence and is critically shaped by and in a context of violence in social relationships. Inflicting pain on others is the pervasive and fundamental mode of social control. Its primary victims are well aware of this; only those relatively insulated from violence by their privileged social positions have the luxury of underestimating its importance.

Bob Hodge and Gunther Kress, who explicitly share with me the perspective of social semiotics (1988), grounded in the pioneering work on linguistic meaning done by Michael Halliday (1976, 1978, 1985a), are also drawn to the Althusserian view of ideology. There is one aspect of this view which they particularly emphasize and with which I am very much in agreement, however. Human beings as social persons, as 'subjects' (i.e. as opposed to the *objects* they often seem to become in social science accounts of human behavior), are shaped by the way in which we are 'interpellated' (hailed, or interrogated) by the discourse habits of others, that is by the assumptions about what it is to be a person (and specifically a person of a certain gender, age, class, culture and subculture) that are projected onto us as we participate in social interaction with others in our community. This view makes it possible to analyze the social construction of personhood and subjectivity itself (cf. Chapter 5).

While Fairclough, Hodge and Kress all draw on Althusser in these ways, Fairclough and Jim Wertsch (1991) also rely on views developed by Jurgen Habermas (e.g. 1983) which seem to me again somewhat overly optimistic. Habermas, with a keen insight into the role of power in dialogue, has tried to formulate criteria for truly democratic or egalitarian discourse, and many people interpret this project as if changing the ways in which we talk to one another could move society toward more just social relations. This view also tends to segregate the discursive from the material implementations of power. It is not our modes of discourse *per se* that we need to change; it is the power to inflict pain with impunity. Discourse contributes to that power, supports and sustains it. Its forms reflect it, and alternative discourses can in turn be used as tools against that power, principally by competing with the ideological discourses that help legitimate its exercise.

Robbing the wolf of its sheep's clothing does not make its teeth less dangerous, however. While they still have their teeth, wolves will not likely parley on equal terms with sheep.

The sociologist whose work I find most useful today, Pierre Bourdieu (discussed more fully in the next chapter, and see also Lemke 1993c), is also critical of Habermas' views (e.g. Bourdieu and Waquant 1992) on similar grounds. At stake here is our basic view of the relation between what happens in particular everyday events and the larger social-structural relations between genders, classes, age groups, cultures and subcultures. We need a theory of politics in the large to talk about the role of discourse, and of the symbolic values of actions generally, in society. I believe that to combine social theory and social semiotics effectively we need a social theory that recognizes its own status as just another discourse from some particular social viewpoint. We need a social theory that sees all social phenomena, including itself, as being partly the product of how people in a community deploy semiotic resources: how we mean, and what we mean, by every meaningful act.

Fairclough, Hodge and Kress all recognize the need for such a larger social theory, and basically they adopt neo-Marxist positions, views that would fall under the general heading of critical structuration theories (Gramsci 1935; Althusser 1971; Bernstein 1981; Habermas 1983; Giddens 1984). All these theories take social injustice as a central phenomenon to be accounted for, and all attempt to fashion some sort of two-way relation between social events and social structure. All assign discourse or ideology an important role, and all belong to a historical period in which it had long been possible to see social class inequities as unjust and unnecessary, but in which other structural inequities (based on gender and sexual orientation, on age, on cultural and subcultural differences) were only beginning to be theorized. In many ways Bourdieu's sociology is similar, but it provides more fully realized means of making contact with both the bodily or material aspects of social life and with the specifics of our socially positioned habits of meaning-making.

I will return in the next chapter to a fuller discussion of the sort of social theory that a textual politics needs, but here I want to point out that neither Gee nor Wertsch, in their discussion of how discourse shapes our views of the world and is shaped by our position in it, emphasizes the need for a theory of social structure. Wertsch (1991) is writing primarily to an audience of psychologists, especially those who have already begun to back away from universalizing theories of mind and to accept the arguments of cultural and historical psychologists like Vygotsky (1963), Leontiev (1978), and Michael Cole *et al.* (1971) that minds are formed by our social interactions in a community and a culture. He wants them to consider the usefulness of Mikhail Bakhtin's social theory of discourse (which I discuss in the next chapter) as a tool for understanding more precisely how this process occurs.

Where Fairclough, Hodge and Kress rely on sociological theory, Wertsch (and Gee 1990) draw more on cultural anthropology to connect discourse to social life. But both Wertsch and Gee do so by invoking the psychological notion of mental cognition as a sort of bridge between the two. Cognitive psychology sees discourse as a product of the speaking subject, an expression of more fundamental mental states (beliefs, attitudes, feelings) and processes. Cultural anthropology sees discourses as characteristic of cultures and subcultures, of communities rather than individuals. This double view leads Gee to distinguish, as I have above, two senses of the word discourse: discourse as what we are actually saying (and doing), and Discourses (capitalized) as our social habits of different people saying (and doing) the same sorts of things in the same ways time and again. Gee uses a notion of the 'socio-mental' to let the social into the mental world (a theme developed in much more detail in Wertsch's account), so that Discourses (which are social and cultural) can shape discourse (whose production is still taken to be mental).

Gee's social model of Discourses as 'identity kits' owes much to social role theory in traditional American functionalist sociology, and in fact carries it a step in the direction of Bourdieu's notion of *habitus* (see Chapter 2). It ties Discourses to the roles played by individuals, however, rather than to activities and systems of social practices involving many participants, just as it ties discourse to the speaking individual. This perspective arises partly from the American cultural emphasis on individualism, but also more specifically from cognitivist discourse in a mentalist framework. We will see in Chapter 5 that the notion of the human individual becomes highly problematic in social semiotics, and that we cannot assume the existence of a human 'mind' until we can say how it too is brought into being through the discourses and social practices of a community.

Wertsch struggles with this same key problem. His view of mind is radically transformed from the traditional concept. Following Bateson, he sees mind as inherent in human interaction with the social and material environment, as shaped by social processes (cf. Vygotsky 1963), and as embedded in the systems of meaning which Geertz (1973, 1983) and many others see as defining *cultures*. He usefully appropriates the insights of Bakhtin to fill out this picture, but leaves out one important element in the Bakhtinian model: the social habits that shape the discourses of different social 'voices' are themselves the product of larger sociological relationships (Bakhtin's principle of *heteroglossia*, to be discussed in Chapter 2). In this view the *voices* or *Discourses* that give shape to minds and discourse are not independent of one another; they always already have relationships which are fundamentally sociological ones, and which we need a sociological theory to understand. This is especially true of the value orientations of our discourses: what they construe as being good or bad, desirable or undesirable (see Chapters 3 and 4).

Although I have suggested some points where my views may differ from those of Wertsch, Gee, Fairclough, Hodge and Kress, anyone who reads both their work and my own will see how deeply in agreement most of our fundamental perspectives are. We draw on many of the same sources, we frame many of the same questions, we come to many of the same conclusions. I have not written this book to argue with them, but to support them and the many others whose work and views I will make use of. I want to show what more needs to be done, what else needs to be taken into account, what other directions we need to explore.

In Chapter 2, I will take up the basic problem of how to integrate discourse into fundamental social theory by identifying a common strategy in the work of many key theorists (principally Bakhtin, Foucault, Halliday, Bernstein and Bourdieu) which suggests a conceptual bridge between the social event and the social system. I believe this strategy points towards a solution to the classic 'micro–macro' problem of modern social science.

Chapters 3 and 4 illustrate textual politics at work. They analyze how discourses are used for political ends, from socially and politically situated positions, and further develop such key notions as heteroglossia and value-orientation. Chapter 3 deals with the language of social controversy: how what appears to be the same argument comes to radically opposed conclusions in the discourses of a fundamentalist demagogue and an advocate for the civil rights of gays. Chapter 4 traces the successive transformations of a somewhat dubious piece of statistical research in education into a strongly political policy statement, illustrating and analyzing the ideology of technocratic discourse.

In Chapter 5 we return to the fundamental problem of the semiotic construction of persons and subjectivity, and the potential ideological functions of our own academic and folk discourses about the nature of the human mind. Here we will also consider issues of the social construction of gender and personal identity, and the relations of the discourses of the bodily and material to those of the cultural and semiotic.

Chapter 6 will argue that we cannot understand human social and cultural systems of action and meaning apart from the material ecosystems in which we are participants, nor the dynamics of ecosocial systems without taking into account the beliefs and values of human communities. Modeling human social systems on many scales, from individual development to long term social and cultural change, requires understanding the nature of complexity in self-organizing systems, both material and semiotic.

Chapter 7 will look to the future: to the possibilities for a postmodern textual politics, not simply as an analytical framework, but as a political agenda. It will offer some disturbing theses on the role of violence in social systems, adult oppression of the young, post-democratic and post-humanist values, and what ought to replace print literacy and school curricula in the postmodern world.

As if that were not more than enough, *Textual Politics* ends with a 'retrospective postscript' called 'Making Meaning, Making Trouble'. It presents an edited and updated version of a 10-year-old essay (Lemke 1984) which frames many of the issues discussed in this book and rounds out the discussion of such topics as the contextual theory of meaning, communities as dynamic open systems, and the ways in which ideologically functioning discourses inhibit social change while social change happens anyway. Long out of print, many people have asked me to include it in this volume. It shows the development of my views on these subjects, and it will provide readers new to them with some helpful background.

Chapter 2

Discourse and Social Theory

Requirements for a Social Theory

What we say, what we do, and the sense we and others make of our words and deeds mark us as members of a community. Our viewpoints and our habits of action define the historical period in which we live, the cultural traditions that have shaped us, and the typical life experiences within the community of people of our age, gender and social position. Our *discourse*, what we mean by saying and doing, deploys the meaning-making resources of our communities: the grammar and lexicon of a language, the conventions of gesture and depiction, the symbolic and functional values of actions, the typical patterns of action that other members of our community will recognize and respond to. In different historical periods, in different cultural traditions, for people of different ages, genders and social positions, both these resources and the typical, recognizable patterns in which people use them are different.

In order to understand how the discourse of every moment shapes the changing resources and patterns characteristic of a community, we need a general social theory. We need it to help us identify the kinds of differences in how people talk and act, and to relate these different patterns of behavior to one another. We need to understand what the different possible positions in our society are, how they differ in terms of people's actions and their meanings, and how they imperfectly fit together to make the whole of a diverse community.

Equally, we need a general social theory to help us understand how the discourse habits of the community around us both shape our own discourses and viewpoints and provide us with resources for saying and doing things that are new but still make sense to others.

A social theory is of no use to us for these purposes if it is only a static picture of how some one community seems to some one observer at a particular moment of its history. The role of discourse in society is active; it not only reconfirms and re-enacts existing social relationships and patterns of behavior, it also renegotiates social relationships and introduces new meanings and new behaviors. Social systems change. The social theory we need must show us a *dynamic* community; it must show us how and why social relations are always changing, and also how they can seem, for certain periods, to remain relatively fixed.

The social theory we need must also be a *critical* theory; it must describe social processes in ways that show how power is exercised in the interests of the powerful, and how unjust social relations disguise their injustice. Discourse functions ideologically in society to support and legitimate the exercise of power, and to naturalize unjust social relations, making them seem the inevitable consequence of common sense necessity.

Finally, and most fundamentally for our purposes, a social theory must show us how to connect each individual social event with the larger patterns of social relationships that persist from one event to the next. We need to be able to relate the *discourse*, the words and deeds of the here-and-now, to the *Discourses*, the social habits of speech and action in the community as a whole. We need a *unitary* theory which integrates and connects microsocial events with macrosocial structures and processes.

In short, we need a social theory which is dynamic, critical and unitary. These three requirements are actually closely interdependent on one another. It is the relation between events and social systems that makes communities dynamic; when we connect the discourse of each event with the Discourses of the community, we see the motor of social and cultural change. When we focus on how change occurs, we find we need to connect individual events with larger patterns in social systems. But we cannot do either of these things if we do not look critically at our own common sense assumptions to see how they are themselves part of the culture around us, how they function ideologically to lead us away from conclusions that might be dangerous to the status quo.

However much we pride ourselves on being objective social scientists, or pretend to be merely observers, we are all *inside* our social system. We are all *positioned* within that system so as to have only one point of view on it, or only a limited range of viewpoints during our lives. None of us are simultaneously both male and female, old and young, rich and poor, powerful and powerless, literate and illiterate, straight and gay, European, Asian and African. Our traditions, our theories, our assumptions, our interests, our values, our logic, our language, our experiences, our discourses are all characteristic of where we fit inside this larger system. We cannot get outside of it (except perhaps to move inside some other system), so we must be able to account for why we see the system as we do. Pierre Bourdieu, for all that he holds back from some of the more radical implications of this basically postmodern view (cf. Lyotard 1984; Harding 1986), calls this the principle of *reflexive* sociology (Bourdieu and Waquant 1992).

Social Theories of Discourse

If discourse plays a critical role in social dynamics, then social theories about discourse should point the way to a dynamic, critical, unitary social theory. Unfortunately, most theories of discourse are not social theories. Indeed most theories of discourse are mainly linguistic and psychological, paying relatively little attention to the question of who says what when, why, and with what effects. The social context of discourse and issues of discourse as social action are largely ignored. Instead discourse is mostly seen as the product of autonomous mental processes, or it is simply described as having particular linguistic features.

Why is this? Granted, some people are simply interested in linguistic description for its own sake, and others want to use discourse as a tool for understanding what they call the mind, but why are our theories of linguistic description, and our theories of mind, ones that ignore the social functions of language, the social origins of human behavior, and the social position of the linguist or psychologist? The answer, I believe, lies in the ideological functions of the discourses of psychology and linguistics in our own society and its history. Social perspectives on any human phenomenon are potentially dangerous to the interests of power.

In modern times, in European cultures, we have preferred theories that claim to be universal, theories that do not admit that they may see the whole world, but can only see it from one culture's viewpoint. We have constructed a notion of 'human nature' based on our own views of what is worth paying attention to in the activities of humans. We have rooted our psychology in a fanciful connection to biology and the unity of the human species. We have rooted our linguistics in this psychology. We have taken our modest successes in the atypical domains of physics and chemistry (where the objects of interest do not have the kind of complexity for which cultural differences in viewpoint can matter very much; cf. Harding 1986; Lemke 1993b; Salthe 1985, 1993) and used this to make plausible our impossible claims about the universality of our views of language and mind.

We have not questioned the fundamental assumptions of our own cultural tradition: whether an objective science of matters human and cultural is possible in principle, whether the notion of mind as associated with both a biological organism and a social person is tenable, whether social systems can usefully be thought of as being composed of individuals as such, whether our subjective experience of ourselves as actors and perceivers is the product of the discourses and practices of our culture rather than a universal human given.

Some, but not many, have asked whether our taste for universalizing theories may have arisen from the need of European societies to justify their domination of other cultures by force in the past few centuries, or from the need of upper-middle class, middle-aged, European males to legitimate their domination by force of workers, peasants, women, children, elders, slaves and various cultural Others in their own society. It is not just common sense, but science as well, especially the sciences of the human and near-human, which we must subject to skeptical, critical examination to determine their ideological biases.

We will return to these questions in more detail in Chapters 5 and 7. Our task here is to identify the modern exceptions, the major theories of discourse which have emphasized its social dimensions. I want to discuss particularly the work of Mikhail Bakhtin, Michel Foucault, Michael Halliday, Basil Bernstein and (though not a discourse theorist) Pierre Bourdieu. Each of them seems to have arrived at what I see as the same basic solution to the problem of connecting discourse to Discourses, events to larger social relations and processes. Each has also contributed greatly to our resources for analyzing the social functions, including the ideological functions, of discourse.

Bakhtin and Heteroglossia

I begin with the work of Mikhail Bakhtin (especially 1929, 1935, 1953) in part because he was the first of these five to try to construct a social theory of discourse, and so his work seems to us today the most original, even idiosyncratic. He worked as part of a group of scholars in the period immediately following the Russian Revolution, a time when Marxist ideas were widely respected, and when there was a temporary crack in the monolithic ideology of European culture. In this period, Vygotsky (e.g. 1963) began to ask about the social origins of mind, standing the received wisdom of psychology on its head. Bakhtin, along with V.N. Voloshinov, P.N. Medvedev and others wanted a theory of language and literature that saw it too as having a social origin and character, and not as being merely the autonomous product of individual minds.

What, for Bakhtin, are the fundamental elements of language as a social phenomenon? Words? Sentences? Speakers? None of these:

> The actual reality of language/speech is not the abstract system of linguistic forms, nor the isolated monologic utterance, nor the psycho-physiological act of its implementation, but the social event of verbal interaction implemented in an utterance or utterances. (Bakhtin 1929/1986: 94)

An utterance, a moment of discourse, as a *social event*, as an act that contributes to the social activity of discourse: this for Bakhtin is the starting point. What of the *meaning* of this event, however? For Bakhtin our meanings do not arise in individual acts of will in which we are the sole determiners of our utterances, because a verbal act 'inevitably orients itself with respect to previous performances in the same sphere, both those by the same author and those by other authors' (p. 95). The utterance always originates in and functions as part of a social *dialogue* (whether the other participants in this dialogue are considered to be actually present or are only implied):

> The linguistic significance of a given utterance is understood against the background of language, while its actual meaning is understood against the background of other concrete utterances on the same theme, a background made up of contradictory opinions, points of view, and value judgments. (Bakhtin 1935/1981: 281)

This is a view of meaning that came later to be called the principle of intertextuality (cf. Kristeva 1980; Lemke 1985, 1993d) because it sees the meaning of each particular utterance or stretch of discourse as arising in the relations *between* sayings and social viewpoints, and not in relations among linguistic forms as such, or among speakers as individuals. We make sense of every word, utterance, or act against the background of (some) other words, utterances, acts of a similar kind. This implies, of course, that it is very important to understand just *which* other texts a particular community considers relevant to the interpretation of any given text.

In what he says, Bakhtin distinguishes between a narrower, formal linguistic, or semantic view of meaning and a broader more social view. The former depends on features of the language itself, and we will later call it the semantic *meaning potential* of the utterance as a linguistic form. It tells us what this utterance *could* mean, across a variety of contexts, in so far as it is interpreted consistently with very general principles of grammar and word meaning. The latter is what the utterance actually does mean, however, as a social act, in the context in which it is used here and now. That context in turn depends on a whole social system of utterances made in various times and places, a system of texts written or said from different viewpoints, embodying different opinions and values. The notion of the *utterance* for Bakhtin is a bridge between the linguistic and social, the event-meaning and the larger social systems in which that event has its meaning for us.

Bakhtin went on to develop this view of the utterance into a more general view of discourse as always implicitly *dialogical,* as always speaking against the background of what others have said or written in other times and places. He describes the struggle to make a word or utterance one's own, to place it in a new context as a new social event, so that its meanings are as much our own as another's. Along the way he began to see that the background against which an utterance means is not simply a set of isolated, unrelated utterances. He saw the diversity of language, how the utterances of people from different times and places and different social positions were systematically different:

Language is unitary only as an abstract grammatical system of normative forms, taken in isolation from the concrete ideological concep-
tualizations that fill it . . . Actual social life and historical becoming
create within [a language] a multitude of bounded verbal-ideological
belief systems . . . [within which] are elements of language filled with
various semantic and axiological content, and each with its own different sound. (Bakhtin 1935/1981: 281)

What he calls at this point 'bounded verbal-ideological belief systems'
he elsewhere glosses as the 'social languages of heteroglossia' or as distinct
social *voices*. He illustrates what he means by referring to the stratification of
language in actual use into a variety of

social class dialects, languages of special groups, professional jargons
(including those of lawyers, doctors, teachers, and novelists), genre
languages, the languages of generations and age groups, of the authorities, of literary and political movements, historical epochs, etc.
(1935/1981: 262–3, cf. 289)

All the languages of heteroglossia . . . are specific points of view on
the world, forms for conceptualizing the world in words, specific
worldviews, each characterized by its own objects, meanings, and
values. As such they may all be juxtaposed to one another, mutually
supplement one another, contradict one another, and be interrelated dialogically. (1935/1981: 291–2)

Here Bakhtin is articulating his critical insight that the various social
voices, the various characteristic discourses of different social groups, have
specific, ultimately sociological, relations to one another. All the social relations of groups, their alliances of mutual support, their conflict in opposition
to one another, are created, recreated, negotiated and changed in the social
dialogues of our discourse with one another.

What Bakhtin calls social languages or voices we have been calling Discourses, or now more formally, *discourse formations*. There are the persistent
habits of speaking and acting, characteristic of some social group, through
which it constructs its worldview: its beliefs, opinions and values. It is through
discourse formations that we construct the very objects of our reality, from
electrons to persons, from words to 'discourse formations'. We necessarily do
so from some social point of view, with some cultural system of beliefs and
assumptions, and some system of values, interests and biases. We do this *not*
as individuals alone, but as members of communities, and however we do it,
whatever discourse formations we deploy to make sense of the world, *our*
formations always have systematic sociological relations to *their* formations.
We speak with the voices of our communities, and to the extent that we have

individual voices, we fashion these out of the social voices already available to us, appropriating the words of others to speak a word of our own.

In the theory of heteroglossia, all the key elements of a social theory of discourse are present, including a dynamic model:

> Language and languages [i.e. heteroglossic discourse types] change historically primarily by means of hybridization . . . the crucible for this mixing always remaining the utterance. (1935/1981: 358–59)

The notion of hybridization is that particular utterances, even though the product of a single speaker, may contain within them elements of more than one dialect or discourse formation, thus producing new possibilities, which, if taken up by other speakers, can lead to linguistic and cultural change.

How has Bakhtin built his bridge between the event (the utterance) and the social system of heteroglossia (the social relations of various constituent groups in a society)? First by the principle of intertextuality, that the meaning of an utterance or event must be read against the background of other utterances and events occurring in the community, and second by introducing an intermediate notion between the social event and the system of social relations, the social language or voice characteristic of a particular group in the community.

The principle of intertextuality needs to be further specified. We need to understand just *how* members of a community read one text against the background of some, and not other, texts to construct its meaning. The principle of heteroglossia will need ultimately to tell us more both about how different social groups come to speak and act differently, and about the relations between the discourse habits of a group as such and the discourse habits associated with the various activities in which members of the group engage. Bakhtin's principles are foundations on which we can build such a social theory of discourse.

I doubt that I would have recognized the significance of these principles when I first read Bakhtin in the early 1980s if it had not been for the familiar ring they had. I had already encountered, I realized, these same principles in different terminology in the work of Halliday, Bernstein, Foucault and Bourdieu.

Halliday and Bernstein: Register and Code

Bakhtin's notion of the social languages of heteroglossia was modeled on the diversity of the regional and social dialects of Russia in his time, and so for him these forms of discourse were associated specifically with the groups of people who used them. The British linguist Michael Halliday, some 40 years later, was trying to describe the linguistic differences associated, not with different communities of speakers, but with different activities in social life. We all recognize, as did Bakhtin, that the language of mathematics is different from the language of sports or politics. Halliday sought to characterize these differences more specifically, or, as he would say, more delicately.

Unlike Bakhtin, however, Halliday had at his command a very powerful semantic analysis of the grammar of his own language (English). He recognized that the language of a sports report, a sales transaction, and a newspaper editorial differed not simply in their vocabulary, and not simply because these uses of language are more likely for people in some social positions than others, but because the frequencies of occurrence of many grammatical and semantic features in these texts were skewed by the nature of the different activities in which language was being used.

From this recognition came his now well-known theory of *registers*: the functional varieties of language, characteristic of particular activities in which language is used, defined by systematic differences in the probabilities of various grammatical and semantic features in the texts of each register (Halliday 1977, 1978; see also Gregory 1967). Where the *field* of the activity differed, as say between politics, sports or mathematics, there were characteristic differences in the frequencies of say action verbs vs. relation verbs, or active vs. passive voice; where the *tenor* of interpersonal relationships (including intimacy and power relations) differed, there were corresponding differences in mood (interrogative requests vs. imperative commands, say) or in modality (simple polar verbs vs. modal auxiliaries indicating possibility or doubt); and where the differences were those of *mode*, as between speech and writing, or the language of participation vs. that of observation, there were differences in how information in one clause was highlighted or backgrounded and linked to information in other clauses (thematization, cohesion, etc.).

Though register theory was initially only about differences, about variation in linguistic features from one sort of activity or situation type to another, people quickly found it useful to speak of *the register* of this or that activity. More delicate analysis (e.g. Gregory and Malcolm 1981) showed that while Halliday's arguments apply statistically to the whole of a text, within a text, as we move from one section to another, there is smaller scale (*phasal*) variation in how the text constructs its meanings. Texts have internal semantic structure, which further reflects the detailed functions of each particular stage in the activity that gave rise to the text, or which the text is describing or enacting.

Halliday, along with Ruqaiya Hasan (e.g. Hasan 1984b; Halliday and Hasan 1989) and Jim Martin (1985, 1992), have since tried to work out more detailed connections between register variation and the internal structures of texts of different kinds. These kinds, or *genres*, also identified by Bakhtin (1953), from familiar literary ones such as sonnets and folktales (e.g. Propp 1928) to expository genres like the scientific research article (e.g. Bazerman 1988) to spoken genres such as those characteristic of the dialogue of the sales transaction (e.g. Mitchell 1975; Ventola 1987) or the dialogue of the classroom (e.g. Lemke 1990a) are again all characteristic of activities rather than of groups of people as such.

Halliday's social theory of discourse suggests that our uses of language are inseparable from the social functions, the social contexts of actions and relationships in which language plays its part. Halliday suggests that language be viewed as a system of resources, a set of possible kinds of meanings that can be made, and that we then examine which kinds of meanings actually get made in the course of which human activities, by which social participants. This is what is meant by seeing language as a *social semiotic*, a resource to be deployed for social purposes.

This view is consistent with the key principles we have identified from Bakhtin. It makes it possible to identify a number of the grounds on which a community may find one utterance or text relevant for the meaning of another (that it is of the same register, or the same genre; that it was constructed in the course of the same kind of activity, etc.; cf. Lemke 1985). It also introduces an intermediate notion between the text or utterance and the social system: the system of registers and genres in a community. Implicitly it shifts the emphasis toward seeing the fundamental elements that define the community as its system of activities or social practices, rather than viewing it directly as a system of different types of individuals.

There is obviously one link missing, however: how are we to understand the differences in language-using habits between those of different ages, genders, social classes, subcultures, etc.? Halliday was greatly concerned with this question, and in the 1960s and 1970s both he and Ruqaiya Hasan collaborated with Basil Bernstein, a sociologist working in the field of education, in order to forge this missing link. Bernstein (1971, 1975) called it *code*, or later, semantic coding orientation. It was greatly misunderstood in its day, especially in the United States, where great efforts were being made at that time to show that all social dialects, especially those of oppressed African-Americans, were powerful resources for meaning-making, and not merely clusters of random mistakes in grammar. Bernstein tried to point out something that is now largely taken for granted: that the schools expect people to use language in certain ways, and that these are by and large the ways of the upper-middle class, putting the members of other social classes at an automatic relative disadvantage.

Bernstein argued, as has now been well established by the later work of Hasan (e.g. 1989b; Hasan and Cloran 1990), that the communities formed by members of different social classes learn to use language differently, so that even in what seems to be the same social activity (say, mothers questioning or scolding their children), even after we have taken register difference into account, there are further differences in the frequencies and characteristic combinations of grammatical and semantic options that are taken up by members of different social classes. Hasan has shown similar sorts of difference according to gender as well.

These are not small differences. They stand out in plots of Hasan's data so strikingly that statistical tests of their significance are hardly necessary (though of course they have been done). These differences are not simply statistically significant, they are socially significant, as the large body of research on language in education shows (e.g. the pioneering study of Shirley Heath 1983, and the many studies done by Bernstein's research group, 1971, 1975, 1987).

Bernstein is a sociologist and he was not interested in merely describing linguistic differences. He wanted to embed them in a more general social theory in which one could see how differences in social class position led to differences in habits of language use, which in turn tended, in the context of a society and particularly an educational system shaped by those of the more powerful classes, to assign children of the less powerful classes to jobs and lives in which they would not wield power. Bernstein, too, sought to connect discourse to larger social relationships and processes. While his model emphasizes the reproduction of social relationships rather than social change and social dynamics, it otherwise represents an impressive general synthesis (see Bernstein 1981). Here once again we find an intermediate notion, *code*, or semantic orientation, that serves to bridge between the event and the larger social system.

So far, all of these social theories of discourse have begun from the discourse side, that is from the text or utterance, and sought to explain its features by their social origins or functions. We turn now to two theorists who are mainly interested in the larger social system, but who have also introduced intermediate notions very similar to those of Bakhtin, Halliday and Bernstein in order to connect that system to specific texts of discourse and action.

Foucault's Discursive Formations

Michel Foucault saw himself primarily as a historian, not as someone who sought to retell the past as it had been, but as someone who tried to describe how we today construct our continuities and discontinuities with many pasts. The texts and artifacts of the past are objects in our present-day world, and it is by way of our present-day notions of similarity and difference, continuity and discontinuity, that we construct their historical meaning in the present day, and for the present day, by construing relationships among these objects and ourselves.

For most historians, the primary objects of the past are texts, written documents surviving in various archives. Modern scholars have also learned to read paintings and statuary, architecture and battlefields as texts as well. Historians, like anthropologists, are philologists; they need to find ways of reading texts even though they are not members of the communities that made these texts and in which the texts had their original meanings. Those original meanings are not recoverable; we can never know if we have reconstructed them or not. We can still learn from them, however, learn from the ways in which they are different from the texts we make today. What is critical in this enterprise is how we put together different texts – diary, a set of tax records, a chronicle, a taxonomy of diseases, a treatise on alchemy, a record of a trial for witchcraft – which texts go together, and why, and how?

Foucault sought to build a general model of how our picture of the past, of our continuities and discontinuities with it, depends critically on our sense of the possible ways in which texts can be combined. He was building, in one sense, a general theory of intertextuality for the practice of history, and so in part for the practice of social science. Of all the theorists considered here he is the one most concerned with change. He reflexively situates his own discourse inside the systems he analyzes, at least in so far as he recognizes that how a historian looks at texts is itself part of a discursive formation built over historical time out of foundations that may include those same texts. When Foucault points out the ideological functioning of some way of speaking, he usually does so because, having seen its historical continuities and discontinuities with other ways of speaking, he can no longer regard it as a natural or inevitable product of common sense necessity (e.g. Foucault 1980).

Foucault's major theoretical statement is *The Archeology of Knowledge* (1969) and this is usefully read in the context of his analysis of the emergence of social science discourse in the modern world (*The Order of Things*, 1966). Foucault's analysis of the principles of intertextuality is thoroughly postmodern (despite misunderstandings of it in the 1970s as a version of structuralism) and probably the most sophisticated possible in our time. Only its failure to engage with linguistic analyses of discourse limits its usefulness. It is not possible to know in terms of linguistic features of texts exactly how to interpret many of Foucault's theoretical principles, and while he sketches the general principles, there are no explicit examples to show us actually how to analyze the relations of specific texts. These are of course implicit in much of the rest of his work, but we have to recognize that his notion of a *discursive formation* cannot be equated exactly with any linguistically defined notion of a *discourse formation*.

For our purposes, however, this is not necessary. We are interested in how Foucault uses the notion of the discursive formation to help bridge between texts and social systems, and we can see that *functionally* the discursive formation is an intermediate notion of exactly the same kind as the others we have identified. Here, for example, is Foucault's version of the principle of general intertextuality:

> At its very root the statement (énoncée) has a dispersion over an enunciative field in which it has a place and a status, which arranges for it possible relations with the past and opens up possible futures

... There is no free, neutral, independent statement; a statement always belongs to a series or a whole, plays a role among other statements, is part of a network of statements ... There is no statement that does not presuppose others; that is not surrounded by a field of coexistences, effects of series and succession, a distribution of functions and roles. If one can speak of a statement as such, it is because a sentence or proposition figures at a definite point, with a specific position, in an enunciative network that extends beyond it. (Foucault 1969: 99)

The enunciative field or network specifies, roughly, the rules of use of a statement in various contexts in relation to other statements. Another way of saying this is that statements tend to be used together in certain typical patterns (discursive practices) and to form systems (discursive formations) that relate statements to one another according to a variety of principles.

A discursive practice can be defined as ... a body of anonymous historical rules, always determined in the time and space that defined a given period, and [which determines] for a given social, economic, geographical, or linguistic area, the conditions of operation of the enunciative function. (1969: 117)

A discursive formation for Foucault is defined by four kinds of relations among statements: those which determine what sorts of discursive objects (entities, topics, processes) the discourse can construct or talk about; those that specify who can say these things to whom in what contexts; those that define the relations of meaning among statements, including how they can be organized to form texts; and finally those that tell us what the alternative kinds of discourses are that can be formed in these ways and how they can be related to each other as being considered equivalent, incompatible, antithetical, etc.

Foucault's notion of the discursive formation is thus more powerful than any of the notions we have encountered previously because it includes the rules for how these others are to be related to one another (i.e. what kinds of heteroglossic relations can exist among these narrower notions of discourse formations).

Finally, we need to hear Foucault on discursive change:

A change in the order of discourse does not presuppose 'new ideas', a little invention and creativity, a new mentality, but transformations in a social practice, perhaps also in neighboring practices, and their mutual articulation. I have not denied the possibility of changing discourses: I have deprived the sovereignty of the subject of the exclusive and instantaneous right to it. (1969: 209)

That is, discursive change is cultural change, it is systemic change. It is not the province of individual action, though it may originate in an individual event; it requires that a social community change its ways of speaking and doing.

We see that for Foucault as well as Halliday the focus is on social practices, habits of activity characteristic of a community, not on individual acts of intentionality. For Foucault, the discursive formations that tell us what people are saying and doing in a historical period are systems of doings, not of doers as such. Foucault provides a discussion of what he calls the 'subject-positions' defined by a discourse formation, the social roles of the speakers of these discourses. He seems to suggest to many people that we can use the notions of discourse formations to define individual subjects in so far as they are participants in a discourse. We will return in Chapter 5 to this complex question.

For now the important point is that one can give, as Foucault does, very complex and subtle accounts of social relationships and their historical changes in terms of discourse formations. By reading Foucault against the background of Bakhtin, Halliday and Bernstein, we can see once again how intermediate notions of a particular kind help to connect texts or events and the social systems in which such texts can occur, do occur, and make sense.

If there is one element of this synthesis that is still rather weak, it is the problem of how to relate discourse formations seen in overview as characteristic of societies and their cultures with the actual lives of individual people who enact these discourses, and in enacting, potentially change them. Bernstein has begun to give an account of this process: how we are each socialized into the discourse patterns and habits, the coding orientations characteristic of our social class, gender, subculture, etc. The theorist who has made the fullest effort to provide a general theory of how people of different social categories acquire their social habits, however, is probably Pierre Bourdieu.

Bourdieu and Discourse Habitus

By now it should be getting pretty clear just what all these intermediate notions that bridge between texts or events on the one hand and larger social systems characteristic of whole communities, on the other, have in common. They are all notions of what is *typical* in a community: typical habits and patterns of discourse and action. Every text or event is unique, but it can also be seen as an instance of some kind or type of text or event that recurs in a community and is recognizable as such. Most general are what we might call *activity formations*, the typical doings of a community which are repeatable, repeated, and recognized as being of the same type from one instance or occurrence to another, such as a baseball game, a train ride, writing a check or making a phone call. We could also call these *action genres*. Among the special cases of action genres are *speech genres* and *written genres*, but these are clearly also definable as the products of the activities that produce them. Genres are specific in their properties, having definite beginnings, ends and stages along the way. Notions like register and discourse formation can be made a bit more general to handle kinds of language apart from such neat packaging, and so also can activity formations.

What is important here are the relations between text or event and formation or genre on the one hand, and those between formations or genres and larger issues of social structure and process on the other. Every text or event takes its meaning in part from being seen in the community as an instance of one or more formations. We interpret it against the background of other instances of the same formations to see how it is distinctive and we contrast it with instances of other formations. Different formations (codes, genres, registers, voices of heteroglossia, discursive formations) are not just different, however. They have systematic relations to one another, and those relations define and are defined by the larger social relationships of classes, genders, age groups, political constituencies, and significant social divisions of every kind. The model is recursive; each level is defined by its relations to the other levels in the model. So, for instance, social class is defined by the fact that not all activities in the community are equally likely to be practiced by all people. People are defined by the activities in which they participate, and significant social categories of people by the intersections of groups of related activities, including the discourse practices by which we label people as members of social categories.

Models of this degree of complexity and recursiveness appear to be necessary when dealing with human social systems (see the final section of this book, 'Making Meaning, Making Trouble', and also Chapter 6 for some of the reasons why, and for a fuller discussion of how the various levels of the model integrate with one another).

A social theory which has the requisite degree of complexity (except perhaps for underplaying the role of discourse and the inherent dynamic features of the system that lead to its continual changes) is Bourdieu's (1972, 1990b) theory of social *habitus*. Bourdieu has made some special contributions to social models. One of these is his efforts to link social abstractions like the habits, attitudes, preferences, dispositions and actions characteristic of a social class, gender, age group, etc. to the actual life-trajectories of bodily persons.

Bourdieu has noticed, as have many others trained as he was in social anthropology, that members of different cultures not only talk differently (using different languages, discourse formations, coding orientations), but they even *walk* differently. They carry themselves differently, with a *body hexis* distinctive to their culture (and gender and age group, etc.). This suggested to Bourdieu that cultural and subcultural dispositions of all kinds are literally *embodied* in people. Bourdieu here rejects the great Cartesian split which seems so clearly to function ideologically in the discourses of the human sciences. He takes something usually thought of as belonging to the domain of 'mind': how we perceive things, how we feel about them and react to them, our habits and preferences and attitudes and dispositions to action (including to discourse) and makes them matters of *body*. By the same move, he renders unnecessary the dichotomy between matters characteristic of groups, communities, social categories like gender and age, etc. and matters characteristic of individuals. He speaks of culture as directly embodied in persons. Persons with such dispositions to action embodied in them tend to act in ways that reinforce these dispositions, or in many cases complementary dispositions, in others. Thus social relationships also become embodied. Cultural habitus for Bourdieu is an embodied system of sociologically structured and structuring dispositions.

We acquire these dispositions in the course of living our lives, interacting with the social and material (especially the human-made) environment, which consists of other people acting out of these dispositions and the material effects of such actions in the world. We do not all acquire the same dispositions of course, for we live different lives, have different characteristic experiences, participate in different activities with different frequencies, and occupy different roles in the activities in which we do participate. The dispositions of the habitus are more alike for those who lead more similar lives, and progressively become less alike for those who typically engage in different roles and different activities (Bourdieu 1979, 1984). Habitus can be as specific as the dispositions acquired by a trained athlete or dancer, dispositions specific to their sport or their style of dance training, or it can be as general as the dispositions that distinguish males and females, or workers and managers.

Bourdieu's other special contribution is his emphasis on the distinction between synoptic and participatory views of human activity. Synoptic views stand outside of the process of enactment of an activity, generally describing it after it is finished, or as an ideal formula that applies to the typical case. Participatory views (I also use the term *dynamic* view in this sense) look at human action from the viewpoint, not of an outside observer, but of a participant, for whom every aspect of the ongoing action is contingent, dependent on the next move, the next response or reaction, and so on the various strategies by which we get through the activity, bringing it to some sort of, usually conventional, conclusion. The notion of habitus or embodied cultural disposition also links these two perspectives together. The habitus is what shapes our responses to the myriad unpredictable contingencies of the moment, and shapes them in such a way that, on the whole, when the synoptic accounts are totaled up, things have turned out in the way typical of goings-on in our community. The habitus mediates between a synoptic view of activity formations characteristic of a community and a dynamic view of the processes by which these activities are actually enacted on specific occasions by human actors.

We should not be surprised then that Bourdieu has extended Bakhtin's notions of heteroglossia in much the way that I have in my own work (cf. Bourdieu 1991; Lemke 1988c and next chapter). He regards the social relationships among discourse voices as being structured by, and in turn contributing to the structuring of, the social relationships of power among different positions in the social field (defined by social class, by age, by gender, etc.).

Bourdieu's basic metaphor for this is an economic one. He construes an economics of linguistic transactions in which utterances or discourses are the products that producers offer on a market to potential consumers. Each producer, by virtue of membership in a subcommunity or position in the larger web of social relations (what I will sometimes call a *caste* or subcaste), has some linguistic habitus, some embodied system of dispositions to speak in a particular way. The link to material embodiment is most evident in the case of social 'accent' or norms of pronunciation, and from there to social dialects (including lexicon and grammar), semantic coding orientations (cf. Bernstein 1981, 1987; Hasan 1989b, 1990), and even genres and discourse formations, is a reasonable progression.

So a speaker speaks partly in ways typical of his or her social position and caste membership in accent, in grammar and lexis, in semantic dispositions, and in likelihood of using particular genres and registers to produce discourses of recognizable types with definite viewpoints on their subjects. Bourdieu also recognizes that this process of discourse production maps forms and contents onto one another, so that in the finished product we can no longer distinguish them. In fact, in many cases there are no intertexts, no alternatives available in which we could see the same content in a different form, or vice versa, since we cannot in general find just any social or political point of view combined with any statement about the world.

Bourdieu provides us with a way of connecting the relations among the contents and viewpoints of various discourse formations, or social voices of heteroglossia, with the relations among the social positions of their authors. Since his view of linguistic habitus includes, as it should, interpretive, or consumer, dispositions toward discourse as well as producer dispositions, he can also show us that we all *evaluate* the worth of discourses, and even of utterances, from our own social viewpoints. These evaluations are part of the meaning a linguistic act or text has for us, a critical part of its/our textual politics. We evaluate some accents as better or more prestigious than others, some dialects as better, some realizations of the norms of a discourse type as better. In doing so, we hear and read (and ourselves produce) language always against the social background of these evaluations.

While evaluations may differ from one caste to another in a society, there are generally *dominant* norms of evaluation, which are those of the dominant caste, and which are to some extent accepted as natural by members of other castes. In any case, everyone knows up to a point what these dominant norms are and speaks and evaluates at least in relation to them if not always strictly according to them. They are facts of social life and they are what they are because of the overall power of the dominant caste to maintain their dominance in discourse as in all else.

Bourdieu takes this so much for granted, referring only to the 'field of power', as the social background for these relations among discourses and their evaluations, that we do not seem to get in most of his work any very explicit grounding of textual politics in the politics of coercive power. Bourdieu's view of power is multiplex; there is economic power, symbolic power of many kinds, social influence, and each grounded in its own sort of capital and in caste-specific dispositions to acquire and use that capital. Like most of us, however, Bourdieu looks little at the most primitive forms of capital: physical strength, weapons and the dispositions to use them to control the behavior of others. Because there are so many other ways in which social control of behavior is exercised in modern society, we prefer to overlook the most basic one, and so we may miss the important ways in which coercive power grounds the efficacy of all other forms of power, and the role of bodily materiality in this as well.

Bourdieu's sociology seems generally well suited to help us bridge from particular texts and events to larger macrosocial structural relations, particularly from the intermediate formations themselves (of which Bourdieu has relatively little to say) to, on the one hand, the materiality of situations and human participants (by way of the embodied dispositions of the caste-specific habitus), and on the other, the relationships of social power among significant social groups. It is inevitable, however, in this picture of the relationships between discourses and the social positions of their authors, that Bourdieu's discourse also is limited by his social position. I have already suggested that as an upper-middle class intellectual, he may be overinclined to emphasize the role of symbolic capital and less disposed to focus on that of coercive power.

Whether it can be laid to his own social positioning or not, we should also be aware that Bourdieu's view of social processes, however dynamically he sees the constitution of social structure, remains basically a static view. He is not concerned primarily with long term historical change, or indeed with radical and revolutionary change. It is indeed hard to imagine anything but the most gradual and piecemeal changes in social life as Bourdieu describes its basic mechanisms. I believe as well that his discourse embodies a masculinist disposition, which, while very sensitive to the general social domination of females by males, still tends to see all of social life as a competitive struggle for profit and distinction in a way particularly characteristic of masculinist perspectives in our culture (see also Lemke 1993c). It is not surprising either that little attention is given to the viewpoints on social life of the very young or the very old, currently still the most invisible of the basic biases of our intellectual culture.

The social theories of discourse presented in this chapter fit together like the pieces of a puzzle. They develop essentially similar approaches to the roles of intertextuality, cultural formations and the web of social relationships in the discursive construction of meaning. Taken together, they also point to additional factors which need to be better theorized: the materiality of meaning-making processes, the discursive construction of individuality and subjectivity, the role of coercive power in the social order, the politics of our own theories. We will return to these basic issues in later chapters. It is time now to move on to some specific texts, to analyze how they mobilize the resources of language and discourse to accomplish social, and very distinctly political, ends.

Chapter 3

Discourses in Conflict:
Heteroglossia and Text Semantics

Basic to the textual politics of any text are the discourse patterns that, from somebody's point of view, stand opposed to it. There are very few matters in a complex and diverse society about which there is only one discourse. Each different social or political point of view, each school of thought constructs its own discourse formation; it speaks of the matter in its own way. Although many discourse formations try to seem autonomous and self-sufficient, attempting to create the ideologically functional impression that they are simply presenting their viewpoint in the most natural way possible, it is always possible to detect in them what Bakhtin called their implicit dialogue with other points of view, other discourses on the same subject.

It can in fact sometimes be difficult to tell whether two different discourse formations are indeed talking about 'the same thing' or not. Since each of them constructs the subject matter by what they have to say about it and how they say it, there is always a sense in which they are *not* speaking of exactly 'the same thing'. If one discourse says that the *freedom fighters* are being kept in a *concentration camp*, while the other says that the *terrorists* are being held in a *prison* (cf. Mansfield 1987), the reader has to do some substantial work to construct a unity between these discourses. It is not enough simply to substitute some words in one for apparently corresponding words in the other; the semantic *relationships* between *prisons* and *terrorists* are not the same as those between *freedom fighters* and *concentration camps*.

Even more importantly, we interpret the meaning of what each of the two discourses says in relation to two different sets of *intertexts*. Using one set, we may conclude that the terrorists are prisoners, and also criminals, and suppose therefore that they have had a trial and been found guilty of specific violations of civilized law (though in fact in the discourses in question these suppositions are often unwarranted). Using the other set, we may conclude that someone's freedom is being threatened by people who act with no regard for civilized jurisprudence but intern people without trial. Reading one discourse we are led to side with the authorities, reading the other, to side with those defending themselves from oppression. Are these discourses really talking about 'the same thing'?

Is *abortion* the 'murder of an unborn child' or the 'termination of an unwanted pregnancy'? Is there a *neutral* discourse here? Or would any pretense of neutrality, as in a scientific or medical discourse about abortion, still be seen by some discourse communities as an abdication of moral responsibility? If *children* were being *murdered*, who would accept a dispassionately clinical discourse as morally appropriate (cf. the pseudo-scientific accounts of 'experiments' performed on Nazi concentration camp inmates). In highly polarized discourse communities, where even a 'neutral' position may represent a special interest (that of the medical community's assertion of its special prerogatives, or similarly, say, those of the journalistic community), that we most clearly see textual politics, and heteroglossia, in action.

In these extreme circumstances, every speaker or writer is forced to choose sides, or is taken by one side or another as having done so. Every utterance, every text, represents a political act because it cannot ignore the polarization of the community. Admittedly, these are extreme cases, but they illustrate a universal phenomenon: we cannot make meaning outside the system of discourses of our community, not as speakers and writers nor as listeners and readers. Every text requires that we bring to it a knowledge of other texts (its intertexts) to create or interpret it, and members of different social groups (whether defined by gender, age, social class, religion, political affiliation, occupation, etc.) will in general bring different intertexts to bear, will speak with different discourse voices and listen with different discourse dispositions.

Heteroglossia in Bakhtin's original sense meant simply the diversity of social languages, socially defined discourse types in a community. In a more fully developed social theory of the role of language and discourse in society (as in Chapters 1 and 2) however, we need to understand that these different discourse voices are not simply different; they are also systematically related to one another, and related in ways that depend on the wider social relations between the subcommunities that use them.

Discourses, in the sense of recurring discourse types or formations, are not simply the product of our dispositions and our deployment of lexis and grammar. They are also themselves a resource to be deployed (a *symbolic capital* in Bourdieu's terms). As writers and as readers, whether we explicitly refer to discourses other than our own or not, we make use of the existence and widespread currency of other discourses because we must always take them into account, must always be at least implicitly in dialogue with them.

How do we deploy these resources? How do we write and read meanings differently against the background of intertexts from different and competing discourses? Ultimately we do it by the lexical, grammatical and semantic means at our disposal (in speech we have also the resources of sound, e.g. of a sneering or a mocking accent, and in general we also have the resources

of other, especially visual, semiotic systems: caricatures, 'scare quotes', etc.).
What are those means and how do we use them? We need to have good
answers to this question in order to go beyond generalities and specifically
link what is said and how it is said in one discourse to the different semantic
patterns constructed in another discourse. Then we can ask how it happens
that these discourses have come to be as they are, and come to be used by
some people rather than others, people who have particular social relations
to one another as members of particular social groups.

If we are to have a social model of discourse as part of a general theory
of social processes, then at some point we have to get very specific about what
is actually said and done in a particular social event or text. Since so much
of our viewpoint toward the world and social issues is constructed in language, and since we know more today about how language works than we do
about any other system of semiotic resources, linking the phenomenon of
social heteroglossia to the actual semantic patterns constructed in particular
texts is an important task. That is what I will try to do in this chapter.

Heteroglossia and Text Semantics

Before we actually begin analyzing the two texts I want to present, we need
first to head off some potential, and common, misunderstandings. First, the
heteroglossic relations between two texts cannot be deduced solely on the
basis of what is said in the texts. Heteroglossic relations are, above all, social
and political relations. They must be construed, or constructed, by someone,
from some point of view. This is of course done with reference to what is said
in the texts, but it is perfectly possible for two texts to be counted as instances
of compatible discourse formations from one point of view in the community
and as instances of totally opposed and incompatible discourses from another viewpoint.

So what we have to examine here are two interdependent uses of
language:

1 the discourse's construction of 'the way the world is' (its *ideational,
representational* or *presentational* thematic) meaning and its viewpoint
toward this state of affairs (its *orientational* or *attitudinal* meaning), and
2 the discourse's (and our own) construction of the heteroglossic relations between it and other possible discourses.

The latter is a meta-discursive use of language (i.e. discourse about discourses).
This can get complicated!

All these constructions employ the same basic resources: the semantic
resources of language. What are those resources? In one sense we can say

that they are the resources of lexis (words) and grammar (wording). In another sense we can say that they are all the possible kinds of meanings that can be made with language, i.e. that can be made through words and wordings. If we allow this to include texts of any length, then we pretty much have all the meanings made in the community. (In practice of course, we need to take into account the total context of use of language, including associated actions and visual representations.) If we initially restrict ourselves to the meanings that can be made with a single grammatical clause, it is possible, as Halliday has done (e.g. 1978, 1985a), to sort out the semantic resources available to us into three major kinds.

The first of these, Halliday's *ideational* (or *experiential*) resources, deal mainly with specifying what kind of process or relationship we are talking about (material action, sensory perception, identity, location etc.), what the participants in the process or relationship are (agents, beneficiaries, targets, sensors, phenomena, locations etc.), and various relevant circumstances (time, place, manner etc.).

The second kind Halliday calls *interpersonal* resources. They enable us to specify the kind of speech–act relation between speaker and addressee (statement, question, command), and the attitude or stance of speakers both toward addressees (friendly, formal, hostile) and toward the ideational content of their own discourse (certain or doubtful, pleased or displeased).

The third kind are *textual* resources. They enable us to shift the starting point and relative prominence of information within the clause, and to connect the meaning of what is said in one part of the clause to what is said in another (or even in a different clause).

We do not make meaning just with single clauses, however. We make meanings by combining clauses into long spoken chains of clauses, or the sentences and paragraphs of conventional writing. Of course language gives us the means to do this as well, the means to create, or at least suggest to the reader, a continuity of ideational, interpersonal and textual meaning. Any resource that enables us to project *continuity* obviously also allows us to construct *changing* patterns of ideational meanings, interpersonal stances, and textual organization and informational prominence. Some of these larger, complex patterns become socially institutionalized in the sense that they come to be repeated, with variations, in recognizable ways from one text to another, one occasion of discourse to another. They come to be discourse formations, genres, text types.

What I call *text semantics* (Lemke 1988a, 1989c, 1994b) deals specifically with such patterns of continuity and change in clause-level meaning across texts. In addition to my own work, there is a substantial literature making use of Halliday's analysis of clause-level semantic resources (e.g. Halliday 1977, 1982; Gregory and Malcolm 1981; Hasan 1984a, 1988; Thibault 1986, 1991; Martin 1989, 1992; Ventola 1991; Halliday and Martin 1993). It is possible, with some caution (Lemke 1983a, 1989c, 1992a), to *separately* trace out the patterns of ideational meaning that run through a text, and then to see in relation to them how interpersonal–attitudinal and textual–organizational meanings are also brought to bear. The caution is because these three kinds of resources are intimately interdependent on one another in real text; all three kinds of resources contribute to all three kinds of meaning-making. It is only in a very specialized sense (Halliday 1978; Martin 1992; Hasan 1994) that each kind of resource has as its primary, original, or most direct semantic function the making of a particular kind of meaning.

I prefer to define the kinds of meaning as primary, and then to look at how all the different resources contribute to their construction, continuity, modulation and change across a text (Lemke 1989c, 1990a: Ch. 8, 1992a). I also somewhat generalize Halliday's original typology in order to describe what I see happening most typically in text semantics. We construct with the semantic resources of language (and in more general contexts with the resources of other semiotic systems as well) three simultaneous kinds of meaning:

- *Presentational*: the construction of how things are in the natural and social worlds by their explicit description as participants, processes, relations and circumstances standing in particular semantic relations to one another across meaningful stretches of text, and from text to text;
- *Orientational*: the construction of our orientational stance toward present and potential addressees and audiences, and toward the presentational content of our discourse, in respect of social relations and evaluations from a particular viewpoint, across meaningful stretches of text and from text to text;
- *Organizational*: the construction of relations between elements of the discourse itself, so that it is interpretable as having structure (constituent, whole–part relations), texture (continuities and similarities, with differences within these), and informational organization and relative prominence across meaningful stretches of text and from text to text.

You will probably have noticed that these definitions (they are really only descriptions) present these meanings as made not only within a text but also 'from text to text', and this is very important.

All meaning is intertextual. No text is complete or autonomous in itself; it needs to be read, and it is read, in relation to other texts. *Which* other texts? Each community, each discourse tradition, has its own canons of intertextuality, its own principles and customs regarding which texts are most relevant to the interpretation of any one text (cf. Lemke 1985). In our own community, texts are more relevant for one another's interpretation the more they share the same patterns of presentational meaning. Among such texts, those that also share the same orientational stances, or are considered instances of the same discourse formation or heteroglossic social discourse, are considered more relevant or appropriate intertexts, other things being equal. Purely organizational dimensions of meaning-making in texts are least considered, but since genres tend to combine particular organizational conventions with some rather than other presentational meanings and orientational stances, they are never entirely irrelevant either.

This viewpoint has some far-reaching implications. For one thing it no longer considers words as such to have meanings. Words have meaning *potential*, a range of possible meanings that we abstract from all their actual uses, but their relevant meaning potential in a given text is always severely restricted by the *pattern* of presentational or orientational meanings they help to express. Their actual, specific meaning for us in a given text depends critically on that pattern. These patterns, which in the case of presentational meanings I call *thematic patterns* or *thematic formations* (Lemke 1983a, 1990a) are fundamentally intertextual. The same patterns recur from text to text in slightly different wordings, but recognizably the same, and each wording can be mapped onto a generic semantic pattern that is the same for all. I take these thematic patterns, appropriately modified or subclassified where necessary to take into account the dependence of presentational meaning on the orientational stance of the discourse (in which case I will call them *heteroglossic discourse formations* or voices) as the irreducible units of text meaning.

Text meaning is not reducible to or recoverable from word meaning potential alone. Text meaning is made by using thematic patterns as the direct meaning-making resource. Thematic patterns include the semantic relations which words (or more abstractly the *thematic items* which the words express) consistently have from one text to another, or from one part of a text to another. Just as a word has only a general meaning potential which is narrowed by its context of use, and especially by the words it is grammatically linked to, so even the semantic relations between two words still represent only a potential range of meaning relations. It is only when we have a full pattern, usually consisting of many thematic items with relatively constant semantic relations (which are now their thematic relations) that we can reasonably identify the kinds of definite meaning that we ordinarily associate with words.

Another way to say this is that texts and thematic patterns are elements of the system of meanings, they are units of meaning, they have meaning. Words as such are not units of meaning and do not 'have' meaning. They are, rather, elements of the system of grammatical resources which we use to construct meanings. Lexis and grammar, wordings, are the tools, the resources; we use those tools to create meanings. An utterance, a social act of meaning-making, is a text. It has meaning, or has meaning construed for it, on the basis of the thematic patterns we take it as instancing on that occasion.

A clause is also a unit of grammar, but, like a word, it can realize an utterance, can be the whole of a text. It is *as* utterance, *as* text, that we make single words or clauses mean, and not as isolated lexical or grammatical units.

Of course thematic patterns are not the whole story. They are just the most linguistically and culturally salient contextualizations of a wording in terms of which it has meaning for us. Even more culturally (but not linguistically) salient is the context of situation, what is happening socially and materially in terms of events and actions, of which the utterance or text is an integral part. Wordings have specific meanings for us in relation to this sort of context as well. For example, 'G' day!' or 'Fuck you!' are utterances for which the presentational thematics is largely irrelevant and only the orientational-attitudinal meaning of the social situation really counts. In a more specialized sense, as I have already said, it is not the thematic pattern alone, but the whole discourse formation, including the attitudinal stance of its heteroglossic voice, that provides the critical linguistic context for the meaning of an utterance or text, constructed from words and wordings.

Text semantics is also not in principle reducible to the formal analysis of propositions or their truth values. *Meaning* is a more fundamental category of analysis than *truth*. 'Truth' is just one of the meanings we can make about a proposition, and it is not a meaning we can make about questions, commands, requests, offers, etc. unless we turn them into statements or propositions. Propositions do not even exhaust the meanings that can be made with a single clause, much less text meanings. Propositional formal semantics is based on a particular linguistic trick. Any statement, say 'John is coming', can be embedded in another clause, say: 'It is . . . that John is coming.' Halliday refers to this kind of embedded statement as a *fact* and contrasts it with similar constructions (Halliday 1985: 227–51). In the framing clause I have chosen, what can fill the blank are Attributes of embedded clauses, or, loosely, of propositions. Truth-value theories of propositional semantics are based on privileging just one of these Attributes, truth.

In the semantics of English, however, abstracted from all the discourses in which such constructions appear, we discover that there are many such Attributes which propositions can have, and that they are all *evaluations*. We can meaningfully say, for example, that it is good, useful, unfortunate, unusual, important, appropriate or likely that John is coming, but we do not meaningfully say that is it red, large, abstract or grammatical that John is coming. Systematic analysis of the kinds of orientational meaning we can make specifies pretty much what sorts of predicates are evaluative and in what ways. There are a small number of different kinds of evaluations (Desirability, Probability or Warrantability, Necessity or Obligation, Usuality, Significance, etc.) that turn up not just in the evaluations of embedded statements, but all over the grammar and lexicon of English (e.g. modal auxiliary verbs, modal adverbs, verbs of mental process, etc.; see Halliday 1985: 332–41; Lemke 1989c, 1992a, and in preparation; Martin 1992: 412–15, 533–6).

Among the many evaluative attributes (or predicates) that an embedded statement (or proposition) can have are those in the class we could call Warrantability, Probability, or relative Certitude. It is one of several classes of attitudinal stance a speaker can take toward the content of his or her own discourse. Within it there falls in a particular option (whose existence follows a general pattern also found in the other classes), a particular kind and degree of evaluation of this sort, expressed most commonly by the attribute *true*. *Truth* is just a common foot soldier in a much larger semantic army, just one among many attributes of propositions deriving from the system of orientational and attitudinal stances our culture and language allows speakers to take toward the presentational content of their own discourse. It can hardly be a candidate for the ground or basis of all meaning. The fact that historically it has been, and for many philosophers today still is, should make us look critically at the wider discourses in which it is embedded, and inquire into their ideological functioning. That is not our task at the moment, however.

Discourses in Conflict

I want to use two texts to illustrate how to contruct heteroglossic relations between discourses from an analysis of their different text-semantic patterns. These texts belong to two different social communities, each of which sees itself as opposed in social interests and viewpoints to the other: Christian fundamentalists who regard homosexuality as sinful and oppose full civil rights for gay citizens, and secular gay activists who oppose both the views of Christian fundamentalist groups and their right to write these views into law. There are clearly differences of values between these groups, and there are also differences, as we shall see, in how they present the-way-things-are-in-the-world.

Each of these texts shows its author to be aware of the divergence between his discourse and the discourse of the other community. Our analysis will show more specifically how that divergence arises from differences in thematic patterns and value orientations toward them, and how each discourse internally constructs its heteroglossic relations to the other. (This viewpoint, by the way, makes talk about 'authorial' belief or intention merely a customary metaphor; authors may make meaning in the context of the production of a text, but readers do this work in the context of interpreting it. Similarities in the meanings made on these two occasions are characteristics of the community's meaning-making practices, and not characteristics of authors, readers, or texts as such. Cf. Lemke 1989b on the semiotics of object-texts vs. meaning-texts.)

To appreciate more fully the larger system of heteroglossia in which these texts are interpreted in the community at large, we should also be aware that these are only two of many social discourse voices on the subject of homosexuality and gay rights. Fundamentalist Christian discourse, while relatively monolithic, still shows considerable diversity on these matters, including outright support of positive gay relationships (e.g. Johnston 1983). The larger community of mainstream Christian denominations has a very wide range of views, in relation to which those of the fundamentalist text we will read are fairly extreme. On the side of the gay community, the second text represents a fairly mainstream, majority view, but there are also some gay Christians who regard their homosexual orientations or actions as sinful, and some gay activists who would take a more radically critical view of the basic values of mainstream Christian discourse. Each of these communities has its own Discourses, and reads any text in relation to its own system of intertextuality, which in turn embodies its own beliefs and evaluative attitudes.

We will see that these texts explicitly invoke still other discourse formations about homosexuality and gay civil rights, ones that originate in still other communities: medical, psychiatric, psychological, sociological and legal discourses. We will see that in most cases it is not necessary to know a particular intertext in order to interpret the text we are reading: any (co-thematic) intertext of the relevant discourse formation will probably do just as well. It is the relevant thematic patterns we need to be familiar with, and the value stances associated with them by particular social discourse voices.

Text 1: The Discourse of the 'Moral Majority'

To suggest			1Aa
that	homosexuality is a sickness		1B
or that	it	is a physical condition	1Ca
		caused by biological facts	1Cb
rather than	an emotional and mental condition		1D
is highly blasphemous.			1Ab
The Bible tells us			2A
that	the cause of homosexuality is sin.		2B
	A person is not born a homosexual;		3A
	he becomes one according to his sinful will.		3B
A person lets sin and the devil take control of his life.			4

Our first text is the fifth paragraph of what its source (Liberty Home Bible Institute, n.d.) calls a 'commentary', presumably on the Christian *Bible*, though possibly on its topic, homosexuality.

I want to begin with a *dynamic reading*, taking the text phrase by phrase and attempting to see how we might make sense of it as we go, that is as we unfold the text in linear time. Normal visual reading is not generally quite so strictly linear, since we can and sometimes do see and process 'ahead' in the text when it is laid out visibly before us. The dynamic mode of interpretation is more usual for spoken language, but it is useful as a general analytical technique. It should always be complemented by *synoptic reading* in which, as literary criticism does, we interpret each part of the text in relation to the whole, frozen outside of the stream of time and the action of reading or hearing. Both modes of reading are extremes and somewhat artificial, and each produces different insights into text semantics and textual politics. We will read the second text in this chapter more synoptically.

I am also somewhat artificially extracting this text fragment from its surrounding text. For a dynamic reading, only the preceding text is relevant; for synoptic, both preceding and following text is. Our purpose here is to examine the process of meaning-making, rather than to achieve the fullest explication of the meanings that can be made with this particular text. As we get into the fragment, we will look back at the role of whatever precedes the phrase currently in focus.

'To suggest . . .' is a beginning [1Aa] which *projects* (Halliday 1985: 227–51) some discourse to follow (i.e. [1B], [C], and [D]), whether we take this to have been actually uttered or merely 'thought' (i.e. constructed in language without public utterance). It embeds the projected clause(s) in an infinitive phrase that stands here as a potential subject for some predicate. The *suggestion* we are about to hear is a suggestion about which something further, the predicate, will then be said (i.e. [1Ab]), completing a grammatical and semantic structural unit, the 1A clause. As is customary with beginnings, we are being set up for what is coming. The specific semantic content of this setting up comes from the semantic class of the verb 'suggest'. It is a verb, as we have seen, of mental or verbal process (cf. Halliday 1985: 106–12, 129–31) which contrasts with others such as 'assert' in a way which in fact constructs *orientational* meaning as well as *presentational*. That is, not only are we told that someone may be doing something (*suggesting*), but the writer has chosen to characterize this action for us in a way that makes the implied Sayer (*Suggester*) seem somewhat tentative about whatever he or she is about to say.

When we find out later [1Ab] that the writer considers such a suggestion a terrible thing to have made, we realize, retrospectively, that to have *asserted* it would have been even worse, that the negative evaluation of it is actually strengthened by choosing the word *suggest* (as if 'even to suggest, much less to assert . . .' is terrible), and that using the infinitive here allows this terrible deed to remain at least in the realm of the hypothetical (irrealis). As it stands, there is no actual Sayer identified; the infinitive requires no grammatical subject in this role. We will be left to wonder just who might suggest such a terrible thing.

At [1Aa], however, we do not yet know that this suggestion will be terrible, only that a supposition is being made that such a suggestion is possible. With [1B] we begin to hear the suggestion, 'that homosexuality is a sickness'. *Suggestions* are not normally a thematic topic (except possibly for linguists and philosophers), but *homosexuality* certainly is. There are in the community, and available to actual and potential readers of this text, quite a range of possible discourses about homosexuality, each of which constructs a particular set of thematic formations (statements about who is doing what, how one matter is related to another, etc.) and also constructs a set of orientational stances toward these thematic states-of-affairs (i.e. that they are possible or real, desirable or terrible, normal or surprising, etc.). Each of these discourses creates its own defined 'ideological-axiological' world in Bakhtin's terms (see Chapter 2, and recall that his 'ideological' would be better translated as 'ideational', i.e. thematic or presentational in my terms).

The bare proposition, a presentational or thematic semantic clause, [1B], does not yet tell us the stance of the writer towards it. We can well imagine at this point that he agrees with it, since it certainly seems, as expressed, to be a variant of the thematic evaluative pattern: /HOMOSEXUALITY IS SICK/, which is mainly orientational-attitudinal (i.e. we don't like homosexuality, we think it is bad) in its usage, but which still has to express some presentational meaning (namely that it is a characteristic or attribute of homosexuality that it is 'sick'). [1B] foregrounds the thematics a bit more, saying that it is 'a sickness'. It constructs an Identification relation (cf. Halliday 1985a: 112–28) between two thematic items, /HOMOSEXUALITY/ and /SICKNESS/ and at the same time (Halliday shows how usual this is, 1985: 115–18) a relation of Token to Type, that the one is a specific instance of the more general other.

It will turn out, however, that in this writer's discourse, while homosexuality is certainly considered bad, it is for reasons that are to be strongly distinguished from anything having to do with sickness, and the view that homosexuality is a kind of sickness is something to be rejected in the strongest terms. This text shows very well the importance of analytically distinguishing the presentational or thematic content of a discourse from the attitudes it constructs toward that content. Both of these basic discourse functions are performed in every semantic unit of the text, often by the same words, but it is still useful to distinguish them as distinct aspects of the meaning we make with the text.

The next clause constructs a thematic proposition that we can represent as:

/HOMOSEXUALITY — Tok/Val — [PHYSICAL CONDITION]/

where I am using a notation (Lemke 1983a, 1990a) based on Halliday's analysis of identifying clauses which relate a Token (the instance) to its Value (the type, class, or general case). Dynamically, in the text up to this point, we are still in the dark about the attitude to this possible state-of-affairs, and might well read it in isolation as a plausible and neutral element of a scientific discourse on the topic. We also need to take into account, however, the *organizational* dimension of meaning in this text. Clause [1Ca] is not isolated, but is grammatically and cohesively (cf. Halliday and Hasan 1976) linked to [1B] and to [1A].

The parallelism in wording between [1B] and [1Ca] is matched by the semantic parallelism in the thematic content of the two clauses, further strengthening their cohesion (cf. Hasan 1984a on cohesive harmony). The organizational relations here are signaled most explicitly by the conjunctions 'that . . . or that . . .' interpretable as being logically linked by *alternative-or* rather than *disjunctive-or*. That is, [1B] and [1Ca] are to be read as two different ways of saying more or less the same thing, rather than as mutually exclusive of one another. This makes sense in a thematic universe (i.e. in terms of intertexts) in which:

/SICKNESS — Tok/Val — [PHYSICAL CONDITION]/

The relevance of this thematic formation (i.e. thematic pattern shared by many such intertexts) is reinforced by [1Cb], which specifies this as a physical condition 'caused by biological facts', which would certainly be a commonplace of such a physicalist or medical discourse. So, in this possible discourse world, it is clear that if we consider homosexuality to be a sickness, we could clearly also consider it to be a physical condition caused by biological facts, since that is more or less what a sickness is in common sense discourse. So [1B] and [1Ca–b] are to be taken as two suggestions of more or less the same thing for the purposes of this text.

If we wish to interpret a little further, we might in fact wonder what further specific discourses are relevant to the implied thematic connection that 'homosexuality . . . is caused by biological facts.' Many readers might immediately read this against the background of many familiar intertexts, that is through the thematic pattern or formation of texts in which it is specifically *genetic* biological facts that might be said to cause homosexuality, but we have as yet no warrant in this text for doing so.

[1D] is introduced by the clearly disjunctive (more precisely *replacive*, Halliday 1985: 207–10) conjunction 'rather than', which sets up a thematic *contrast* between mutually exclusive alternatives. The specific alternative here is 'an emotional and mental condition'. Again the grammatical and lexical parallelism of the alternatives is very strong, 'homosexuality is a . . . condition' in which what is contrasted are the specifiers or *classifiers* of 'condition': /PHYSICAL-BIOLOGICAL/ vs. /EMOTIONAL-MENTAL/.

The text has now set up for us a contrast that we recognize as a common one in many possible intertexts. What the text has grammatically and lexically constructed for us is the salience or importance of this possible contrast for this text, for its discourse world.

When clause [1A] finally concludes with [1Ab], 'is highly blasphemous', the orientational meaning, the evaluative attitude toward the thematics that precedes it, is finally (and from the dynamic reading point of view, *retroactively*) established. I will not go through the complex process by which this happens grammatically (see Lemke 1988c for more detailed analysis of both these texts), but only point out that while what is 'blasphemous' grammatically is 'to suggest . . .' that semantically, it is the thematic proposition(s):

/HOMOSEXUALITY — Tok/Val — [PHYSICAL-BIOLOGICAL
CONDITION]/   (1)

on which the strongly negative evaluative attitude of /BLASPHEMOUS/ falls, transmitted to it, as it were, by the grammatical and cohesive links in the text, which at the same time reverse the effect on the other embedded proposition:

/HOMOSEXUALITY — Tok/Val — [MENTAL-EMOTIONAL
CONDITION]/   (2)

which is to be evaluated positively according to the discourse of this text (i.e. it is good to /SAY/ so, not necessarily good that it /IS/ so).

Even more importantly, what has been accomplished here in a single complex sentence is to set up and to *oppose* to one another (cf. Lemke 1988c) two different intertextual thematic formations (ITFs), that of texts which assert or assume (1), and that of texts which assert or assume (2). It should be clear that these two ITFs do not *have* to be set up as being *opposed* to one another; they could in some other text or set of texts be treated as *consistent* or compatible with one another, even as being simply *variants* of one another. That is obviously not the case in Text 1, however.

The word 'blasphemous' is striking. It occurs in a highly focal place in the sentence, in the most prominent New Information site and role (Halliday 1985: 274–81). It belongs, like most evaluative attributes (see Lemke, in preparation), to a semantic cline that is gradable by degrees, and it is of very high negative degree in Desirability just as a lexical item, and further strengthened by 'highly'. This extreme evaluation has the effect of even further contrasting the ITFs of (1) and (2) as *opposed*.

Of course it also has a thematic force of its own, a presentational meaning. That meaning has to be construed in relation to some set of intertexts, to some ITF in which we are likely to meet /BLASPHEMOUS/ in the company of the other thematic items in this text. This word has a fairly restricted distribution among ITFs; it belongs most often to texts we notionally classify as speaking a religious or theological discourse. We will see that this text goes on to construct such a discourse, so that we can at some later point be more certain that this is not merely metaphorical hyperbole. In fact the very next phrase of the text takes us into this *theological* ITF.

[2A], 'the Bible tells us', has, as do all clauses, its thematic meaning, which here is parallel to and also subtly in contrast with [1Aa]. *Tells*, contrasting with the parallel *suggests*, is another projective verb of Saying; orientationally, it is much higher on the scale of Warrantability. This is reinforced by the Sayer here being 'the Bible', which in this construction, in this ITF, is an authoritative Sayer. The Saying 'tells' is also *realis*, contrasting with the more irrealis *to suggest*. [2A] also does more attitudinal work in relation to [1Ab]. To blaspheme is to speak against or in contradiction to God; what the Bible says is, in this discourse, the very contrary, God's own word. So just as [1Ab] cast its negative evaluative attitude over [1B–C], so we expect that [2A] will introduce thematic propositions which are not only authoritative (high on Warrantability or certainty) but also present beliefs that it is Desirable to hold. We can thus further expect them to develop a discourse about /HOMOSEXUALITY/ (the *theological* ITF) which will contrast with that of [1B–C] (which from now on I will label as the *biomedical* ITF).

The grammatical organization which links [2A] and [2B] establishes [2B] as part of the approved thematics of the *theological* ITF. (Note that it might be more fully glossed as US Fundamentalist Christian Anti-Homosexual Theological ITF; as we are analyzing it here, it is specific to this text, but this text was produced in and is mainly consumed by a subcommunity for whom many similar intertexts are available, and for whom it would be read in relation to this common intertextual pattern.) Presumably [2B] and [3A–B] are also part of this ITF, but notice that [3A] is in fact a negation of /Persons are born homosexual/, which can easily be read as an instance of the *biomedical* ITF, in which it would be linked to [1C] by the common thematics of genetic biological determinism.

The cohesive parallelism of [3A] and [3B] again sets up a contrast between the denied *biomedical* thematics of [3A] and the approved *theological* (i.e. 'Biblical') thematics of [3B]. In fact [3B] for the first time gives us a thematic proposition about homosexuality from the viewpoint of this *theological* ITF which is recognizably framed in religious terms ('sinful'). [4] augments this, elaborating it with further signs of theological discourse ('sin', 'the devil'). In terms of orientational meaning, we have not only the heteroglossic opposition of the *biomedical* and *theological* ITFs being carried further here, and the construction of approval for the *theological* and condemnation of the *biomedical*, but we also have, within the *theological* thematics of [3B] and [4], further evaluative attitudes toward the state-of-affairs they present.

Becoming a homosexual, according to [3B], is the result (contrast with the causal explanation in [1Cb]) of 'sinful will', and in this discourse clearly the negative evaluative attitude toward the cause is extended to the effect. In [4] this is even stronger as far as the negatively valued cause is concerned ('the devil'), though one perhaps needs the semantic linkage between 'will' in [3B] and 'lets' in [4] to see why [4] does not in fact exonerate the homosexual of sin as the victim of a superior power, 'the devil'.

I can well imagine that some readers even at this point are a bit confused about the text's theological logic. Full understanding does require familiarity with the ITF through other intertexts (discussed in Lemke 1988c), in which it becomes clear that what is at stake here is whether the homosexual has willfully chosen this path (the claim of this *theological* ITF) or whether such persons have indeed no control over the matter (which is the conclusion the text would draw from the opposing *biomedical* discourse formation).

In Figure 3.1 I have tried to indicate some of the complexity of the heteroglossia in this text. There is one authorial speaking voice which ventriloquates (a Bakhtinian term) two discourse formations about /HOMO-SEXUALITY/. It does this by using two meta-discourse moves (in [1A] and [2A]), which are contrasted with one another. By this means, and others, it constructs two thematic formations about the topic, approving one and disapproving the other, sets these two ventriloquated voices (the one it identifies with and the one it rejects) in heteroglossic *opposition* to one another, and constructs within each a causal explanation for homosexuality, one of which does not morally condemn it, the other of which does. Figure 3.1 shows the meta-discursive component and the heteroglossic *opposition* of the two ITFs, as well as their internal thematics and how these contrast semantically. It does not show the other attitudinal meaning constructions, and it deliberately abstracts away from the particular textual organization of the ITF thematics (see Lemke 1983a for why this is useful).

I want to turn now more briefly to Text 2 to see how the heteroglossic relations among ITFs reflect, and help to constitute, the social relations among subcommunities. The texts of a community's dominant discourse formations construct relations of *Alliance, Opposition,* etc. (see Lemke 1988c) among various thematic views of the world, including the views of other communities and *their* discourses. So, from each text's or community's point of view, there are systematic relations among discourses, which we can see as essentially sociological and ultimately political relations. It is an essential feature of how these relations are constructed in discourse (first emphasized by Bakhtin) that they always involve *value judgments* about the discourse of others, and by extension, about other communities. So deep is the connection between the presentational and the orientational dimensions of meaning-making, between what we say the state of affairs is and how we judge it, that even saying that something *is*, is always already a judgment (of Warrantability). It may well be that in making meaning from a viewpoint, it is impossible for discourse not to imply judgments on all the Orientational dimensions, including Desirability.

Text 2: The Discourse of Gay Rights

Text 2 (see Figure 3.2) is drawn from the fourth to seventh paragraphs of an article published in the leading US gay magazine, *The Advocate* (Johnson 1984). Under the title, 'Gay as Religion: Free Thought in a Free Society', Johnson argues that restrictions on the civil rights of gays that are based on

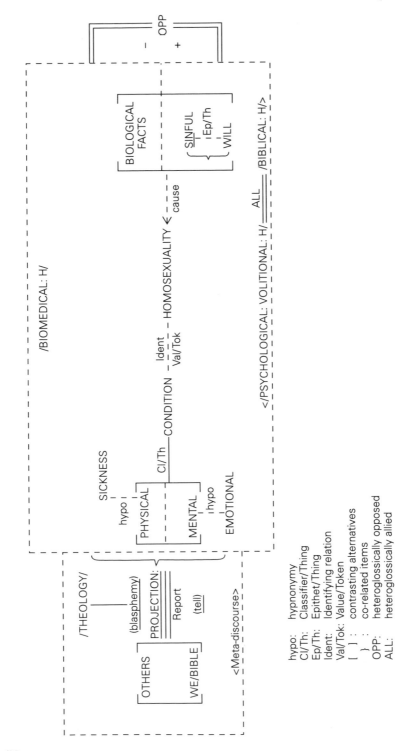

Figure 3.1

the religious objections of some Christian denominations to homosexuality contradict the constitutional separation of church and state in the US.

It is perhaps so obvious that we no longer take note of it, but the ideological basis of the right these denominations claim to write their particular beliefs into the common law is simply the presumption of their universal validity. Modernism, in order to supplant an older, religious worldview, found it necessary to adopt the principle that its truths too were inherently universal. Its truths, grounded in a scientific-rationalist worldview, were to take precedence over those of religion wherever the two were in conflict, but modernism could not challenge the principle that whatever was true was *ipso facto* universal. That step is only possible in the postmodernist view appropriate to a world in which no one cultural group has the power to enforce a claim to universality (though each may privately believe it). Moral relativism and moral tolerance are uneasy modernist allies, potentially corrosive of the fundamental modernist claim that *real truths* (i.e. those grounded in modernist science) *are* universal. Only the thin shield of the *fact/value* dichotomy prevents moral relativism from subverting scientific absolutism, the ground of modernist legitimacy. As we will see in later chapters, postmodernism gives up the defense of this ultimately untenable disjunction.

Meanwhile modernism continues its ancient war with religion, and particularly with absolutist, today 'fundamentalist', Christianity. As a result, there exists at present, in our own community, a readily invoked heteroglossic *opposition* between modernist, scientific discourse formations and surviving, pre-modern religious discourse traditions. (Of course 'mainstream' Christian discourse long ago made its accommodations with modernism, which is why it is the 'mainstream', and why it marginalizes and disparages fundamentalism.) In Text 1 we have seen this opposition at work between the *biomedical* and *theological* ITFs. In Text 2 the viewpoint is reversed, but a similar heteroglossic opposition is still constructed.

In lines [4A] and [4Ba] two consecutive words of the text, the informationally focal final word of [4A], 'religious', and the thematized first element of [4Ba], 'scientific', are not immediately or directly contrasted with one another. It is only against the background of the widespread cultural construction of their opposition as worldviews that we initially sense an incipient contrasting of thematic formations here. To see actually how this text constructs two ITFs and a heteroglossic opposition between them, we need to identify recurring thematic-semantic patterns in the text, and to listen as well for the evaluative stances the text's own voice takes toward them (see Lemke 1988c).

Without pursuing the analysis in detail, we can still readily see that this text constructs two discourses about /HOMOSEXUALITY/: one it labels that of *science*, the other that of *fundamentalism*. In the first, homosexuality is 'a normal variation'; in the second, it is a matter for 'serious objection'. In the first, claims are based on 'scientific observation'; in the second, on 'revealed' texts or 'superstitions'. Textual organizing and structuring devices such as

TEXT DISPLAY 2

	In 1984 the only remaining serious objection to homosexuality is religious.	4A
	Scientific observation and modern statistical surveying show	4Ba
that	homosexuality is a normal variation of sexual behavior in human beings	4Bb
	... ((SCIENTIFIC OBSERVATION)) has changed the way the modern world views sex.	4C
	We look scientifically.	4D
	We no longer look to ancient 'revealed' texts	4Ea
	to find facts about the world.	4Eb
	We look to the world ...	4F
	With that shift in methodology,	5Aa
	Old superstitions have been debunked ...	5Ab
	Thanks to ((SCIENTIFIC OBSERVATION)),	5Ba
	it can be shown	5Bb
that	homosexuals are not incarnated demons or witches,	5Bc1
	not criminals or spies ...	5Bc2
	Today homosexuality is understood to be a psychological condition,	6Aa
	a quirk of personality ...	6Ab
	a simple personal characteristic.	6Ac
	There is no evidence	6Ba
that	active homosexuals are mentally disordered or socially dysfunctional.	6Bb
	...	
	Certain religious groups, however, demand,	7Aa
	in spite of the evidence,	7Ab
that	this particular trait be singled out for special condemnation and blame.	7Ac

Figure 3.2

the uses of 'remaining/modern' [4A, 4Ba], 'changed/modern' [4C], 'look/ no longer look' [4D–F], 'shift' [5Aa], and 'today' [6Aa], set up the contrast between the two thematic formations. There is also textual parallelism, foregrounding specific thematic constrasts (e.g. 'texts/world' in [4E–F]).

Just as Text 1 used such expressions as 'blasphemous' and 'the Bible tells' to mark what was Warrantable and what was Desirable, what the text voice affiliated with or rejected, so Text 2 uses 'scientific' and 'superstitions' in the same ways. Note once again that simple clause or sentence-level grammatical analysis is not sufficient to analyze the range of thematic propositions to which these attitudinal markers apply. A complex text-semantic analysis is necessary, operating at the level of the thematic formations themselves (details in Lemke 1988c). A diagram of the main ITFs and their relations is given in Figure 3.3.

Just as in Text 1 it was not possible, in isolation, to interpret the meaning-contribution of clauses [1B–D] to the text, so in Text 2, for example, line [6Aa]: 'Today homosexuality is understood to be a psychological condition', seems, in isolation, to belong to the same thematic pattern as, say, [1D] from Text 1: '[homosexuality is] an emotional and mental condition'. In the context of the discourse formations that are being constructed and constrasted in these texts (and which define large sets of intertexts with similar thematics and viewpoints), however, these lines in fact instance completely different discourses about homosexuality. Line [1D] is interpretable in Text 1 only as an instance of its *theological* ITF, and as meaning /NOT-BIOLOGICALLY-DETERMINED/ but /WILLFULLY-CHOSEN/, whereas [6Aa] in context means roughly that homosexuality is a 'simple personal characteristic' rather than something 'demonic' 'criminal' or 'mentally disordered'. [6Aa] belongs to the *scientific* ITF of Text 2.

Note also that the *fundamentalism* discourse of Text 2 is not identical to the *theological* discourse of Text 1, nor is *biomedical* identical to *scientific*. If we really want to read these two texts in relation to one another, to *make* them intertexts of one another, then we need to look to still wider cultural discourse formations to do so. That is, we need to be able to use the larger social system of heteroglossia, the thematic, attitudinal and sociological relations among many texts in our community as a resource. We need, for example, to acquaint ourselves with the specific discourse of 'facultative psychology' that fundamentalists use as an alternative to mainstream 'liberal humanist' psychology in interpreting [1D]. We need to examine the possible relations between the discourse of biological determinism of homosexuality (which Text 1 opposes) to the 'Kinsey Report' science that seems to represent more closely the scientific worldview of Text 2. We need to understand the similarities and differences between how fundamentalist views of homosexuality are set forth in their own texts and how they are described by text voices opposed to their discourse.

We are now deeply involved in *textual politics*. The interpretation of these texts, from the meanings of particular phrases to the force of their overall arguments, depends critically on where we situate ourselves among the discourse viewpoints of our community. Which intertexts do we use to interpret these texts? What kinds of relations do we make between them? What discourse patterns do we construct that seem to us validly invariant from one text to another? Textual meaning is not separable in principle from the rhetorical contexts of production and use of a text. If the meaning of any fragment of a text, from a word to a sentence, is defined to be the *contribution* of that fragment to the meaning of some larger unit, then we can see the

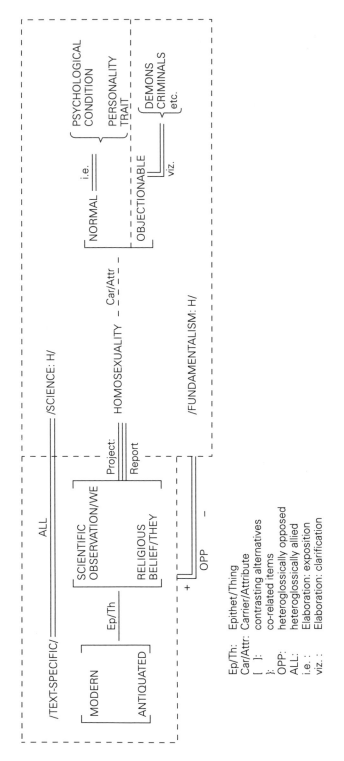

Figure 3.3

pointlessness of trying to circumscribe 'the meaning' of such fragments in isolation. Even when we resort to some notion of their most probable, frequent or 'unmarked' meanings, we are simply privileging *some* common contexts of use over others. The probabilities of co-occurrence of wordings and their larger textual, situational, and intertextual contexts is itself an essential resource for meaning-making. The very notion of meaning is vastly diminished if we neglect to model just *how* the meanings we make with wordings depend on these wider contexts.

Much the same holds true at a higher level. The social meanings of texts and discourses cannot be usefully isolated from their social contexts of production and use. Who speaks these ITFs, when, to whom, for what purposes, in whose interests and with what effects (not uniquely, but *typically*)? Ultimately we may concern ourselves with individual speakers, addressees and sequences of social events, but we can usefully do so only in relation to the typical patterns of such things in our communities. What *kinds* of persons speak these discourses? What subcommunities do they belong to? What are the interests of these communities? How do their interests and agendas conflict with those of other communities? What discourses do these other communities speak and on what occasions, with what typical effects? How are larger scale sociological relations between these communities, including relations of power and domination, enacted, maintained, strengthened, challenged, resisted and changed through these kinds of social events, these kinds of discourses? This is the very heart of textual politics.

I hope that the examples I have briefly presented in this chapter forcefully raise these issues. We will be deeply concerned with them in the rest of this book. In the next chapter I want to analyze portions of a few texts that reveal some central discursive ideologies of our contemporary society. In this chapter the texts may have allowed a certain distance; for most of you the issues and viewpoints were probably somewhat marginal to your central concerns, the discourse communities perhaps not ones you consider yourselves members of. In the next chapter, the central issue is the relation between discourses of expert knowledge and discourses of social policy. For most of us, it will hit very close to home – I hope.

Chapter 4

Technical Discourse and Technocratic Ideology

Introduction

In Chapter 3 we looked at some of the details of text semantics. We saw in microcosm the intimate interplay of thematic (*presentational*), attitudinal (*orientational*), and structural-cohesive (*organizational*) dimensions of meaning-making. All these aspects of meaning depend on the intertextual patterns through which we interpret our texts. Those patterns in turn characterize the discourse communities we belong to and their heteroglossic relations to other discourses and communities.

In this chapter we are going to examine further the political uses of discourse formations. We will document a single instance of a widespread and increasingly dominant political strategy in modern society: the transformation of discourses of expert knowledge into discourses of social policy. We will see that the political advantage of this *technocratic* strategy to those who practice it is that it presents policy as if it were directly dictated by matters of fact (thematic patterns) and deflects consideration of *values* choices and the social, moral and political responsibility for such choices. This strategy is associated with the political interests of a particular segment of a dominant élite (managers and experts), and its use represents a bid to wrest policy control from an older segment of that élite (owners of capital).

We need to consider first some of the characteristic features of *technical* discourse, particularly *thematic condensation* and *monologic orientation*. We will then see how transposing these discourse patterns and the value system associated with them from technical reports to policy recommendations enables technocratic discourse to accomplish its ends, at least with some readers. Finally, we will consider the sociological and political relations among the various communities that participate in the system of heteroglossia which links technical and technocratic discourse to more values-oriented policy discourses, both conservative and progressive.

The central text in our analysis will be a special publication of the United States Department of Education, entitled *What Works: Research About Teaching and Learning* (US Department of Education 1986), produced and widely circulated during the Reagan Administration. Despite its disclaimers, it has a clear political and ideological stance, and presents 'research findings' as objective facts that presumably have clear implications for action. It is mainly a technocratic text, but it also reveals some of the internal conflict among American conservatives between the new technocrats and the older conservative establishment.

In citing its 'Findings', *What Works* also cites the research from which they are drawn. Two of these research source texts will be included in our analysis. They were written by Herbert Walberg (1985), a prominent researcher in the field of education, who is best known for reanalyzing the results of large numbers of small research studies by statistical methods (research 'syntheses' or 'meta-analyses'), and for attempting to analyze educational 'productivity' by analogy with the methods of economics used in industry. One paper, by Walberg and two co-workers (Graue *et al.* 1983), reports one of these 'research syntheses' (on the role of parents in their children's educational success or failure). It was written for an audience of researchers and is almost purely technical in its discourse features. A second paper, addressed to an audience of education and policy leaders, mixes technocratic and technical discourse to make policy recommendations based on Walberg's research (Walberg 1985).

These three texts form a tightly linked intertextual set. Not only are they co-thematic (presenting the same thematic state of affairs about the world they construct), but each one explicitly cites its chronological predecessors in the text-chain. The texts differ however in the audiences they address, the values they emphasize, and in many specific features of their linguistic *registers* (for details see Lemke 1990b). They do not belong to quite the same genre, and we will explore some of the typical relations among the members of this *genre system* (Bazerman 1994 and cf. Lemke 1985 on co-actional texts).

I will focus on only a few thematic strands that run through these texts: mainly those that deal with the purported culpability of parents for their children's failure in school, and those in which conservative and middle-class social values are most in evidence, though always disguised as results of 'objective research'. Let's begin by examining some of the features of technical discourse as represented by the first paper in the text-chain.

Technical Features and Technocratic Functions

Consider first some of the most commonly noted grammatical features of technical discourse (e.g. Huddleston *et al.* 1968, Halliday and Martin 1993).

For example, there are relatively few processes of direct action (Halliday's Material Processes; cf. Halliday 1985 for the terminology of systemic functional grammar as used here and always capitalized) compared with abstract relations. Other types of Processes tend to be expressed as Participants in these relations (nominalization). Animate agents, especially the human researchers, tend not to appear. This often results from using agentless passive clause structures. The nominalized processes on the other hand are frequently reified and used as agents in the place of human agents. So for example, we find near the beginning of the research synthesis article (Graue *et al.* 1983: 351; hereafter *Synthesis*: 351): 'Enough of these programs have been evaluated to provide an overall assessment of their effectiveness'. There is no agent which has done the evaluation (and it certainly would not be Graue *et al.*); the process 'assess' is nominalized as a participant, as is the process-derived epithet 'effective'.

Just after this sentence, we find: 'Many large-scale sociological and economic studies show weak and inconsistent associations of educational outcomes with school-resource proxy variables'. This gives a first example of the ubiquitous 'studies show' or 'research proves' formula in which the process 'study', minus its (fallible) human Actor, is reified and made to do what the same or some other human Actor actually does. As Halliday (1967) and others have pointed out, nominalization is quite a useful grammatical strategy in Indo-European languages, whose resources for qualifying nouns (cf. the long noun phrase following 'show' above) and for setting them in abstract relations to one another far exceeds its machinery for doing this with processes directly represented by finite verbs. Nominalization is, I believe, only the most obvious special case of a more general feature of technical discourse that I will call *condensation*.

In brief, nominalization allows an entire activity, a Process complete with its typical Participants and Circumstances, to be understood merely by naming it with the process noun. The whole implied activity can then be qualified and related to other activities in a highly condensed manner. The complete activities, and thus the complete meanings, are only recoverable by readers familiar with the thematic formations of relevant intertexts in which the activities are explicitly presented. Discourse types that rely heavily on this strategy divide the world of potential readers into initiates and the uninitiated to a much greater degree than do other kinds of written expository texts.

Technical discourse is also dominated by third person forms. No 'I' speaks to a 'you', no space for dialogue, disagreement or differing points of view is opened. Even the solidary (inclusive) 'we' is absent, and only the authoritative authorial (exclusive) 'we' of multiple authorship is allowed. The world of technical discourse is a closed world which admits no criteria of validity outside its own. In Bakhtin's terms, it is a pre-eminently 'monological' discourse.

In its own terms, technical discourse minimizes its use of the interpersonal, exchange and dialogical resources of language because it claims to be a value-neutral, objective reportage of the facts. It claims to present facts, speaking for themselves, and not merely the inferences and judgments of researchers. Its general conclusions are meant to be universal, within the limits set for the subject. They are no more expected to make use of deictic Person than of deictic Tense; they are presented as true for all time and outside human dialogue or opinion, independent of the particular human agent who has happened upon 'the facts'. This historically and culturally specific ideology, which I will loosely call positivistic in the discussions below, is no more necessary to scientific practice than the discourse features I have sketched here are necessary to scientific discourse. Early science often made use of the Dialogue genre, and argued science as philosophy and theology had been argued before it. The features of technical discourse that the scientific community rationalizes in terms of their limited technical functions have also been shaped historically by a cultural ideology that sustains the role and image of science in society (cf. Latour 1987, 1988).

Both condensation and monologism in technical discourse serve to establish and maintain a social élite, its claims of privilege and its access to power. These strategies, once confined to technical and scientific discourse, have with the increased power and visibility of science come to be adopted into managerial and bureaucratic discourse, from which technocratic discourse itself emerges. I will return later, when we have analyzed some specific examples, to the general sociology of these discourses. First, let us consider in more detail what I consider to be the functionally pre-eminent characteristic of technical discourse: its extreme reliance on thematic condensation.

Thematic Condensation in Technical Discourse

For our first example, consider the second citation from *Synthesis* given in the previous section: 'Many large-scale sociological and economic studies show weak and inconsistent associations of educational outcomes with school-resource proxy variables'. We might ordinarily say that this clause 'presumes a great deal of background knowledge', but of what does that 'knowledge' actually consist? It consists of a pattern of meanings, semantically realized in language, and held in common by this text and by many, many others. In fact it consists of several such intertextual thematic formations. What are we to make, for instance, of 'large-scale' in relation to 'sociological and economic studies'? We must have read other texts in which it is made clear that 'large-scale' in the thematic formations where such studies are talked about refers not at all to spatial extension, but to the large numbers of 'subjects' or 'cases' that are included in a statistical analysis. Lexical items have a wide range of potential meanings in relation to other lexical items (cf. Hasan

1985, 1986a), but their actual use-meanings in a text depend more directly on their place in a particular thematic formation, that is their field-specific semantic valences (Lemke 1983a, 1990a). 'Weak' and 'inconsistent' here also have such field-specific meanings, and it is only familiarity with the thematic formations of statistical research methodology that enable us to read 'weak associations' as 'statistical correlation coefficients in the range 0.0 to about 0.4'.

What are we to make of 'educational outcomes' unless we know that a statistical correlation must be between two quantities, and that the outcome of education is most often quantified by student test scores? Again, this 'knowledge' is simply familiarity with a repeated pattern of semantic connections between lexical items and their field-specific near-synonyms (together, abstractly, the *thematic items* of a formation), always expressed in language (though also expressible through visual semiotic representations and specialized extensions of natural language semantics such as mathematics). Finally for 'school-resource proxy variables' we need quantities that can stand in for estimates of the educational resources of a school. This last is not as easily retrieved from intertextual sources as was student test scores, and in fact examples are given in the remainder of the sentence: 'such as expenditures per pupil and school size'. These in turn also assume familiarity with further thematic formations, not just those that tell us that the nominalized 'expenditures' is an instance of the thematic formation <SCHOOL OFFICIALS— SPEND—MONEY—FOR—ITEMS>, but the narrower set of intertexts from which we could learn that schools with more pupils generally are considered to have greater educational resources.

Of course, all discourse makes sense in relation to some such set of thematic intertexts, but in technical discourse the degree of condensation, that is, the number of unexpressed thematic items and relations that are needed to make sense of those that are expressed, is much greater than for other discourse types. To illustrate, let me take as our second example of thematic condensation the single most important sentence of *Synthesis* (as defined by the criteria of the genre of the technical research article), its main conclusion:

> The main conclusion of the present synthesis is that school-based home-instruction programs are consistently favorable and have, on average, large effects on children's academic learning.

Note, in passing, the absence even here of an authorial human Actor to draw the conclusion. It is as if 'of the present synthesis' were a 'subjective genitive' in classical linguistic terminology, as if the synthesis draws its own conclusion about itself. Elsewhere in the article we are told what 'school-based home-instruction programs' are. This nominal group, whose principal thematic item is 'home-instruction' condenses many variations on the theme: <PARENTS—

[PROCESS]—CHILDREN—AT HOME>, where the Processes themselves condense activities like reading aloud, discussing a TV program, setting aside time for homework, etc. Obviously we might take 'children's academic learning' to be similarly complex, but in fact it is just a local synonym for students' test scores – until it is extracted from its context here, when it will be taken by all readers who do not know its exact origins to mean much more than it does.

Note that even 'test score' condenses a complex process in which someone writes down questions and problems, students answer and solve them under particular conditions, a teacher or someone else decides what answers are correct and in what degree, and a quantitative scheme is set up that usually counts each separate question as of equal numerical value to each other, and someone adds up the number correct and perhaps applies a formula to convert the result to a standard form. Expand the condensation 'test score' into such a narrative and dozens of critical questions arise concerning the values and validity of the practices. Condense it all down to 'test score' and there is perhaps only a general reservation about the importance of test results in education. Go further and relexicalize it (in the context of a thematic formation already in use in the text) as 'children's academic learning' and all trace of the critique-evoking potential is lost (except perhaps for those who hate children, are against learning or are anti-academic).

We have hardly yet touched the major condensations of this sentence. What do we make of 'consistently favorable'? To whom and in what ways? To expand this we need to refer to the first sentence in the 'Results' section of the text (obligatory in this genre): 'Calculations showed that 91 percent of the comparisons favor treated groups'. These 'calculations', here reified grammatically as an Agent, are nowhere explicitly described in the text, and must be inferred by the expert intertextually. A less intertextually expert reader can still construe the rest of the sentence on the standard thematic pattern of statistical research methodology: <COMPARE—NUMERICAL INDEX—OF TREATED GROUP—WITH NUMERICAL INDEX—OF CONTROL GROUP>. 'Favor' has to mean that the index, usually the mean test score, of the treated group is greater than that of the control or untreated group. 'Treated' means that in <PARENTS—[PROCESS]—CHILDREN—AT HOME> the Process was the 'treatment'. Note, by the way, that there is no end to possible thematic expansions; there are no ultimate, irreducible 'semantic primitives' (except perhaps those that underlie grammatical relations). Any thematic item can be, and to be construed *must* be expanded through a thematic formation. What is at stake in highly condensed discourse is the accessibility for readers of the appropriate formations and the issue of *which* formations the text proposes as being adequate for (canonical) expansion.

That leaves us with 'have large effects', which here does not have its most common meaning, for 'effects' is used in this article and in this sort of research generally in a specifically quantitative sense. For example, the title of Table 4, which covers a full two and one-half pages of this 10 page article and which to the technically expert reader contains most of the specific content of the article (far more than the less than one-half page devoted to explicit discussion of its contents), is: 'Analysis of Variance and Covariance of Effect Sizes'. The table lists, among other data, these 'effect sizes' to two decimal places. What then is meant by a 'large' effect? Large compared to what? In fact, as established in the other article by Walberg (1985), and used in *What Works*, it means large compared to the quantitative 'effect' of socio-economic status in similar studies. This is in fact indirectly stated in *Synthesis* (p. 351) at the outset:

> Other research suggests that specific and alterable behaviors of parents toward their children such as intellectual stimulation in the home environment are still more strongly predictive of cognitive development than are such proxy variables as family SES and size.

Again 'research' is making the suggestions, and 'suggests' is itself a lexical realization of low modal Warrantability (contrasting, for example, with 'show'; see Chapter 3), reminding us of the proper cautiousness of truly 'objective' research. We see again the 'home instruction' thematic pattern, and the quantitative comparison comes now in the form 'more strongly predictive of', which fits with yet another thematic formation of statistical research and can be paraphrased as 'are more highly correlated with' and 'have larger statistical effects on outcome measures of'. An entire semester course or an introductory statistics textbook is condensed in the network of thematic formations needed to make these connections explicit. To complete even this bit of the picture, we would also have to be able to expand 'cognitive development' (except that again it is just another synonym for test scores) and 'family SES', which is someone's guess at a single quantitative measure of socioeconomic status.

If you have not yet made sense of the article's main conclusion, it is that the reason why the children of the poor do badly on tests in school is much more because their parents do not give them proper intellectual stimulation (and a few other things, such as middle-class social values, see below) than because of the social position of their family and its poverty, or the lack of resources in their neighborhood's schools. Condensation does a remarkable job of hiding the implicit ideology in this thesis, even from relatively sophisticated readers of purely technical discourse. Indeed it is hidden so well that separate articles by Walberg (e.g. Walberg 1985) were needed to bring it into policy discourse.

What functions does this high degree of condensation serve, other than making it easier to construct relations among nominalized processes and process-defined quantities? Most obviously, it makes every scientific text critically dependent on the canonical thematic formations with which it assumes the reader to be familiar. (Note that it is only the common semantic patterns, not specific individual intertexts that are needed.) Technical discourse is opaque even to the intelligent reader armed with a good technical dictionary, unless he or she is familiar with the semantics of the needed formations. Even an acquaintance with the historical texts in which these formations originated may not help, for they have been revised in each generation, and codified in 'canonical' form in the textbooks. As George Markus (1987) has pointed out, there is no hermeneutics of natural science, in the sense that technical texts are not 'open to interpretation' the way philosophical, literary or most other texts are. For most texts of significance in our society, it is necessary to decide *how* they are to be read, including how they are to be read intertextually in relation to other specific texts. Technical texts exist within a system of reading practices that specifies uniquely one and only one canonical interpretation in terms, not of specific other texts at all, but directly in terms of standard intertextual thematic formations.

A taste for brevity, for mathematical expression, and for condensation are all part of the technical mode of discourse, one which can presume that all licensed readers will read a text in terms of the canonical thematic formations. Canonical reading is what makes high degrees of condensation, including mathematical expression, possible without losing the reader altogether. It serves another obvious function, however: to make technical discourse the exclusive property of an initiated élite. To be self-taught in theoretical science or advanced mathematics is extremely rare compared to what is possible in other fields. To read and use technical discourse one *must* have learned the canonical formations. In history, in literature, even in most of the social sciences, you can learn from reading original source texts. In the natural sciences, and all truly technical fields, the textbook has become essential.

Of course, the textbook is not enough in most cases. Very few people learn science from textbooks without teachers, and very few learn it even with teachers. Someone must translate the language and semantics of the technical thematic formations into more familiar terms, as good teachers (and few textbooks) do (Lemke 1990a). Someone must open the door from the inside. Technical élites are maintained not by the secrecy of their discourse, which they proudly publish to all the world, but by their control of the education which supplies the thematic keys to interpreting it.

The opacity of *technical* discourse to the uninitiated permits *technocratic* discourse to use the prestige and mystique of science to win advantage in policy debate, but it also obliges the technocrats to transform technical discourse into something that is comprehensible to a wider audience. This transformation frees elements of technical discourse from their canonical contextualization and redefines them in ways that better serve technocratic values and interests. We turn now to an analysis of value orientations in technical and technocratic discourse, and the value implications of the technocratic appropriation of technical discourse.

Analyzing Orientational Meaning

As discussed in Chapter 3, *orientational* meaning includes all those aspects of meaning in a text or discourse by which it orients itself toward potential addressees, toward its own presentational content, and in the social system of heteroglossic discourse voices of its community generally. Orientational meaning is most fundamentally about social relationships: how one discourse voice constructs its relationships to others. The social phenomenon of heteroglossia, that different subcommunities speak with discourse voices that take particular evaluative stances toward their own and others' constructions of reality (i.e. their presentational meanings), unifies the processes of establishing relationships to addressees and audiences with those of taking evaluative stances toward the ideational content of our own and others' discourses.

Let's begin with a focus on how a text constructs an evaluative stance toward the ideational content it is presenting: how texts say and imply in their situational and intertextual contexts what they regard as good and bad, desirable and undesirable, proper and improper, warranted and doubtful, normal and unusual (see Chapter 3 and Lemke 1989c, 1992a, in preparation).

Orientational analysis asks how a positive or negative value of some degree is assigned to a thematic item, relation or formation. How are chains of positively and negatively valued elements constructed across texts? How are value-laden items or formations linked in terms of their values? How are whole formations set in value oriented relations of alliance or opposition to one another (as in the analysis in Chapter 3)? What happens to the value orientations of thematic elements when they are shifted from one formation or discourse voice to another – as for example from technical to technocratic discourse?

Let's examine the second paragraph of the *Synthesis* article with a specific aim: to identify two value chains and the discourse strategy by which they are cross-linked. This will provide a sense of how, over much longer stretches of text, global orientational patterns are woven from simple value strands (for the notion of semantic chains in a text, see Halliday and Hasan 1976, and for the ways in which these are interconnected through a text, Hasan 1984a and Lemke 1994b).

Look first at the value chain for high/low correlations, expressed in a number of different ways here:

Many large-scale sociological and economic studies show *weak and inconsistent associations* of educational outcomes with school-resource proxy variables such as expenditures per student and school size, and *relatively moderate and consistent amounts of variance associated* with student background variables such as socioeconomic status (SES) and family size (McDermott 1976). Other research suggests that specific and alterable behaviors of parents toward their children such as intellectual stimulation in the home environment are *still more strongly predictive* of cognitive development than are such proxy variables as family SES and size (Walberg and Marjoribanks 1976).

(Graue *et al.*, 1983)

This orientational semantic chain, the <CORRELATION> chain (consisting of the italicized phrases in the text), shows a clear progression from negative through low positive to high positive value, strictly within the technical value orientation. In this kind of technical discourse, high correlations ('association' 'associated variance'), large-scale studies and high predictivity are positively valued and their opposites are negatively valued. Each element in this chain, regarded now as a thematic element, defines a relation between two other elements. One of those elements is in each case a positively valued member of a second thematic chain <LEARNING>, represented in the first two instances of <LEARNING—CORRELATES—[to DEGREE]—WITH—[FACTORS]> by 'educational outcomes' and in the third by 'cognitive development'. In fact all these mean no more than 'test scores'. The other element in each case belongs to a third thematic chain <FACTORS>, which is constructed by this text (i.e. it is not already part of a canonical ITF). Its members would hardly be recognized as forming a chain on purely lexical or general semantic grounds, or even intertextually within this field of research. It is constructed by being put into a common semantic relation to the other elements of this little formation. Consider the elements of this crucial third chain now in terms of value orientations:

Many large-scale sociological and economic studies show weak and inconsistent associations of educational outcomes with *school-resource* proxy variables such as *expenditures per student* and *school size*, and relatively moderate and consistent amounts of variance associated with student background variables such as *socioeconomic status* (SES) and *family size* (McDermott 1976). Other research suggests that specific and *alterable behaviors of parents* toward their children such as *intellectual stimulation in the home* environment are still more strongly predictive of cognitive development than are such proxy variables as family SES and size (Walberg and Marjoribanks 1976).

(Graue *et al.*, 1983)

What we see now in value terms depends on whose value system we assume. From the point of view of a parent, we might expect that the first three *factors* would be fairly strongly positive. Socioeconomic status is good when it is high, bad when it is low (as assumed also in the text's orientation), and larger or smaller family size is considered better or worse depending in part on social class and ethnic tradition. The suggestion of altering parents' behavior toward their children is likely to be regarded rather negatively on its own terms, and intellectual stimulation in the home will be good, with a priority depending on the family's own values.

What is happening in this text, however, is that technical value orientations are being used to rerank the value priorities of other thematic items. The high technical value of strong <CORRELATIONS> is being equated in this text with the importance of a <FACTOR>. When this is linked thematically to a common 'good' <LEARNING>, it denigrates the value of what is 'not important to learning' and elevates what is important, but now 'important to' is being defined only as 'strongly correlates with'. The resulting ranking of factors runs counter to what we can expect (and the authors would probably expect) to be the values of parents, and even of many other educators. We are told that money spent on education has relatively little to do with students' learning and that lower class students don't do much worse than upper-middle class students in school. The authority of 'many large-scale . . . studies' is offered for these assertions. A critical reader might well consider the absurdity of these studies' conclusions as authority for doubting the reliability of social science research.

If the implications of 'alterable behaviors of parents' are not likely to be positive for parents (who are of course not expected to be reading a research journal article which would be opaque to them), this notion is nonetheless highly valued technocratically. It represents an instance of the transformation of a technical value into a technocratic one. 'Alterable behaviors' are valued in technical discourse not just because of their high correlations with test scores, but directly, as I will explain below. The particular example here, 'intellectual stimulation', is likely to mitigate any negative reaction to 'alterable behaviors' on the part of a middle-class reader, but to see what is meant we need a little contextual help (from elsewhere in this text):

> Poverty and family size, themselves correlated, both predict less intellectual stimulation in the home environment as well as lower levels of cognitive development (Walberg and Marjoribanks, 1976).
>
> (Graue *et al.*, 1983)

This may seem to contradict what was said in the main paragraph, but initiates in statistical methods will see that it need not. What is clear in this sentence, so full of negative valuations, is that 'research shows' that there is a serious lack of intellectual stimulation in poorer families. Similar statements about the lack of full language development in poor homes turned out to conceal enormous ignorance of dialect and discourse style differences that correlate with social class. Since most intellectual stimulation in middle-class homes is verbal, the same ignorance may be at work here. In any case, it should now be clear that what is being said in the text raises very controversial values issues, and that different value systems are indeed in conflict in reacting to the text's apparently 'objective' technical statements.

I want to complete the analysis of the positive value status of 'alterable behaviors' in these discourses. Just below the last cited sentence, we read:

> Although poverty and family size are not easily changed on a mass scale, the behaviors of parents may be favorably altered, if instructional materials are made available.
>
> (Graue *et al.*, 1983)

In the technical discourse of research, a factor or variable that can be altered or 'manipulated' is positively valued because it means that experimental studies can be done that systematically vary that factor. Otherwise one must simply hope to find cases where the factor takes on different values, with no hope of systematic experimental control. When this principle is carried over into the technocratic discourse of social engineering, 'alterable' factors are valued over those 'not easily changed' for a different reason and in a different sense. From a political perspective, conservatives and technocrats alike find it not in their interests to contemplate the extremely large capital expenditures, or the radical transformations of class relationships, necessary to change the effects of socioeconomic status (SES) or eliminate poverty. It is in their interests to say that there is a cheaper way, and to give great emphasis to 'research findings' that support this position, and none to those that might discredit it.

At this point we clearly need an examination of technocratic discourse itself, for which we can turn to some of the texts that appropriate the conclusions of *Synthesis*.

Technocratic Discourse and Its Ideology

In the Introduction to *What Works*, Chester Finn, Jr, then Assistant Secretary for Research and Improvement in the Department of Education, sets out a brief version of what I take to be the principal ideology of technocratic discourse:

> If we would have [our] actions be as well-informed as possible, in situations where we do not have knowledge we can reasonably allow our actions to be informed by 'true opinion', by what informed people judge to be the 'most likely story'. In this volume, as you will see, we draw upon the knowledge and opinions of both modern scholars and of distinguished thinkers of earlier times.

The value-laden thematic chain here includes 'well-informed', 'informed', 'true opinion', and 'knowledge'. These values of technical discourse are transposed here to support the premise of a technocracy.

Technocratic discourse argues for action and policy based on particular opinion regarding what it calls 'facts' and from which it draws necessary or obvious consequences without explicit discussion of value choices. Its value system is an implicit one, largely fashioned from the transposed values of technical discourse, but made to serve the interests of a managerial class. The technocratic élite claims a right to rule on the grounds of its ability to use expert knowledge to solve social problems.

As in *What Works*, however, technocratic discourse does not wish to be read as just one more opinion regarding policy. It wishes to place itself 'above the fray', as a supplier of 'facts', neutral and objective, free of all interests and values except truth, which *all* parties *must* take into account in deciding policy. In their prefaces to *What Works*, President Reagan and then Education Secretary Bennett emphasize that the proper role of the US government is merely to supply information, not to influence local educational policy decisions. Here is Finn's version of this theme:

> *Why does the report contain so few specific recommendations about actions that should be taken?*
>
> ... The appropriate design and implementation of [education] policies, practices, and actions will differ according to local conditions and it is not the place of the federal government to interfere. ... The purpose of this volume is to provide reliable information that people can, if they wish, put to use in various ways. In most instances, the reader will rapidly be able to visualize some implications for action of findings that we have included.

A recommendation can be phrased grammatically as a description just as easily as an order can be worded as a question. If it is so easy for readers to 'visualize some implications for action' of what are presented as research 'Findings', it is because they are presented in a discourse frame that makes them directly readable as prescriptions. Here are a few examples from the text:

> Children get a better start in reading if they are taught phonics.
>
> The most effective way to teach writing is to teach it as a process of brainstorming, composing, revising, and editing.
>
> Student achievement rises significantly when teachers regularly assign homework and students conscientiously do it.

This is the dominant pattern in the wording of 33 of the 41 statements of research 'Findings' in *What Works*. For comparison, the only one of the 41 that reads as a neutral description is (p. 33):

Children's understanding of the relationship between being smart
and hard work changes as they grow.

The 'value-plus-practice' pattern seen in the other examples is a special
case of the general value-construing strategy that characterizes technocratic
discourse. The practices are recommended indirectly through the 'Findings'
because they are said to have a proven (or at least empirically supported)
causal relation to some otherwise positively valued 'good', such as 'achievement', 'success', 'learning', 'higher test scores', 'more effective education' and
so on. If the correlations are not interpreted as causal relations, the implications for action and policy are weakened significantly (see example below).

Technocratic discourse relies as much on the 'hard sciences' as on the
soft, and its model for argument is based on positivistic science's claims to
identify true causes. In every case, technocratic discourse begins with an
action it covertly wants to recommend as policy, and then cites 'research
evidence' and 'studies' which show that this action is a necessary cause of
something else that is positively valued by those to be convinced. No argument is made concerning the value of the outcome nor any as to value
choices regarding means. The argument is only that the covertly recommended means are necessary to the unargued ends. What is argued for is
only the value of the evidence by which this necessity is established ('reliable
research') and the value of basing action and policy on expert knowledge.
This form of argument is a regular discourse pattern in technocratic texts.

Another distinctive feature of technocratic texts is the way in which they
incorporate condensations from technical discourse without requiring that
the condensations be expanded in order for the text to be meaningful to the
reader. As we have seen, technical condensations require canonical intertextual
expansion by a trained expert reader, and render technical texts opaque to
all other readers. When they are incorporated in technocratic texts, however,
a sense is constructed for them that does not require a reader even to recognize them as condensations. In fact, the technically expert reader who
does so and expands them intertextually may well find that the arguments
which seem so convincing on the surface (i.e. without the expansions) are
entirely unconvincing with them. I will present an extended example of this
in the next section.

A third distinctive feature of technocratic texts is that they are less
monological than are technical texts. Although they do not raise value-choice
issues, they may pose thematic alternatives between what they would call
'different interpretations of the same facts'.

The final characteristic feature of technocratic discourse that I wish to
note here is its pervasive denigration of common sense. This theme establishes a value orientation in both technical and technocratic discourse in
favor of reasoning and explanations in technical terms that are comprehensible
only to the initiate and against common sense accounts accessible to everyone. I have studied this feature as it appears in the discourse of scientific

education (Lemke 1983b, 1989a, 1990a). It functions there to undermine the confidence of students in their own ability to reason in domains where a technical discourse has been set up, and discourages them from trying to bring their ordinary experience to bear on such matters. In general, it helps to establish a heteroglossic opposition between 'science' and 'common sense' (with a strong value bias in favor of science) that is ideologically useful in getting the public to defer to the 'scientific knowledge' of a technical élite (cf. similar analyses in Latour 1987).

We need look no further for an instance of this theme than the discussion in *What Works* of classroom education in science:

> Scientific explanations sometimes conflict with the way students may suppose that things happen or work . . . Unless a teacher corrects [their] intuitive assumption by having the students perform an experiment, and see the results, the students will continue to trust their intuition, even though the textbook or the teacher tells them [otherwise] . . . In this way experiments help students use the scientific method to distinguish facts from opinions and misconceptions.
> (US Department of Education 1986: 23)

The value loadings here set 'scientific explanations', 'experiments', 'scientific method' and 'facts' against 'students may suppose', 'intuitive assumption', 'intuition' and 'opinions and misconceptions'. Note that science 'explains' but students only 'suppose', that teachers and textbooks 'correct' and 'tell', and that 'opinions' are linked to 'misconceptions' when both are opposed to 'facts'. Above all it is negatively valued that students should 'trust their intuition', which is opposed to having them 'use the scientific method'.

In reality, students do not usually change their common sense ways of reasoning about events just because they have seen an 'experiment'. Contrary to the ideological claim of Positivism, the 'facts' do not speak for themselves, nor do they judge between rival theories. Until students have mastered the teacher's and textbook's technical thematic formations, they will not even be able to discern which features of the experiment are relevant to the technical argument. One does not just 'see the results'. We see as meaningful only the meaning-patterns we construct using some social formation, commonsensical or technical (see Lemke 1990a for analyses of such cases, especially pp. 144–8).

The general principle, common to technical and technocratic discourse alike, which is operating here is that there are unobvious, hidden causes knowable only in technical terms which are the true explanations of phenomena. The consequence of this viewpoint is to oppose technical discourse and common sense, valuing the former and devaluing the latter. Technocratic discourse can then use this principle to claim the 'rightness' of the 'necessary actions' it puts forward in the form of 'causes' and through which it seeks to dominate policy.

Technocratic Discourse Strategies: The Case of 'Home Curriculum'

In Walberg's 1985 article addressing educational policy leaders (hereafter *Productivity*), we can find (p. 24) a statement in the value-plus-practice format, founded on his own technical results in *Synthesis* (Graue *et al.* 1983) regarding the 'alterable curriculum of the home':

> ... school–parent programs to improve academic conditions in the home have an outstanding record of success in promoting achievement. What might be called, 'the alterable curriculum of the home', is twice as predictive of academic learning as is family socioeconomic status. This curriculum refers to ... joint critical analysis of television viewing and peer activities, deferral of immediate gratifications to accomplish long term human-capital goals ... [among a list of at least seven specific practices for parents]. Cooperative efforts by parents and educators to modify these alterable academic conditions in the home have strong, beneficial effects on learning.

We find in this extract the value-labeling: 'outstanding ... success ... achievement', and later 'strong, beneficial effects', and the obviously recommended list of practices. The positive value terms are taken for granted, and the list of practices is linked to them because they are 'a curriculum' that 'promotes' and 'is ... predictive of' these valued outcomes, in fact 'twice as predictive' as a factor (socioeconomic status) that stands here for an alternative policy. The value argument lies entirely within the realm of (transposed) technical values (note again the positive value of high degrees of correlation). The argument for the value of the practices links them quasi-causally to the valued outcomes, but no argument is made concerning the value choice implications of the practices themselves.

The list of recommended practices in fact is notably biased towards middle-class values and against at least what middle-class people imagine lower-class values to be (e.g. immediate gratification, uncritical televiewing, lack of supervision of peer activities). How 'alterable' are the 'behaviors of parents toward their children' when those behaviors reflect class and social group values that differ from those of upper-middle class people of northern European descent? There are many other value systems in the world that do not regard higher test scores as more important than children's happiness, free play and independence, or even amusement, that see negative consequences of excessive parental supervision and abhor a preoccupation with critical analysis and the philosophy of 'delayed gratification' that sacrifices human happiness to capital accumulation. Apart from all these questions, how effective can these prescriptions actually be if they are based solely on statistical correlations, outside the framework of a detailed explanatory theory? A brief look at this question will provide us an opportunity to observe the effects of concealing condensations in the transformation of technical to technocratic discourse.

In *Synthesis*, whose findings provide the 'evidence' for Walberg's technocratic policy argument, the bulk of the research results appear only in a supercondensed form, the article's statistical tables. A *technical* reading of those tables shows, for example (Table 4: 358), that of the approximately 120 studies of home-intervention programs on which all the claims are based, only 22 lasted even as long as one semester, and 94 lasted less than six weeks. Any educational researcher knows that the claims being made on the basis of this data are meaningful only if long term improvements in academic performance can be achieved. Any special interest by parents in students' work is likely to produce a short term improvement which may not last, or may hit a plateau fairly quickly. Table 4 shows that as the programs lasted longer, the size of their effects decreased, with those lasting the full semester having an effect size *no larger at all* than the benchmark, socioeconomic status differences, and a significant probability of actually not being any higher than the comparison group which was not in the program at all. This last information is contained in an asterisk, whose explanation is several pages earlier, but would have been noted as a matter of course by an expert familiar with this technical register. In reference to these rather important 'facts' the text says only (*Synthesis*: 355): 'Programs . . . lasting five to six weeks rather than shorter or longer lengths of time showed larger comparative effects on average.' Reference to the table shows that this is true, but refers to only three of the 120 studies, and represents a radical departure for those three from the otherwise smooth and expectable downward trend of effects with increasing length of the program, as would be expected if the effects were small and temporary. It is far more likely that those three studies represent a statistical fluctuation, a fluke, with their effect sizes from three to six times bigger than those in the immediately adjacent categories of time length for the interventions, than that they represent a 'magic length' of time to produce the largest possible effects. The technically expert reader brings to a critical reading of technocratic discourse just this capacity to expand the condensations in a technical text on which technocratic claims are based. Other readers generally do not.

By the time this matter finds its way into the technocratic policy discourse of *Productivity* (p. 25), it has become:

> Although the average effect [of the programs] was twice that of socioeconomic status, some programs had effects ten times as large . . .
> Since few of the programs lasted more than a semester, the potential for those sustained over the years of schooling is great.

This last claim is either disingenuous or technically incompetent in relation to even a cursory examination of the data in Table 4 of *Synthesis*, on which it is based.

The weakness of the *technical* argument can be glossed over or even reversed in its *technocratic* version because the technocratic discourse does not even alert the general reader to the condensations which, for the technical reader, lie behind it. What we regard as 'the facts' here, or in any argument, depends very much on how we expand the condensations that lie behind any discourse that purports to establish what those facts are. Technocratic discourse not only appropriates the prestige and the 'facts' of technical discourse, but in doing so it also conceals the essential condensations of technical discourse. The deceptions of technocratic discourse do not depend so much on the non-technical reader's inability to expand these condensations (which would be true in purely technical discourse also), but on its making those condensations largely *invisible*. Non-technical readers do not even suspect that there is something important missing, something they need to know to evaluate technocratic arguments. Technocratic discourse takes condensed technical discourse and purveys it to readers as if it were not condensed at all. It is this ultimately simple discourse strategy which enables technocratic discourse to tailor the apparent scientific 'facts' to the needs of its policy arguments.

In *What Works* (p. 7) great prominence is given to research findings about the 'Curriculum of the Home':

> ... What parents do to help their children learn is more important to academic success than how well-off the family is.
>
> Parents can do many things at home to help their children succeed in school. Unfortunately, recent evidence indicates that many parents are doing much less than they might... When parents of disadvantaged children take the steps listed above, their children can do as well at school as the children of more affluent families.

Just below, in very small print, three articles by Walberg are cited in evidence. Here, the condensations are entirely hidden, except for the citations and what they imply to the expert reader. For all others, and certainly for the readers to whom *What Works* is addressed, there is nothing apparently missing, no opacity as in truly technical discourse to signal that we need to know something more in order truly to understand what is being said to us.

Whatever élitist function condensations may serve in technical discourse, concealing them in technocratic discourse only further enhances the power of the technocratic voice. Having read the surface message of this particular text, why should we be concerned to provide more financial resources to poor school districts when the parents could be solving the problems by acting more middle-class with their kids? Why should we take seriously sociological arguments that educational opportunites must be biased against the poor, when it's just a matter of 'alterable' parental behavior patterns?

All of us, particularly educators who recommend *critical literacy* and reflective reading practices, need to understand just how difficult it is to read technocratic discourse critically. This discourse strategy works to make its own ideology a public reality; only technical experts can function as critical participants in this mode of social policy discourse. Only readers who know where the technical bodies must have been buried can see such texts as the graveyards of informed public political discourse that they surely are.

Technocratic and Value-Centered Discourses in Conflict

Orientational meanings do not simply define the evaluative stance a text takes towards its own thematic presentations. They also operate to position the text and its discourses in the larger system of social heteroglossia. So far we have examined the technocratic strategy to see how it creates an effective rhetoric by ventriloquating technical discourse. *What Works*, however, is not a purely technocratic text. It is the product of an ideologically conservative government, attempting to shape social policy in education against the long prior dominance of more liberal political discourse. *What Works* is tightly enmeshed in the net of social heteroglossia. It is constructing an opposition between its own voice and that of liberal discourses about educational policy. It is appropriating and ventriloquating the voice of technocratic research on education, while attempting to maintain the dominance of its own tradition-alist conservatism over technocratic discourse in general. It is caught, along with many of us, in the contradictions between older value-centered political discourses and the newer, fact-centered technocratic ones. Texts like this one both reflect and help constitute the sociological and political relationships among communities which speak these diverse discourses.

The following extract is from the Forward by Secretary Bennett to *What Works* (pp. v–vi):

> We must remember that education is not a dismal science. In edu-cation research, of course, there is much to find out, but education, despite efforts to make it so, is not essentially mysterious . . . I would like to demystify a lot of things that don't need mystifying.
>
> Most readers will, I think, judge that most of the evidence in this volume confirms common sense. So be it. Given the abuse common sense has taken in recent decades, particularly in the theory and practice of education, it is no small contribution if research can play a role in bringing more of it to American education. Indeed, the reinforcement these findings give to common sense should bolster our confidence that we, as a people, can act together to improve our schools.

The negative value chain here includes: 'dismal', 'mysterious', 'mystifying' and 'abuse' and is set against the positive chain, 'demystify', 'common sense' 'reinforcement' and 'bolster our confidence'. The resulting value contrast tends to construct a heteroglossic opposition between the authorial voice and another unidentified one that 'mystifies education' and 'abuses common sense'. There can be little doubt that the heteroglossic work being done here is to create an alliance between conservative political discourse and common sense discourse about education, perhaps best called traditionalism, while setting both in opposition to what can only be an implied alliance of technical discourse on education ('the so-called experts' we might hear) and most probably liberal political discourse.

While the text voice here seeks an alliance between itself and the common sense views it attributes to its readers (while covertly intending to shape those views through the 'Findings' that follow it) it must at the same time ventriloquate a technocratic discourse that, as we have seen, is grounded in the denigration of common sense. Secretary Bennett's theme elaborates an initial tone set by President Reagan in the cover letter, on White House stationery, that introduces the book. It concludes:

> I am confident that with the benefit of such knowledge and renewed
> trust in common sense, we Americans will have even greater success
> in our unstinting efforts to improve our schools and better prepare
> our children for the challenges of today's world.

The theme of 'renewed trust in common sense' has no direct relation to anything else in the cover letter, or to any of the themes in the body of *What Works*, its 57 pages of 'Research Findings' and 'Comments', or to a general sense of the point of the book, whereas every other phrase and clause in the short letter clearly does. The word 'renewed', which itself carries a positive valuation ('renewal' is good, and was a winning theme in the 1984 election campaign), subtly signals the heteroglossic opposition of *something* to common sense and, by accentuating the role of 'trust' in common sense, opposes whatever that might be.

In the context of these framing discourses by the President and the Secretary, Dr Finn and other technocrats within the Administration need to be careful to affirm that research supports, rather than contradicts, the value-based conclusions about educational policy that traditional conservative discourse holds. In fact, as we have seen, the main body of *What Works* is pre-eminently technocratic in positing research findings alone as the basis for action and policy, without reference to other values, conservative and traditional or not. It only adds, in Reagan's, Bennett's and Finn's prefaces that these actions and policies are by and large the same as those values would favor. Finn himself straddles the fence on this issue, and the staff who have written the body of the text speak with a purely technocratic voice.

The conservative strategy here is to establish a heteroglossic opposition between technical and common sense discourse, but favoring common sense. It can then tolerate, and even welcome, technocratic discourse that favors its own value-based opinions, while at the same time insulating its constituency from other technocratic discourse that uses research views which do not agree with its policies. Research that supports us is 'true opinion' which 'confirms common sense'; research-based discourse that opposes us 'mystifies' education and 'abuses common sense'.

The strengths of this conservative strategy are that it can count on an alliance between its own values and common sense discourse, because the long historical hegemony of its values has shaped common sense discourse, and there is a strong antipathy among non-experts to the arrogance of the technical and technocratic denigration of common sense and common people. The social 'hegemony' (cf. Gramsci 1935) of a particular class, its dominance over education and official public discourse of all kinds (cf. Althusser 1971), favors the acceptance of its values and ideology by all classes, even though they serve only its own interest in maintaining its dominance. These values and ideological uses of thematic formations become integral to many of the discourses of non-dominant groups as well; they become part of common sense.

The class whose interests traditional conservative discourse favors is, historically, the class of owners of capital and property. The weakness of the conservative strategy we have just outlined, however, is its failure to recognize that technocratic discourse carries with it its own values and ideologies, which represent the interests of a new class – a class that is itself bidding to establish its own social hegemony in place of that of the owners of wealth. If technocrats can succeed in convincing people, through *What Works* and texts like it, that research findings support their views on education, then they can substitute, in the guise of those findings, their own views. Common sense does not already have an opinion on everything. New issue-specific discourses must be articulated to define what common sense will say about new problems and issues. Technocrats can articulate such discourses just as well as traditional liberals or conservatives. They can modulate common sense by degrees from existing views that incorporate values favorable to the older hegemony to new views that favor their own interests. The 'touchstone' of 'confirming/abusing common sense' is hardly an effective barrier to technocratic hegemony in the long term.

Both liberal reformist and conservative traditionalist policy discourses have attempted to buttress their value-based arguments with technocratic 'value-free' appeals to 'the facts'. By doing so, both have left the specifics of their positions on new issues vulnerable to being articulated by, and in the interests of, the new technocratic élite of managers and experts. By appropriating and using technocratic modes of policy discourse they have undermined their ability to construct a credible heteroglossic opposition between their voices and those of the technocrats.

The most effective opposition to technocratic policy discourse today comes from absolutist moral discourse, as can be seen in the resurgent religious fundamentalist movements in many parts of the world (cf. the discussion of

US Christian fundamentalism in Chapter 3). This discourse bases social policy squarely on explicit value principles and, if necessary, overrides contradictory 'facts' with appeals to a Higher Authority than science or research. Fortunately, common sense in our own society has long since shifted away from such moral absolutism, and even where it persists, one still finds a healthy skepticism of both religious extremism and its self-aggrandizing leaders.

The reformist impulse of maintream liberal discourse has long made alliance with anti-commonsensical, and so anti-traditional, technocratic modes of policy argumentation. Once strongly values-centered, it too has become vulnerable to technocratic articulations of its positions on new issues. The counterculture discourses of the 1960s, and some of their successors (radical feminist, gay and environmentalist discourses) have rebelled against the technocratic compromises of liberalism, seeking new moral foundations for anti-technocratic policy.

Postmodern intellectual perspectives have begun to enable us to see that all universalizing claims for specific grounds of policy, whether scientific, religious or moral are ultimately empty. What this implies for our sense of political responsibility is far from clear. We will return to this issue in Chapter 7, but before we can do so, we need to explore the consequences of modernist common sense concerning the grounds of all discourse. We need to return to some of the fundamental issues raised in Chapter 1 and Chapter 2 concerning our own intellectual ideologies. We need a basis for talking about the relations of discourses, cultures, values and individual human subjectivity. The most profound implication of a *textual politics* is that by examining the texts of our own community we can come to understand how and why we make the meanings we do, and what other meanings might be made instead. All action makes meaning; critical reflection on our habits of meaning-making enlarges our universe of possible action. To make use of this principle, we need new ways of articulating the relations of discourse and action, meaning and matter, body and mind, species and ecosystem. The next two chapters will barely begin this important and necessary cultural project.

Chapter 5

The Social Construction of the Material Subject

Conflating Material and Social Individuals

Critical discourse in semiotics, literary studies and social theory has been struggling for some years now with what we have come to call the 'problem of the subject'. We have fashioned this problem out of our perplexity over the contradictions between traditional notions of the human individual and newer, essentially social ways of talking about human meaning. Through it we remind ourselves that the postmodern intellectual revolution remains painfully incomplete.

On the surface, the 'problem of the subject' is how to have an active, creative human subject which constructs social meanings, at the same time that this subject must itself be a social construction.

In a deeper sense, however, the problem lies as much with our desires as with our theories, as much with our politics as with our reasonings. We desire the moral comfort that the traditional liberal discourse of human individuality provides: its defense of personal and intellectual freedom against the pressures of social interests. We know, however, that the discourse of radical individualism is fundamentally incompatible with critical politics, constructivist epistemology and social science. We know that it is a discourse rooted in middle-class ideology and supportive of interests, privilege and modes of domination most of us reject. Nevertheless, we have tried, from early in this century, to re-create this object of our desire within the new intellectual arena of critical social theory, and we call our inevitable difficulties in doing so 'the problem of the subject'.

In this chapter I am going to try to dissect the notion of the individual human subject, to expose its internal contradictions, and to define the sorts of discourse constructs that can usefully replace it in a social semiotic theory. This is the subject that thinks, that imagines, that writes, that reads and interprets. It is the central notion around which most of modern psychology, politics, ethics, education, and literary and literacy theory is built. Without a critical analysis of how it is constructed, we cannot build a useful textual politics.

The cultural, ideological, common sense notion of a human individual conflates, that is identifies as indistinguishably the same unitary object or phenomenon, what a variety of scientific discourses in principle enable us to distinguish. Most fundamentally, I believe, the classical modernist concept of the human individual conflates a physical, biological notion of the individual human organism with a social, cultural notion of the individual human person, the social actor, agent, or persona.

The biological organism and the social persona are profoundly different social constructions. The different systems of social practices, including discourse practices, through which these two notions are constituted, have their meanings and are made use of, are radically incommensurable. The biological notion of a human organism as an identifiable individual unit of analysis depends on the specific scientific practices we use to construct the identity, the boundedness, the integrity, and the continuity across interactions of this unit. The criteria we use to do so – DNA signatures, neural micro-anatomy, organism–environment boundaries, internal physiological interdependence of subsystems, external physical probes of identification at distinct moments of physical time – all depend on social practices and discourses profoundly different from those in terms of which we define the social person.

The social-biographical person is also an individual in so far as we construct its identity, boundedness, integrity and continuity, but the social practices and discourses we deploy in these constructions are quite different. We define the social person in terms of social interactions, social roles, socially and culturally meaningful behavior patterns. We construct from these notions of the personal identity of an individual the separateness and independence of that individual from the social environment with which it transacts, the internal unity or integrity of the individual as a consistent persona, and the continuity of that persona across social interactions.

We obtain the common sense notion of a human individual only by a complex process of conflation: mapping the social-biographical person onto the physical-biological organism. This, too, is accomplished by our cultural patterns of discourse, and the associated actional practices. Because the classical notion of a human individual is constructed in this way, if we no longer make the traditional metaphysical presumption of a single 'real object' to which each of these discursive systems 'refers' or 'on which' it acts, there is no longer any reason to suppose that 'the individual' constructed by each of these systems of practices coincides with those constructed through the others.

In traditional modernist discourse there was a unitary individual: biological organism, psychological personality, social persona, subjective identity, psychosocial agent, all in one. The biological organism, defined as a material object amenable to the discourse of physics, chemistry or biology, was the ultimate warrant for the 'reality' of the individual and the ultimate guarantor that all other discourses (psychological, social, legal, ethical etc.) about 'it' referred to the same, well-defined entity. The total discourse of the human individual uncritically conflated a biological organism as a physical object with a separately defined social persona, identity and personality.

From the postmodern viewpoint this was a massive sleight-of-hand. Even within the natural sciences there is no guarantee that physical, chemical and biological definitions of an 'organism' coincide for all purposes. Each uses essentially different criteria and practices to specify its defining attributes, continuity over time and spatial boundaries. When we consider the criteria and practices that define the temporal continuity of a personality or the biography of a social agent, we can find scarcely any overlap between what is meant by the material vs. the biographical continuity of what we are supposed to assume is the same entity.

Physics defines an individual material object, biology a structurally individualized organism, psychology an individual mind or personality, sociology an individual social agent. There are biographical individuals, historical individuals, and subjective individual identities – and there is no longer any reason to suppose that all of these coincide in defining the same unitary entity for all discursive purposes.

What reason was there ever to suppose that they did? It will take a better archeology of the discourses of the individual than any we yet have to answer that question properly, but we can make some reasonable guesses. A long European cultural tradition distinguished 'body' and 'soul' along an axis separating mortal from immortal, earth from heaven, secular from sacred, the rights and privileges of crown and nobility from those of church and clergy. The soul was partly secularized into the notion of 'mind' and the body scientifically reformulated as the 'organism', but it was the social notion of an economic individual, free to act as an agent of its own interests, that was of paramount importance for a new middle class. That individual needed 'rights', primarily the right of private property and the liberty to use it to maximize the advantages of the property-owning classes. Thus was born the political individual and ultimately the social individual.

It was from this essentially ideological notion of the bourgeois individual that the later psychological and sociological notions developed. The unity, the incontestable reality of the individual was essential to maintaining a claim for 'its' inalienable rights. Its reality had to take precedence over the reality of corporate social entities such as clans, fiefs, villages, guilds, parishes etc. The individual had to be made more 'real' than other economic and political claimants, so that its 'rights' could be asserted above theirs. There were, of course, many contradictions right from the start. Political rights were frequently granted, not to individuals as such, but to economic categories of individuals (property-holders, not surprisingly), not to personalities ('all men of good temper'), or to organisms ('all able-bodied men'). 'Free men' were defined in relation to slaves by the laws of property. Women, children and people of non-European cultures were neither truly individuals in the dominant political and economic sense, nor even canonically human. Propertyless adult males suffered the same fate.

The historical course of bourgeois ideology since its beginnings has led it to valorize the individual as a creative and feeling subject, a rational and problem-solving mind, and a responsible social actor. The evident tension, not to say contradiction, among these ideals has not led many to question the intellectual usefulness, much less the ideological uses of the core notion of 'the individual' itself. The growth of social institutions and their increasing power to prescribe every aspect of social activity collectively has led us to rely on the notions of individuality and individual rights in the face of real and imagined institutional tyrannies. The prescriptive institutions of the bourgeois past, the family, the guild, the local church and court, were ones the powerful individual had a chance to influence or control. The modern institutions of the state and its apparatuses, and the statist multinational corporations, have achieved a scale so far beyond the individual that these late bourgeois institutions are destroying individual bourgeois power *en masse*, even while they serve to magnify the power of a few individuals (themselves regulated as never before in the exercise of that power). Power itself is shifting from the property-holders, the owner-class, to the new technocrats, the manager-class.

The dangers are not just to power derived from property, but to all freedom of action, all nonconformism, all intellectual and social change. In such a world intellectuals particularly are loath to deconstruct the basis of our traditional defense against the power of social institutions. To expose the individual as a social construction is to deny its claim to absolute rights, to pave the way to its total subordination to institutional interests. But *not* to analyze how the social practices by which we constitute human individuality prevents us from seeing how those very practices contribute to human exploitation, and from being able to formulate liberating alternatives.

I want to examine the notion of the material individual first, along with the social meanings that attach to the material body. Then we will analyze the social and biographical subject and some of the anomalies that point up contradictions in the traditional unitary notion of the individual. Finally, we will consider the social construction of subjectivity itself and possible directions for a developmental social semiotics of the subject.

The Material Individual and the Semiotic Body

All objects and systems, including the material individual, must be constructed across time and across the changes that inevitably take place in their constituents. The biological organism replaces its cells, replaces even the atoms of which those cells are made, but so long as certain looked-for patterns of continuity, certain theoretically motivated invariances over time can be constructed, we consider it the 'same' individual organism biologically. 'Sameness' is always likeness in some special respect that is defined by our theories, by our culture, by our interests. An organism or any physical object is definable as an individual only by the social practices by which we distinguish it from other objects, define its boundaries in space, and establish its continuity in time. *Which* features we single out as distinctive, which criteria we choose to use to define the boundary, and which invariant patterns over time are significant depend on whether we wish to analyze the object as physicists, as chemists, or as molecular, cellular, developmental or evolutionary biologists.

An individual is definable as a material system by the construction for some analytical purpose of one of the many different possible boundaries that might enclose the system. It is not that there is a system already *there* to be enclosed. There may be matter there, or energy, but we create the *system* as a system by defining its boundary. Of course we do not draw the boundary arbitrarily. We *choose* the parameters relevant to our *interests*, and then we construct the boundary through the points where those parameters change significantly. These boundaries can never be absolute, however; there is always *continuity across* the boundary in real physical and biological systems. There are always, certainly for biological systems, critical biochemical and biophysical *processes* that transfer matter, energy and information *across* the boundary. The system maintains its persistence in time as a system (i.e. maintains the gradients in the boundary-defining parameters) only through the operation of such processes. This is the thermodynamic definition of a persistent open system (for further discussion see the Postscript to this volume; Lemke 1984; Prigogine and Stengers 1984, and references therein). It is the basis of life, of the possibility of building up an internally ordered system.

The paradox is plain; such systems persist as systems (in terms of the boundaries that define them) only by engaging in exchange processes which must disregard those boundaries, that is by interacting with their environments. More precisely, the system is only definable as an individual because it is a part of a larger 'supersystem' consisting of itself *and* its environment.

Biologically and thermodynamically there are no absolute individuals. Not only are all boundaries permeable, but boundary-violating processes are essential and fundamental to the existence of the system defined as an individual. What we call an 'individual' system is always and necessarily only a theory-defined subsystem of something greater.

There is another way in which we define a material individual. Rather than defining an organism 'from above' by its thermodynamic and ecological relations to other organisms and the rest of its ecosystem environment, we might define it 'from below' as the relevant system for modeling the mutual regulation of organs, tissues and cells. There is however no guarantee that the same system definition will be arrived at by these two methods, and every likelihood that in general it will not. The relevant notion of the individual will not in general be the same for the ecologist and the surgeon.

The scientific definitions of the material individual as physical system or biological organism may have prestige in our community, but they are rarely used by most of us. Body notions, of course, preceded scientific discourse formations. The traditionally named parts of the body, for example, divide an apparently continuous spatial distribution of substance in ways which may be rationalized or in some cases contradicted by biology. They can help us understand the 'cultural body', however, not only its 'ethno-anatomy', but all the symbolic meanings and value conventions attached to the body, to its parts, to different 'kinds' of bodies, etc. by a particular community. This is the body as carrier of social meaning, the *semiotic body*.

When we look at an individual, the distinguishing features we have been taught to identify are as much those of this socially and culturally defined semiotic body (seeing it in terms of its social meaning – 'handsome', 'fat', 'clumsy', 'athletic' – and its ethno-anatomy: 'face', 'torso', etc.) as of the biological body. Even apart from dress and hairstyle, facial expressions are culture-specific, at least in their social meanings, if not also in their anatomical features. It is the meanings we attend to and use, along with an individual's style of movement, tones of voice and voice qualities, and predictable patterns of speech, opinion and action, to define that individual. All these things could change, leaving the same biological organism, but an unrecognizably different 'individual' (as in extreme cases of multiple personality, see below).

Our community teaches us specific, if often inexplicit procedures for identifying, classifying, segmenting and evaluating the semiotic body. We read bodies, and with them, patterns of movement, facial expressions and gestures, body hexis, stance, attitude, somatotype, vocal style, etc. We construct, by these social practices characteristic of our community and the subcommunities to which we belong, socially meaningful, semiotic bodies and their texts. The criteria, the categories, the procedures all have little in common with those of the physicist or biologist. They construct a different sort of embodied individual.

The Social Subject

All the features of the semiotic body may change over time, as do the atoms and cells of the material organism, and yet our social practices can construct not only a physical and biological continuity, but also a separate social continuity of what we may call the *biographical* individual. Over the course of a human lifespan many of these features do change. The infant, the adolescent and the elder may be alike in none of the socially signficant features that define the semiotic body, but through the social practices of 'biography' we construct a social continuity of the individual. We relate, again in ways specific to our culture, the persons of today and yesterday, and we do so not fundamentally on biological grounds, but on social ones. The person who has the same family relationships, who enacts the same social roles, who behaves toward us in the same fashion in particular situations, is an individual-with-a-history, a transtemporal social construction, an entity that can change and yet be regarded as 'the same individual' at 80 years as at eight months.

To analyze the social semiotic construction of the subject, we must begin from the systems of social practices of a community, that is from a notion of its characteristic *doings*. One of the principle patterns of organization of these practices, that is of social acts, is that in which they are related to one another as constituent elements of a larger activity sequence or structure. The meaning relations of the constitutent acts are functional relations: each act serves a function in relation to the others in the context of the whole structure. Meaningful social activities that are recognized as such and are both potentially and in most cases actually repeated (with variations) on many occasions define *participant roles*.

For example, the activity of getting-the-check when dining out is such an activity structure. It has functional elements including locating-a-waiter, getting-his or her-attention, signaling-desire-for-check, waiter-compliance-sign, etc. These elements may be realized by various actual behaviors. The minimal set of participant roles are those for diner and for waiter. The structure as a whole is normally embedded within a larger activity structure such as Dining Out, whose actional elements and interrelations enable us to define other roles for more diners and waiters, and for the roles of busboy, maitre d', chef, coatchecker, etc. These definitions of the roles are specific to one activity structure.

To define the more general social role of, say, a chef, we would need to assemble all the activity structures in which typically we expect a chef to participate, and define the general role as the union of all of these. This is a very high order abstraction that we construct. Similarly, we can define a teacher participant role for a particular activity structure such as that of classroom-question-and-answer-dialogue (cf. discussion in Lemke 1990a), and then consider the constellation of such participant roles that is taken to define the total social role of teacher in a given community.

In an actual enactment of an activity structure we conflate the realization of a participant role with a semiotic body, that is we construct an embodied participant. We construct this-waiter-now or this-teacher-now in terms of what they are doing in the immediate activity structure *and* what makes them distinguishable, notable, individual, signficant and evaluable as bodies (but not yet fully as people) as well as role actors. We can say 'the fat one is the waiter, the thin one the busboy' or 'the waiter is awfully fat, isn't he?' as well as 'this waiter forgot my soup' (role performance). We might note in passing that the soup, or the check, is also a participant, at least in the semantics of our language, but of a special class ('inanimate' or more generally, unable to fill certain 'agentive' roles in both the linguistic and the activity structure grammars). We construct 'objects' in much the same way as 'subjects', both as activity participants first (cf. Greimas and Courtes 1983 on *actants* and use of this notion by Latour 1987, 1988).

The waiter may also be a father, a husband, a student, an actor, a son, and sometimes a football player, a dishwasher, a checkwriter, a typist, etc. If we interpret these roles as participant roles in particular activity structures they cannot conflict, though certain combinations are more or less likely to occur in different communities. If we take them to be full social roles, the possibilities of combination become even more restricted by conventions. We find two further sorts of abstraction on the way to our cultural notion of an individual person.

One is that of the *biographical individual*, a construction that preserves features of the semiotic body invariant over short time-spans to trace out the common embodiment of consecutive (or in rarer cases simultaneous) participant roles in distinct activity structures. Thus the waiter role in getting-the-check may or may not be embodied by the same semiotic body as the waiter in taking-the-order in the same enactment of Dining Out. If it is, we have a partial biographical individual defined as an abstraction from the two situations. In fact, I think people are often in doubt about such continuity, saying, 'Is this guy the same waiter who took our order?' Preliminary construction of a semiotic body may take notice of only a few features, often not enough initially to distinguish 'individuals' who will later be distinguished. We might follow the semiotic body of this biographical individual after closing time to find it embodying participant roles in non-waiter activities, and so going further toward constructing a biographical individual. Over long periods of time, we would begin to rely on the repetition of particular patterns of behavior, enactment of roles, to construct the continuity of the biographical individual even across changes in his semiotic body.

The second abstraction is that of the *social type*. The members of a particular community expect to find certain participant roles rather than others intersecting in a biographical individual. The community in fact produces certain social types of individual. In New York young, good-looking male waiters are often also aspiring actors. They will be found at auditions and casting calls, reading *Variety*, drinking in fashionable late-night bars, etc. as well as waiting tables. They are a social type. The degree of variability in their semiotic bodies (apparent age, handsomeness, height, weight, muscle tone, gracefulness, voice quality, etc.) is rather narrow as compared to the population as a whole. So will be their styles of dress, hair and movement, and these will be correlated with a similarly narrow range of likely activity structures in which they will participate and the corresponding range of social roles we will construct for them.

Most members of a community embody some such social type, and the system of types is a defining characteristic of the community, as much as the repertory of activity structures from which it derives. What links these together is the probability distribution of social activities over biographical individuals. In a given community, not all possible combinations of participant roles are equally likely to be embodied by the same biographical individual. Equivalently, the same individual who enacts any particular participant role is thereby either more or less likely to enact many others. Activities and roles tend to intersect in biographical individuals in the combinations I have called social types. Of course these are combinations whose enactments are relatively close together in time; we can and do construct biographical continuity over longer periods of time, during which the individual may change social type. Phases of constant social type can define 'periods' or 'stages' in the life history of a biographical individual.

Long term biographical continuity is not usually central to the construction of the 'person' in the sense of a *social individual.* The social individual is the socially meaningful entity, the biographical individual as embodiment, or we may now tentatively say as 'enactor' of a specific set of participant roles in particular activity structures, the 'one who does' this and that, the 'practice-defined' person. It is customary to regard the social individual as the intersection of the social category groups of which he or she is taken to be a member. For example, 'a white, middle-class Irish Catholic teenage girl'. This may in effect name a social type, but social semiotics insists that these categories must themselves be 'practice-defined', that is what does one have to *do* to be counted middle-class or Catholic or a girl? When such specifications are made at the level of participant roles in activity structures, both the person's own and those of the actions of others in respect to her or him, they define some very small class: all those biographical individuals who meet the specifications. A social individual is rarely unique in this sense. For significant social purposes, there is nothing about the individual that is not shared by some others.

It is of course possible to specify sufficiently the detailed behavior of a social-biographical individual so as to define a class with a unique member. This is close to the common sense practice; if it looks like (same semiotic body, with movement pattern, voice quality, etc.) the person, and behaves in context like the person (participant roles), it is taken to be the person. The classic problem of how to detect an imposter or 'double' demonstrates the relevant considerations in the construction of the social-biographical individual. The 'perfect imposter' *is* in principle the person she or he impersonates, except for a different *long term* biographical history that may in fact be entirely irrelevant to the person-of-the-moment in all their social interactions. (Institutional status, however, does conventionally depend on the long term biography, e.g. in matters of legal and political rights.)

The movement from the social individual as representative of a social type or of a very small social class to the social-biographical individual of common sense is one that looks at interconnections between the semiotic body and the social individual. The key step is the one which recognizes that while a *type* is defined by *what* it does, a unique token of that type may be defined by *how* it does it. That is, features of a performance of a role in an activity structure that are non-criterial for the role may be made criterial for identifying the semiotic embodiment of the role. Several individuals may all do the same thing, but there are said to be differences in how they did it that are irrelevant to what they did, but that are idiosyncratic to who they are. These differences are the ones we come to construct first for the semiotic body, the 'little things' which become signs of the person as unique individual, their 'identifiers' for us. Naturally, these need not be the same for all who identify the individual. In our culture, special significance is given to the identifiers each of us uses to identify ourselves, the features of our 'subjective identity' or 'sense of self'. These are in principle borrowings and specializations from those used in identifications of/by others.

One of the culturally valued activity structures that we are taught as members of our community is 'introspection' or 'self-dialogue', talking or 'thinking' to ourselves and its close variants for non-verbal semiotics: sensing, feeling, visualizing, etc. A great task for social semiotics is the analysis of the social construction of the emotions and 'inner sensations' of this self-constructed subjectivity. Certainly there is need for a biophysiological component in such accounts, but much more essential is an analysis of the social meanings we are taught to attach to states of our organism: their identities and names ('anger', 'love', 'anxiety' etc.), their social significance and evaluation, and the systematic probabilities that these meaning-constructing practices will co-occur with other, 'outer' social actions, including their visible signs on the semiotic body as read by other members of our community.

Our *personal identity* is constructed by foregrounding certain patterns we make in our inner dialogue and feelings as we set them against the background of what we are taught to take as 'outer' events. Needless to say, what is 'inner' and what is 'outer', what the repertory of human emotions is taken to be, how each is identified from physiological states and signs on the semiotic body, and the nature of 'inner dialogues' as activity structures, all differ from culture to culture and from one subcommunity and social group (age-group, gender category, social class, etc.), even from one biographical individual to another.

We can take this analysis one final critical step further. We can ask how our very sense of selfhood, the notion that we *are* perceiving, experiencing, willing, acting egos, that we are/have 'minds', feelings, perceptions, desires, memories, etc. is itself a construction woven from the warp and woof of cultural semiotic resources (language, categories, values, practices) in accordance with the learned patterns of our community. What we are taught in our culture to call our own minds, our own subjective sense of experiencing and being, is a projection onto the complex, interactive, self-organizing system of an organism-in-its-environment of a cultural model of what it is to think of ourselves according to one community's view of being human.

Social semiotics in this way excludes a separate domain for psychology. Not only for cognitive psychology, but even for the psychology of affect (depth psychology, clinical psychology). It excludes them, not certainly as practices, but as autonomous domains of theory. Cognitive processes need to be analyzed as semiotic practices embodied in a socially constructed subjectivity. We 'think' in the same words and in a register of the same language in which we talk. There is no autonomous semantics of thought, no separate *lingua mentis*, apart from that of social meaning generally. We 'think' non-verbally with the same semiotic resources for meaningful action, be they those of our grammar of visual representation, the forms of body hexis meaningfully available in our community, or the semiotic resources of any other activity structure, which are the same ones also observable in outward action. The 'inner' forms may sometimes be specialized, but they are part of the same total social system of meaningful practices. The same sort of analysis is appropriate for sensation and feeling, whether of light or heat, pain or anger. Until the unity of 'inner' and 'outer' semiotic practices is recognized, it is not likely that much progress will be made in understanding the 'inner', which are so much harder to reconstruct from indirect evidence than are the 'outer'.

Critical Anomalies for the Notion of a Unitary Individual

The prevailing ideology of the individual posits a unitary subject, an unconstructed (because 'natural') individual. We should expect, however, that the social construction of this unitary individual will produce anomalies that contradict the ideology. Let's consider some instructive cases in which the social-biographical continuity and unity of the individual may not entirely agree with the biological ones. These cases are usually marginalized as 'anomalies' or 'exceptions', but the fact that they do occur, and that we can and do recognize and make sense of them, helps to reveal the hidden joins and seams in the construction and points toward the processes by which this notion of the individual has indeed been constructed. They also point us toward new, more powerful discourses about gender, class, sexual orientation and other defining categories of the social individual.

Consider first extreme cases of *multiple personalities*. In these we find several fully developed social persons co-habiting in one biological organism. These social persons are themselves complex constructions, based on their patterns of participation in social interactions. They may even be constructed to be of different genders. They may show different typical patterns of tension in facial musculature, so that they 'look' different. They may have different body hexis and styles of speech and movement. They usually speak in very distinct 'voices'. They can have separate social lives, functioning as separate social individuals.

It is not inconceivable, or it *should* not be inconceivable that such a set of persons in one body form a stable configuration, and that such a complex may *not* be *ipso facto* pathological. This reality is profoundly contrary to the prototypical notion of the individual in our culture, however, and to the various ideological, social and political reflexes of that notion. To take but a single classic example, suppose that one of these social persons commits a serious crime. Is it ethical, should it be legal, to incarcerate the other social persons in that body, who are innocent people, because we incarcerate *bodies* in our penal system (actually organisms) rather than persons?

If there can be multiple persons in one body, can there also be a single social-biographical person distributed over many bodies? Identical twins, especially in their early years, may present such a case, where even for parents they may sometimes be indistinguishable in personality and behavior, may 'switch' with each other, may be named jointly by others and treated by others as if they were a single social persona. A more extreme case, largely rejected by western culture, but well accepted in many others, is that of the reincarnated social person (e.g. the Dalai Lama), who serially inhabits different bodies, but remains the same 'soul' and for many purposes also the same social persona (plays the same social role, is treated as the same person in many ways, etc.). Phenomena of possession and transmigration present similar cultural constructions in this respect, and even the familiar question of whether a pregnant woman is to be constructed as one or as two social persons depends on these conflations.

Less dramatic, but important for developmental theories of personality and subjectivity, which I will discuss further below, are a number of other closely related issues:

How artificial are the constructed unities and continuities of personality across the life-span, or across traumatic events?
In extreme cases, does it not often make as much sense to say that in a single organism's lifetime there are entirely different social persons inhabiting it? Consider cases of sex-change operations, radical psychotherapeutic transformations, or fundamental discontinuities of personality. The bias of our culture is toward continuity, and toward denial of the fundamental mutability of personality, but this seems very clearly to be just a bias. On the other side of this coin, we do not construct continuity of personality, or social personas, for embryos (though some are trying to), nor for corpses (which are thermodynamically alive well after we consider them biologically, or socially, dead), even though we do construct biological and physical continuities in these cases. There is a perfectly good scientific logic for defining continuity from conception to disintegration, or even across reproductive generations. Neither in such alternative schemes nor in the one western culture prefers do the corresponding socially, biologically and physically defined 'individuals' begin and end at the same moments in time. Even within the domain of the biographical person in our culture, how well could we really match infant,

early adult and late senile personalities of the same organism in a double-blind, randomized trial?

How useful is it to define the developing, interacting, social persona as a system whose boundary is co-terminous with that of the biological organism?
Many proposals about the nature of the social person, from those of Gregory Bateson (e.g. 1972) to those of Leontiev (e.g. 1978) and the activity theorists, show the value of defining the unit of analysis not as the body-bound individual, but as a larger system including informational pathways and social interactions linking 'us' with the artifacts and tools we use and with the whole of our non-human and inanimate environment as well as the social dyads and groups in which we participate.

To what extent, for example, is it artificial to assert that the same organism functions as the same social person in all dyads, in all groups, in all social contexts? Many characteristics of behavior that are assumed to be properties of the body-bound 'individual' are in fact context-dependent and so are more usefully conceived of as properties of a larger system that includes the immediate context. If these are taken away, how much is left as properties of the individual, valid in *all possible* contexts? If we take into account variations across all possible *physical, chemical and ecological* contexts, and across all possible such contexts over the *developmental history* of the individual, what indeed is conceivably left as specific to the individual as such? We need alternative models of human development that can draw the boundary between the individual and its material and social environments differently for different purposes of analysis.

How effectively does the traditional 'two sexes, two genders' model account for the full range of human diversity that we allot to these categories?
The prevailing dogma of 'one organism, one social individual' maintains that an individual's sex or gender is natural, given and biological, and that there are two genders/sexes: male and female. Moreover, culturally one particular gender, masculine or feminine, is mapped onto one particular biological sex, male or female. Biological sex is itself not a unitary construct, however. There is chromosomal sex, for which we have not only XX and XY but XXY and XYY and other rarer genotypes; there is anatomical sex, the human phenotypes, which include hermaphrodites and other sorts of intersexuals (see Fausto-Sterling 1993). Cultural ideology prescribes two and only two genders, and projects this onto biological discourse, where its inadequacies have become apparent, not just for other species but even for humans.

Anomalies produced by conflating cultural views about social persona with scientifically defined biological organisms are even more evident in the case of transsexuals: those social persons who construct for themselves, and may have socially constructed for them by others as well, a gender identity that does not map canonically onto the biological sex identification that is made for them by quite unrelated criteria and practices (everyday or medical).

As an example of the social and political dilemmas produced by these anomalies, consider that transsexuals are not usually homosexual in the ordinary sense. That is, the preference is for sex partners of the opposite gender identity. There is no unambiguous two-way classification possible here, however. If a man-in-a-woman's-body desires women, is 'he' heterosexual or is 'she' a lesbian? If s/he desired men, would he be gay or would she be straight? If a woman-in-a-man's-body desires women, is s/he a heterosexual? Certainly not in exactly the same sense as a woman in a woman's body who desires men. The inadequacy of the prevailing ideology should be apparent here.

Analyses of such cases requires us to construct a much more complex gender system for our culture, one that recognizes far more than two possible gender identities, and multiple possible combinations with more than two possible biological sex identifications. Even if we try to define gender independently of biology, we would have to consider that gender systems are more likely triadic than dyadic (with masculine, feminine and neuter poles in a continuum of variation), and that the characteristics for each triad are different between middle and working class, among lesbians, gay males and heterosexuals, for different racial/ethnic subcultures, and for infants, young children, adolescents, elders, etc. There are dozens of gender types in our community as well as several distinct possible biological sexes, and a very large number of possible combinations of these in practice as well as in theory. The unity of person and organism again breaks down.

The Specification Hierarchy for Human Systems

I believe that the issues raised so far are sufficient to rule out the notion of 'the human individual' as a primary or privileged unit of analysis for any theory of human systems. If we wish to understand how human communities come to be organized as they are, or the role which discursive systems of meaning play in our communities, if we want to build theories of social dynamics or of textual politics, we need a perspective in which the notion of the human individual can be accounted for as a complex construction, not taken as a starting point for analysis. The notions of human subject, human agent, human mind, human cognition all presuppose and privilege a notion that must be thoroughly deconstructed and analyzed if we are to make any progress at all.

We have already taken one step toward doing this. We have defined human communities as systems of doings, of social and cultural activities or practices, rather than as systems of doers, of human individuals *per se*. In the next chapter we will construct a fairly elaborate and detailed picture of human social systems based on seeing every such activity as having both a material, ecological aspect and a cultural, semiotic one. In this picture activities in human communities are interrelated both in terms of exchanges of matter and energy and in terms of relationships of meaning. The fundamental unit of analysis will turn out to be a 'patch', a mini-ecosystem containing human organisms in interaction with their social and material environments according to both cultural and ecological-physical principles. The patch is part of a mosaic of other patches, each with its own unique history, all interacting and forming a larger scale patch in a larger scale ecosocial system. The patches are units of convenience; underlying them are the interconnected doings, the ecological and social processes that link organism to organism, and organisms to environments, and which at smaller scales operate to constitute organisms, artifacts, landscapes, dialects, communities, cultures and social individuals as self-organizing systems.

In this picture what we customarily think of as human individuals are shifted from center stage in two ways. First, as a unit of the hierarchy of processes at various scales, they become merely one level of organization among many, from the molecular and cellular to the social and ecological. Second, as participants in processes on their own scale, they are defined, both as organisms and as social individuals, by these processes, which in turn constitute the levels of organization above and below 'us'. The autonomy of the individual as separate from the systems in which we participate is denied, and so is the special importance of the level of organization from which we happen to view the universe. We cannot be understood apart from our connections to our social and material environments (communication, tool use, foraging, waste disposal, exchanges of goods, pleasures and pains etc.) nor outside a view of the multiple levels of self-organization of systems larger and smaller than 'us'.

Every picture, however, is drawn from some point of view, and it is important to understand just how our notions about the systems we are part of are constructed. For this purpose, a very useful way of looking at how we construct our view of the natural and social world is the *specification hierarchy* perspective articulated by Salthe (1985: 49–50, 166ff; 1989, 1993). As a theoretical biologist interested in how biological systems are defined in ways that are both similar to and yet different from non-biological physical systems, Salthe noticed that many kinds of biological systems can be regarded as 'special cases' of more general sorts of physical systems. As such they are defined by the discourses and scientific practices of biologists in such a way that they have all the same properties that physical systems do, plus additional properties specific to them alone.

This approach can be helpful in examining how the notion of a human individual is constructed. Our culture also defines other sorts of (non-human) individuals: individual electrons, molecules, hurricanes, colonial organisms, ecosystems, etc. Some of the features we associate with human individuality, such as the possibility of identifying individuals and constructing a continuity of identification for them from before to after some interaction with another individual do not exist for, say, individual electrons. Electrons are not defined with the properties necessary for such a construction of continuity to be carried out. Electrons also do not age; it is not possible to tell the difference between a newly created one and one created in the primordial Big Bang. These two facts are closely related (see discussion in Chapter 6). They remind us that for a system to have the properties we associate with human individuals it must be a system of a particular kind. Historically, Western culture assumed that individuals of all kinds had the properties it constructs for human individuals. We are now in a position to see that many of these properties do not apply to more general sorts of systems.

In Salthe's specification hierarchy, which I have slightly extended for our present purposes, and which is discussed in more detail in the next chapter, the outermost, or most general types of systems and objects are those least specified, those with the most general or abstract properties, thus encompassing the greatest range of types of more specified systems, which are subsets of the more general ones. Imagine a nesting of subsets of subsets of subsets etc. in which each inner set inherits the properties of all the sets outside of it, and each step toward the center increases the specification of members in that set by adding further defining characteristics or properties.

The most specified type of system in the hierarchy, the sort to be found in its innermost circle, is the human system. That the specification hierarchy converges on 'us' is not so surprising when we realize that it is a cultural construction, our construction, and is constructed from our point of view on the universe. We have defined all other systems in relation to the properties our culture ascribes to ourselves, as having them or lacking them. In this way the specification hierarchy actually tells us a great deal about ourselves, including some things we might rather not know.

It tells us, for instance, that while the outermost, most general, least specified kinds of systems we know of are, like electrons, elementary dynamical systems that can be described in terms of relatively autonomous individuals ('particles') in interaction, that as we proceed progressively to systems that exhibit more of the characteristics we ascribe to ourselves (memory, individuality, aging, biographical continuity, development, evolution, etc.), that these more specified types must be complex self-organizing systems of dynamical processes in which individuals are only defined by the processes of self-organization themselves. It also tells us that it is such systems (for humans, these are our *ecosocial systems*), not constituent autonomous individuals (which are at best only one level of organization in the system), that ought to be at the center of the hierarchy.

It potentially tells us even more, however. What *kind* of ecosocial system is at the center? That is, from what specific cultural viewpoint about the nature of the universe has the specification hierarchy been constructed? A European cultural viewpoint? A modernist cultural viewpoint? A masculinized cultural viewpoint? A middle-aged, middle-class viewpoint? One can only suppose so, given the history of those who have most influenced its construction.

This is perhaps rather shocking to anyone who may still have been hoping that modern European science might somehow turn out to be universal after all, shaped without class, gender or age bias. I hope at least some readers will long since have realized that this is certainly impossible in general. It is conceivable that some of what our culture has to say about those systems that are farthest out from our central viewing point, those that are least like us and about which we care least how they behave, might be relatively less sensitive to our particular cultural biases than what we say about those that are closer to home. Perhaps our views on electrons will turn out to be less specific to the viewpoint of our historically dominant social caste than our views of, say, primate behavioral biology (cf. Harding 1986; Haraway 1989, 1991), but I wouldn't bet too much on it.

When we come closest in to the center of the specification hierarchy, when we consider the sciences of human ecosocial systems, we can be most sure that anything that is said in any culture, by members of any caste (i.e. group defined by similar life practices and life experiences; in our community principally one that is homogeneous in age, social class, gender type and cultural background), will be highly viewpoint dependent. Our best hedge against the blinders of this inevitable parochialism is to seek out views from vantage points as different as possible from our own and from each others'. This is not, of course, what is currently done in Western society, where a single caste works with all its resources to ensure that only those who speak with its own voice will be heard on such matters.

The Social Construction of Subjectivity

The heart of our modern notion of the social subject is a particular aspect of our experiencing, the sense we have all learned to create that there is an inner 'I' or experiencing center which perceives and wills.

Experiencing is itself both mediated by semiotic resources such as language and visual imagery and formatively shaped in large part by social interaction. If we set aside as unproductive in this context various realist and positivist certitudes about the form of external realities, we can ask how our perceptions are shaped by both our own and others' habitual culture-specific uses of language, visual imagery and other semiotic resources. Those resources do not include just language, with its semantic categories and grammatical role systems, or visual conventions about how objects are defined and spatial relationships construed, they also include the motor activity habits of our culture, learned in primary social interactions: possible doings, from graspings and object-movings, to shape-feelings, person-touchings, face-shapings, limb-articulations and movement patterns, to later and more complex doings like washing our hands, focusing our microscopes and carrying on our dialogues. All of these have semiotic and cultural values; all belong to systems of paradigmatic and syntagmatic relations of meaning. All shift their meanings and forms as we contextualize them in different ways.

An ecosocial systems perspective shows us that we are primitively enmeshed in and depend for our origins and continuing existence on a hierarchy of levels of interaction and transaction with multiple environments. In this perspective it is only the privileging of particular interactional linkages, particular material and semiotic processes on particular scales, that makes it sensible to distinguish an inner and an outer, a Self and an Other. Our cultural traditions do not do this in the same ways when they speak of organisms in ecosystems and of persons in social-semiotic interaction, but they do teach us to do both. From the locutions of our discourse to the patterns of social interaction that define and teach simple and complex cultural behaviors, all work to create a sense of self, of subject-actor-agent. These implicit roles begin in social and material interaction, and are internalized in that mimicry of external interaction with which the brain internally and adaptively deceives itself (cf. Edelman 1992 on the role of re-entrant neural connectivity in consciousness and cognition).

What is this 'self', this core 'ego' or 'I' that we claim to have direct subjective experience of? Since it is itself the experiencer of last resort, how can it know itself as an object of experience? It cannot, irrespective of what our cultural traditions teach us (cf. the paradox of the 'homunculus', e.g. in Edelman 1992). What we do experience is the meaning-shape of our doings, of our speakings, our actings, our hearings and feelings, of our doing and being-done-to, our participation in interactivity. That meaning-shape follows the patterns of language use and other semiotic formations in our community: culture-specific patterns. Nevertheless, our modernist European tradition has sought to universalize even these subjective experiences, asserting that all other humans experience as we do, sense ego and self as we do, construct intentions and goals as we do, even when cultural anthropology casts great doubt on the likelihood of this, given the absence of shared notions about such matters in the explicit folk theories of different cultures. We know as well that our own European history has elevated the primacy of individuality and the individual subject in recent centuries far above the place it held in the past or holds in other cultural traditions. We ought to be highly suspicious of the assumption that our notions of individual subjectivity are human universals.

I believe the most useful assumption we can make is that subjectivity is a learned cultural mode of construing the meaningfulness of primary experiencing, that our notions of the mind, the self, the ego are historical descendants in our own cultural tradition of earlier notions like the soul and the homunculus. We are taught to experience perceptions *as if* there were an experiencing 'I' and an experienced 'other', to imagine actions *as if* there were an imagining 'I' with intentions and goals, and to objectify actions *as if* they were procedures or nouns that could be embedded in linguistic and other semiotic structures used in planning and imagining. Subjectivity is itself a specific learned cultural construction. It has a developmental history, a foundation in social interactions, a prototype in the semantics of natural language and other cultural semiotic systems, and a specific event-by-event trajectory of the means by which it is demonstrated, participated in, scaffolded, inculcated, internalized, used, and finally taken for granted as a directly experienced reality.

We need some latter-day Jean Piaget to write *The Child's Construction of the Sense of Self.* It should tell us how the child (and later the adult), enmeshed in semiotically and materially mediated interactions with other members of a community and with the material environment, progressively recapitulates (always to some degree individuating) a trajectory of development that leads to our constructing the sense of a Self, a Self that looks out through the windows of the eyes, that initiates motor actions by 'will' and 'intention', that 'feels' the sensations which impinge on a body in which it sits, but of which it is not truly a physical part. It will tell the story of how we are taught to think of ourselves as Selves.

Such research will build on present and future work on the semiotic construction of activity, perception, behavior, intention and affect in the semantics of natural language (e.g. Hasan 1986b; Lemke 1988b, 1992a; Halliday 1990, 1992, 1993; Hasan and Cloran 1990; Martin 1992); on the role of narrative in the production of subjectivity and the role of dialogues, first external and then internal, in the construction of the sense of Self and the distinction of Self and Other (e.g. Vygotsky 1963; Leontiev 1978; Bruner 1983, 1991; Bruner and Weisser 1992). It will relate these discursive practices to the more general semiotics of visual images and depictions, and of cultural activities of a still wider variety of types.

We need such a body of research in order to reflect critically on the limitations of our cultural folk models about minds and selves. It may help us to better understand the alienation from the body of a middle-class culture which has traditionally identified bodies with the lower social orders and minds with the higher ones. It may help us reflect on the many scientific dead-ends born of the radical Cartesian split between the mind and matter. It may help us formulate cultural alternatives to the dismal paradigm of ultimately isolated subjects, and re-evaluate the implications of known alternative states of consciousness for the reunification of Self and Other, or the evidence for unconscious dimensions of the Self. Perhaps, in an age of research on artificial intelligence, it will help us see that notions such as intentionality and goal-directedness may be useful components in modeling how some people learn to think about behavior, but that they are hardly candidates for modeling intelligent behavior as such.

In the next chapter we will systematically examine the arguments for an ecosocial model of human communities as self-organizing systems. We will see what it means to make ecosocial processes, the cultural practices and ecological processes of a community, more fundamental constituents of human communities than individual human actors as such. We will lay out the specification hierarchy in more detail, enabling us to see human ecosocial systems as highly specific special cases of more general sorts of dynamical self-organizing systems. We will understand why it is that human organisms and human communities must be defined by their developmental trajectories, as temporally extended constructions, rather than as present-moment structures. Most fundamentally we will argue for the reunification of the semiotic and the material, the cultural and the ecological, in dynamical models of human systems. The resulting framework for an ecosocial dynamics will then enable us, in Chapter 7, to return to the problem of the postmodern subject and its postdemocratic politics, and to consider some of the most difficult and painful questions of our time.

Chapter 6

Discourse, Dynamics and Social Change

Discourse and Cultural Dynamics

What is the role of discourse in the processes of social and cultural change in our community? How do discursive, semiotic practices and other material, ecosystem processes interact to determine its dynamics?

In this chapter I will argue that in order to model the dynamics of such complex systems as human communities usefully we need a unified notion of *ecosocial systems*. We need to understand how the general principles that govern complex, material, self-organizing systems become further specialized in the case of human communities, where physical activity depends on social meaning. To do this we will try to construct a *specification hierarchy*, so that we can see human communities as special cases of more general kinds of complex systems. We will then be in a position to apply what we know about these more general systems to the particular problems of social and cultural change, and we will also be able to see what is distinctive and unique about the kinds of communities where a textual politics matters.

There are fundamental limitations on our ability to model systems of which we are ourselves a part. As observers and theorists we are limited by *scale*; we exist for mere decades, while the systems we seek to model exist for centuries; we can observe only small regions of space at any one time, while social systems extend over nations and continents. We change quickly: maturing, aging, dying; many cultural processes occur so slowly that they may not seem to us to be occurring at all. We are also limited by *position*: we are members of some cultures and societies and not others; we speak some languages, dialects, registers and discourses but not others; we are socially positioned observers, commanding a limited range of gender, age, class and social status viewpoints even within the cultural groups to which we belong.

On the other hand, as evolutionary and social *products* of the systems we study, we are *pre-adapted* to model them as a condition of our own survival (cf. Rosen 1985 on 'anticipatory systems'). As members of social groups we can participate in cooperative enterprises in which multiple observers cover larger areas, command a greater multiplicity of (not always easily shared) social and cultural viewpoints, and (partially) interpret the (incomplete) records left by our historical predecessors. It is as futile to imagine that a single organism can completely model its own ecosystem, or a single individual its own society, as that a single cell can model an organism, or a single molecule model a cell. A social system, a culture, however, might well construct and maintain a model of itself, necessarily incomplete perhaps (see Gödel 1931 and the Postscript to this book), but possibly adequate for certain purposes.

The tools with which we model the ecosocial systems to which we belong, both as material ecosystems and as cultural systems of meaning-making practices, are semiotic tools. They include: language and the discourses we make with language, the semiotics of depiction and the multi-media texts we make by combining visual with verbal resources, and, most generally, the semiotics of action – the meaningful activities we enact and the meaningful artifacts we create of all kinds.

By engaging in physical activities and producing material products that have meaning for us, we make it possible for those meanings to mediate our future actions. What we physically do depends on value choices and meaning choices. Those values and meanings are embodied in the texts, discourses, activities and artifacts of our culture, which we learn to use for ourselves as members of a community. To understand how meaning and material action are unified in an ecosocial system, one task is to spell out a social and cultural theory of meaning. A second is to articulate how it is possible for social and cultural meanings to arise and function in physical, material systems. While these are large tasks that I cannot fully accomplish in this book, I want to sketch out what I consider to be promising elements for such a theory.

More details on my own notions of a social semiotic theory of meaning-making can be found in the Postscript to this book, and there is a somewhat fuller discussion of certain topics in this chapter in Lemke (1994a). The next section of this chapter summarizes rather complex notions from the theory of social semiotics; some readers may wish to return to it after having read the Postscript.

Social Semiotics and Cultural Dynamics

The theory of cultural discourses as social semiotic formations (Halliday 1978, 1988, 1990; Thibault 1986, 1989a, 1989b, 1991; Threadgold 1986, 1989; Hodge and Kress 1988; Lemke 1988c, 1989c, 1990a, 1990b) has arisen from the study of the semantics of texts inspired by Bakhtin's social linguistics (Bakhtin 1929, 1935, 1953) and Halliday's functional semantics (Halliday 1976, 1978, 1985a). Social semiotics begins by disputing the primacy of the sign and the exclusive emphasis on sign systems in formalist semiotics (e.g. Eco 1976). Instead it gives priority to the *signifying act*, and to social signifying *practices* as regular, repeatable, recognizable types of human meaning-making activity. Social semiotics offers the view that socially meaningful *doings* constitute cultures (social semiotic systems), that cultures are systems of interdependent, socially meaningful practices by which we make sense to and of others, not merely in explicit communication, but through all forms of socially meaningful action (speaking, drawing, dressing, cooking, building, fighting etc.). Sign systems are abstractions from such practices (e.g. linguistic signs from speech), and they change as social practices change.

Sign systems are semiotic *resource* systems; they enable us to make meaningful actions (including utterances) by deploying these resources in recognizable, mostly habitual (and marginally creative) ways. The habitual ways in which we deploy them are identifiable as *semiotic formations*: the regular and repeatable, recognizably meaningful, culturally and historically specific patterns of co-deployment of semiotic resources in a community. A particular literary genre of some historical period is a semiotic formation; so also is an architectural style and type of building, a religious ritual, a typical holiday meal, the making of a particular type of costume. All these formations are defined in terms of the regular patterning of *actions*, of *socially meaningful practices* in which members of a community are engaged when producing them.

Discourse formations are social semiotic formations in which the deployment of *linguistic* resources is essential to the social meaning of the result (though other actional semiotic resources are also deployed as part of the formation, for example, gesture in speech, graphics with writing, etc.; cf. Lemke 1987, 1993a). The linguistic (semantic and grammatical) resources specific to a particular discourse formation form a *register* of the language (a specific distribution of the probabilities of deploying any meaning alternative the language provides; see Gregory 1967; Ure and Ellis 1974; Halliday 1978). A particular type of weather report, for example, would be a specific discourse formation, deploying a portion of the register of meteorology, and doing so according to a scheme of organization and sequence, that is, a *genre* (Hasan 1984b, 1989a; Ventola 1987; Lemke 1988a, 1989b, 1990a; Threadgold and Kress 1988; Martin 1989). There are speech genres, and genres of both literary and non-literary writing; there are also, more generally, *action genres*, which need not involve language at all, though their enactment may be guided by use of a discourse formation, as when we 'talk ourselves through' a complex performance or an activity requiring difficult, context-dependent choices.

As we saw in Chapter 2, semiotic formations provide an intermediate level of conceptual analysis between the microsocial (utterances, texts, particular acts and events) and the macrosocial (dialects, institutions, classes, ideologies). More importantly, they formulate the scale from microsocial to macrosocial in terms of *actions* (social practices) and *patterns of relations of actions* (cultural formations) and not in terms of entities and aggregations of entities (individuals, corporate groups, societies). This is an essentially *cultural* view; social systems are systems of *doings*, not of *beings* as such. They are systems of interrelated cultural practices, not systems of socially interacting individuals. The ultimate theoretical constituents of a social system are not interacting dyads, not even individual members, but individual social and cultural practices. Social 'individuals' must be theoretically reconstructed (e.g. Lemke 1988b, 1993b); as we saw in Chapter 5, they can no longer be taken as 'givens' in a semiotic social theory.

The link between formations and *macrosocial* structural relations and their dynamics is provided by another cultural notion: *organized heterogeneity* (cf. Wallace 1970 on 'organization of diversity'). Social and cultural systems are not homogeneous; they exhibit an essential internal diversity. Their subsystems are characterized by complementary or conflicting alternatives (e.g. the social practices of men vs. those of women, of one social class vs. another, one age-group vs. another, etc.). In the case of discourse formations, Bakhtin (1935) labeled this phenomenon social *heteroglossia*, already discussed in Chapter 2. What is important here is to see that it is precisely the systematic relationships between social voices or discourse formations (and more generally action formations) of different social castes that constitute the macrosocial organization of the community, viewed in microsocial terms. It is how different kinds of people talk and act differently that enables us to define genders, social classes, age groups, etc. It is the systematic relations between their different dispositions toward talk and action that tells us about the overall organization of society (cf. discussion of Bourdieu in Chapter 2).

What applies to the discourses of diverse and often conflicting subcommunities applies equally to all their social practices and formations; there is a general system of *heteropraxia*, of specific relations of alliance, opposition, etc. among their ways of doing, each with respect to the others, of which the system of heteroglossia is one very important part. No text can be read, no action interpreted, without taking into account the existence of alternative and conflicting ways of saying and doing within the same total community. No utterance or action escapes making meanings, anticipated or not, in these terms.

The problem of how to usefully represent semiotic formations, particularly discursive, and most especially linguistic, textual formations is a difficult and complex one. How we represent them depends on how we plan to use these representations. There are basically three approaches to this problem, and each brings a needed element.

Formations may be represented in terms of their constituent actions as selections from sets of alternatives with contrasting meanings (paradigm sets), with each selected alternative implying something about the structure and sequence of action as well as the specific acts to be performed. This is a straightforward generalization of the paradigm-and-realization model of language used in systemic linguistics (e.g. Halliday 1976; Fawcett 1980).

Formations may also be represented structurally according to a syntagm-and-realization model as in genre theory (e.g. Hasan 1989a; Ventola 1987), or according to a mixed approach appropriate to the kind of formation being described (cf. the representation of discourse formations by thematic pattern diagrams in Lemke 1983a, 1988c, 1990a). Finally, formations can be represented probabilistically, in terms of the likelihood that two meaningful elements will occur together (conditional probabilities) or that one will follow another (transitional probabilities; see Halliday 1991 and Postscript to this book).

Since semiotic formations deploy resources that form systems of (paradigmatic) semiotic alternatives (often from different semiotic systems, e.g. language and gesture or picture, cf. Lemke 1987; 1993a), and since they are characteristic of divergent subcommunities (heteroglossia, heteropraxia), we can represent them most generally in terms of the conditional probabilities for the co-occurrence of various practices in various contexts, according to the subcommunity, and indeed the culture as a whole. This can be done within the general *relational-contextual* model of meaning employed in social semiotics, which is discussed in more detail in the Postscript.

Any action or activity is socially meaningful only *in relation to* other alternative actions or activities that might have occurred in its place. The specific meaning of an action is interpretable only in relation to the set of socially relevant *contexts* that are constructed for the purposes of that interpretation. Such contexts are generally analyzable into syntagmatic contexts (other parts of the same whole), paradigmatic contexts (alternative parts for the same whole), and indexical contexts (co-occurring wholes on different scales of organization; see Lemke 1990a: Ch. 8 and the Postscript). The very act of meaning-making can be represented as *selective contextualization*; we make sense of a word or a deed by construing it in relation to other actual or possible words and deeds that we construct as the relevant contexts for its interpretation.

All of these various sorts of contextualization relations may be formally represented as *meta-redundancy* relations (Lemke 1984: 35–9; see also Halliday 1991), as discussed in the Postscript. The trick here (adopted from a suggestion of Bateson 1972: 132–3) is to specify the conditional probabilities for co-occurrence of various alternatives in various contexts *hierarchically* so that higher level alternatives (e.g. social class of speaker) co-occur with entire probability distributions linking, say, semantic types of utterances to situational uses (cf. Hasan 1989b, 1994), and not with particular acts or situation types separately. Thus to be a member of a social class subculture is not to use only some semantic strategies available in the language, or even to use them with a certain distinctive probability, but to combine them differently with the demands of situation from what a member of another class might do.

This formal hierarchy of contextualization in social meaning reflects the dynamical hierarchy of emergent levels of organization in human ecosocial systems, as we will see below. The semiotic resource systems of a community are abstracted from the actual patterns of semiotic activity in that community. Semiotic formations show us how these resources are habitually deployed in the community; and the meta-redundancy relations summarize how different formations co-occur with respect to each other. All these analytic forms are abstractions; they all depend entirely on the moment-to-moment happenings in the community.

Semiotic formations are relatively stable elements in the flux of day-to-day social action; they ensure the minimal short term predictability necessary for social coherence. No inertia or active constraining force is attributed to abstract semiotic systems like language, formations such as genres, or meta-redundancy relations, however. If these abstract patterns seem to persist, to change coherently, or to evolve over time, it is because the myriad particular events of human action and interaction from which they are derived are themselves simultaneously elements of material dynamical systems which do persist, change coherently, and evolve over time. If formal semiotic relations exhibit an irreducible hierarchical organization, it is because the self-organizing human ecological communities that enact them do so. Semiotic systems and formations, and thus culture, do not have an autonomous dynamics of their own, but rather a complex interdependence with the material dynamics of social communities.

Meaning systems and cultures change. What was not meaningful before can become meaningful, and this process depends critically on the interdependence between material and semiotic dynamics within a total ecological–social–semiotic system. Human social communities *are* material ecosystems, but they are complex material ecosystems in which meanings – cultural and social attitudes, beliefs, and values – play a role in the material activities that take place within the system to maintain and change it. In order to understand the role of discourses and other meaning-making practices in a community, we need to understand the *general* processes of self-organization in complex material systems, and then to see the semiotically mediated processes of human communities as a special case within this more general framework.

In the next several sections of this chapter we will construct a *specification hierarchy* (cf. Salthe 1985, 1989, 1993) in order to see human ecosocial communities as a highly specific special case of more general kinds of complex self-organizing systems. We will begin from the most general sorts of systems that science can describe, those that have, in effect, the fewest properties, the fewest complications. We will see, as the nature of the systems grows more complex, the emergence of very general principles of the dynamics of self-organizing systems, principles that apply to all the special cases, including our own. We will move on to successively more highly specified classes of complex systems, of which human communities will always be a still more specific special case. At each step we will discern principles that apply to human communities because they apply generally to these broader classes of complex systems.

What is true of all living things is necessarily true of all mammals, and what is true of all mammals applies in particular to all primates, and what all primates have, humans must have too. Of course mammals have, within the parameters that define life, special characteristics that, say, insects, do not have, and humans are primates, but primates with a difference. Our specification hierarchy will be concerned with systems rather than with lifeforms as such, and we will begin it with systems far more general than biological ones, but we will just as surely come to see what human ecosocial communities share in common with other ecosystems, and with all self-organizing systems of every kind, so that we can also see better how we are different and distinctive in terms of the role that human culture and its textual politics plays in shaping us.

We need first, however, to understand what complex systems are and why the complexity of material systems is relevant to understanding cultural systems of actions, discourses and texts.

The Dynamics of Complex Systems

A 'social practice' is a semiotic cultural abstraction, but every particular, actual instance of that social practice is enacted by some material processes in a complex physical, chemical, biological, ecological system. Every action thus enters into two systems of relations, for which our culture has two different sorts of descriptive discourses. As an instance of a social practice, it enters into relations of meaning with other social practices. These are semiotic relations. As a physical event, it enters into relations of energy, matter and information exchange with other events. These are material relations. Every instance of a social practice is simultaneously also an instance of some material process. Every system of social practices, linked in semiotic formations according to their meaning relations, is also a system of material processes linked by physical, chemical and ecological relations.

When we build a building, we quarry stone or cast concrete, we construct doors and walls and windows, we build floors and stairs and shafts, we place ducts and vents – all in accordance with a system of cultural practices that defines for us an architectural style, a desirable design. Our discourses and practices of architecture and design are historically and culturally specific semiotic formations. They specify what buildings and rooms should be like, how comfort and privacy should be provided for, which spaces are monumental, which public, which private, how size, shape and light should co-occur with use and function – in short, the architectural semiotics of our culture.

In doing all this, however, we are also assembling masses with densities, weights, compressional and tensile strengths, electrical and thermal conductivities; we are arranging flows of water and air according to principles of hydrodynamics, flows of heat by principles of thermodynamics, and allowing for material flows of people and goods. We may provide a system of communications capable of handling certain rates of information transfer, a supply of energy that may flow from solar panels on the roof to heating channels in the walls, or from underground generators through cables to electrical connections in every room. These things we do also according to discourses of our community, those regarding science and engineering, but in all these doings, our actions participate in the material ecology of building just as much as they do in the semiotic order of architecture and design. Building both creates an architectural 'text' and materially reconfigures part of the ecosystem. Every action that contributes to building must be understood both for its architectural meaning and for its physical conditions and effects. Every such action is both a material process and a meaningful cultural practice.

Every meaningful social practice can be enacted only through some material processes. The semiotic formations that link cultural practices to one another through their cultural meanings inevitably also couple these material processes together in new ways. Whether in obvious cases such as the construction of cities or the clear-cutting of rainforest, or in less evident ones such as the publishing of books, the imprisonment of offenders, the selection of mates, or the setting of wages and prices, cultural linkages of social practices into semiotic formations produce physical, biological and ecological linkages of material processes. We operate within, and work to transform, our material ecosystem according to semiotic, cultural principles. Reciprocally, the linkages of material processes on which the ecophysical being of the community depends, which indeed *are* the ecophysical being of the community, form the basis for all possible and actual change in our cultural systems of semiotic practices.

The full implications of this fundamental interdependence of cultural practices and material processes cannot be fully appreciated without seeing both as aspects of a unitary *ecosocial system*. Such systems are hierarchically organized at many different scales through complex couplings of processes which feed back to one another to produce entirely surprising, emergent phenomena (self-organization). In the dynamics of complex, tightly coupled systems with strong multiple feedback loops, even small local changes can produce surprising global effects. Semiotic formations, which slightly bias the linkages of material processes according to their semiotic meanings for a human culture, are essential elements in the material dynamics of human communities. There cannot be two systems here, one material and the other cultural, each changing according to separate laws, relatively independent of one another. There can be only one unitary *ecosocial system*, material and semiotic, with a single unified dynamics.

The unity of ecosocial systems is somewhat hidden from view by our failure to appreciate the pervasiveness of the material–semiotic interdependence.

We are partly blinded by the biases of the dominant class in Western society, whose interests favor a view of the world as indefinitely exploitable materially and infinitely flexible culturally. We are also a predominantly urban community for whom agriculture, a primary site of the material–semiotic coupling, seems distant and trivial. We are a machine culture accustomed to simple proportionality of cause and effect (not massive self-amplifications) and stable dynamics (not emergent self-organization). We are a culture reluctant to examine what we do culturally to and with organic bodies (our own, our children's, our enemies', other species'; see Chapter 7). We are only beginning to realize that we are not the lords of creation, but the most recent, dependent, vulnerable and expendable extension of a far older, non-human planetary ecosystem (e.g. Lovelock 1989), and that our survival depends on enhancing, not exploiting, a system that takes no cognizance of our interests and values, except in so far as we long ago adapted to its realities. We are also only beginning to realize that we do not make history and culture exactly as we please, but only within the limits of a vaster, transhuman system, whom we cannot in principle observe or control.

What makes a system 'complex' in this sense? How are the dynamics of such complex systems as human ecosocial communities fundamentally divergent from intuitions about them based on the dynamics of simple, machine-like systems? If we wish to begin from the outermost, most general category of complex systems in our specification hierarchy, we need to consider what many otherwise very different complex systems have in common, for example: a dust-devil (or a tornado), a cell, a developing embryo, a caterpillar–pupa–butterfly, a human organism, a living lake (or rainforest), a living city, an ecosocial system, the living planet.

The study of complex systems is now well advanced in physics and chemistry (e.g. Prigogine 1980; Harrison 1982; Prigogine and Stengers 1984; Jackson 1989) and is beginning to make progress in developmental and evolutionary biology, ecology and geophysiology (see Odum 1983; Salthe 1985, 1989, 1993; Holling 1986; Weber *et al.* 1988; Lovelock 1989; Kauffman 1993). What makes a system truly complex dynamically is not simply the number of variables (or 'degrees of freedom'), but how these variables depend on one another, the pattern of their 'couplings'. The more interdependent they are, both in numbers of interconnections and the strength of the interconnections, the less predictable the future of the system. When the couplings 'loop back' on themselves (e.g. changes in A produce changes in B, which produce changes in C, which in turn produce changes in A again), the system may grow in complexity, generating new global patterns and new information.

All physical systems appear to have some properties in common. They can all be assigned a total mass or energy. If the system can be decomposed into subsystems, in addition to the mass and energy of each component, there is an energy associated with the strength of interaction between components and an energy of their motion relative to one another.

The simplest physical systems, elementary dynamical systems, such as a hydrogen atom (an electron and a proton bound together by their energy of mutual electrical attraction), or two electrons interacting as they nearly collide with one another (mutual electrical repulsion of like charges), have a small number of physical characteristics which completely describe them for all physical purposes. Whenever they exist they have these characteristics, and as we will see, they differ from complex systems in that since they all always have these same characteristics, they have no individuality (each such system is indistinguishable from every other) and no history. They do not age, they have no memory; their past interactions have no effect on their future interactions. 'Past' or 'future' are all the same to them – entirely irrelevant.

Complex systems are different. Physics first studied systems with many degrees of freedom but only weak coupling between their elements (e.g. gases with large numbers of weakly interacting molecules). For systems like this the first symptom of complexity already appears: the Newtonian symmetry between past and future is broken, dynamics proceeds irreversibly and uni-directionally into what we call the future. Each separate internal interaction or collision of molecules is a simple system and could in principle be reversed in time, brought back exactly to its previous state with a finite amount of information and a finite amount of energy. Each collision produces correlations in the subsequent motions of the many other participating molecules, however, which now have further and further collisions, the correlations multiplying rapidly toward a state which would require infinite information to be set into an exact reversal (Prigogine 1980).

This phenomenon of irreversibility was first formulated as the famous Second Law of Thermodynamics: that closed systems tend to the state of equilibrium, the state with the most probable values for any overall macroscopic property of the total system, corresponding to any one of a set of the largest possible number of thermodynamically equivalent distributions of the molecules. Any other state would be much less probable because there would be many fewer molecular combinations corresponding to it; random collisions would rapidly favor the equilibrium state. Equilibrium is also the most homogeneous, most symmetric, least diverse, coolest, lowest energy state of a complex system. It is the final death, the endpoint of decay and decomposition: neutral, inert, exhausted, stable. Spontaneous thermodynamic change moves from the unusual, the specialized, the differentiated, the energetic to the generic, the uniform, the quiescent; from what is uncommon and improbable in a world of random influences that destroy order and organization to the most probable state of no order, no organization; from states high in order and organization ('high negentropy') to those high in disorder and disorganization ('high entropy').

In the real world, however, many complex systems, and all the ones in our list of examples, do not behave in this way. A mass of air with a vortex (dust-devil or tornado) is *more* organized than the turbulent mass of air before the vortex formed, not less. A developing embryo goes from a state of lesser to a state of greater differentiation, away from homogeneity. Mature ecosystems are more complex and differentiated than immature ones, not less. The living planet as a whole is today further from the state of equilibrium than it was four billion years ago, not closer to it. It would be very easy to predict the future of a culture, of an ecosocial system, if it behaved thermodynamically; it would disintegrate, collapse, become homogeneous and incapable of further change. Distinctions would be lost, diversity would disappear, decay would outstrip construction, useless wastes would be more common than useful resources. In fact our history has veered far away from this path to the ecosocial death of equilibrium, placing many buffers between us and the long slide to ruin. *How?*

All our examples are *open*, not closed systems; they all exchange at least energy and information, and usually matter as well, with their environments. The living planet lives because energy flows to it from the sun, is transformed by life, and is returned to space as radiated heat at a lower temperature than it would be by a barren planet in the same orbit. The developing embryo (and child) feeds on the nutrients and organizational information of its external (mother) and internalized (DNA, see below) environments, producing great amounts of waste heat and waste chemicals which must be safely conducted away. The city claims resources of energy and raw materials from its environment and exports back to that environment heat and solid wastes in quantity. In all these systems, the transforming processes (metabolism, chemical ontogenesis, urban production and consumption) are irreversible ones and generate entropy (disorder, matter and energy closer to equilibrium than they began), but the high entropy elements are excreted from the system into the environment, allowing a net increase in the order and organization of the system itself at the expense of its environment.

The unavoidable, irreversible thermodynamic processes that generate entropy (in the form of heat and waste) are called *dissipative* processes, and a system that keeps itself going (and perhaps becoming even more organized and differentiated) by the trick of importing energy, information and resources from and exporting disorder to its environment is called a *dissipative structure* (Prigogine 1980; Prigogine and Stengers 1984) or *dynamic open system* (Lemke 1984). Dust-devils, cells, developing embryos, organisms, ecosystems, cities, ecosocial communities, and the living planet are all dissipative structures. So also are fires, hurricanes, convection cells in heated fluids (e.g. atmospheric circulation and oceanic currents) and even certain inorganic chemical cells that maintain concentration gradients and produce elaborately beautiful patterns (see Prigogine 1980; Berge *et al.* 1984).

We have begun to define the specification hierarchy that converges on human ecosocial systems. Starting from the most general case of all possible physical systems, we are saying that human ecosocial systems are physical systems, but a special kind of physical system. In particular they are complex systems, and among complex systems they are open systems, and among open systems they are certainly dissipative structures or dynamic open systems, which makes them at least minimally self-organizing systems.

The flows of energy, matter and information that maintain these dynamic open systems in existence are thermodynamic *constraints*, they keep the system away from the path to equilibrium by supplying order and safely conducting disorder away. How can such systems come into being in the first place? Once in existence, how can they become even more organized and complex, actually moving further from the path to equilibrium? The answer again is strong coupling. This is most easily seen in the case of chemical reactions involving several different chemicals which tend to form loops of chemical reactions, with some of the initial substances eventually being reproduced in the course of subsequent reactions, thus leading to even more possibilities for the chain of reactions to continue instead of eventually coming to a halt (the path to equilibrium). Such systems of coupled, looped reactions are called *autocatalytic* systems, and they lead to conditions in which the amounts of various substances and the rates of reactions using and producing them depend on one another in *more than proportional* ways (i.e. an increase of 10 percent in some amount or rate might lead to *more* than a 10 percent increase in something else, even, ultimately, in itself!). Mathematically, these are *non-linear* systems, and they do not behave according to the intuitions commonly found in our Western machine culture.

Non-linear, autocatalytic systems are complex in the second degree. They not only show irreversibility, they exhibit the phenomena known as *bifurcation* (e.g. Prigogine 1980; Prigogine and Stengers 1984; cf. 'catastrophe' in Thom 1975) and *chaos* (Gleick 1987; Jackson 1989). Essentially these are systems that can shift unpredictably from one meta-stable non-equilibrium state to another. When they are embedded in buffering, regulating environments (supersystems) they can shift to new states further from equilibrium by *dynamical symmetry-breaking*.

Irreversibility was already a breaking of the symmetry of time in fundamental interactions (which are time-reversible, not distinguishing a 'past' from a 'future'). Bifurcating systems create for themselves possible states with less symmetry (in time, e.g. periodicity, or irregular rhythms; or in space, e.g. gradients or spatial patterns) than they began with. There are always several such states, and if the system spent equal amounts of time in each, the net result would be to restore the original degree of symmetry. This is not what happens, however. As the possibility of the new states is reached (because of a build-up of some internal or external factor), *random fluctuations* determine that the system will become stable in *one* of these less symmetric, less homogeneous, more specialized, differentiated, orderly, organized, further-from-equilibrium states. If the experiment is repeated, it might be another of these asymmetric states that is entered and which then persists, but in each case the system moves further from equilibrium.

Such systems are often called *self-organizing* systems, although it is important to remember that the organizing of the system is the result of interactions with the environment, not an internal and autonomous process. In each new state of the system the internal dynamics are different; there are different rates of reactions, different amounts of chemicals built up, new effects on the environment and new environmental reponses, and new possibilities for still newer reaction pathways to come into being. In this way a new state of the system prepares the way for yet another bifurcation, yet another jump to a still newer state, even more organized and differentiated, breaking more symmetries of the previous state. Again, accidental factors may play an important role. New couplings of reactions may occur in this individual system and not in that, random fluctuations (internal or external) may influence the possibilities of subsequent jumps to new states.

We now arrive on the threshold of a further order of complexity in dynamics, one particularly characteristic of organic and ecosocial systems: the order of epigenesis, evolution and emergence. Systems of this kind have all the properties of dissipative structures and self-organizing systems in general, but they interact with their environments and build up new internal complexity in a special way. They form the next more specified class of systems of which human communities are a still more special case.

Epigenesis, Evolution and Emergence

Electrons and atoms do not age. They have no history, no individuality, no youth, maturity or old age. An atom is already a compound, though not in our sense a complex, system. It has different states, but they are always the same set of possibilities. It does not know irreversibility, it is not a dissipative structure. It is stable. If you shift it to an alternative unstable state, it quickly returns to its original configuration and all memory of the excursus is lost. You cannot tell one atom of oxygen in its stable state from any other; the definition of the state itself specifies all variables, there are no supernumerary degrees of freedom left to record a past history and allow us to distinguish different individuals in the same state. When two electrons collide, there is no way to tell afterwards which electron was which. Electrons cannot be labeled; they have no properties that can be used as a label beyond the properties that define them as electrons. We cannot construct a continuity of identity for an electron across time from before an interaction to after it as we can do for human beings (cf. Chapter 5) or for any macroscopic or sufficiently complex system.

Complex systems are very different, they have so many more degrees of freedom (properties) than an atom, that there are always degrees 'left over' as it were to record history, even if it is only the correlations that reflect the history of past random collisions. Complex systems are individuals and they have a history; it is possible to construct a continuity of individuality from before to after an interaction that changes the system in some way. If such systems have undergone a series of bifurcation jumps to new lesser-symmetry states farther from equilibrium, however, then it is not possible to predict (or model in any way) these future states from a knowledge of prior states, *except* by recapitulating the *intermediate* states, that is the entire *developmental sequence* of bifurcation jumps, leading to that future state. Self-organizing systems thus have a second, invisible history, not just marks of wear and tear, the accumulated memory of past encounters, but the developmental trajectory of changes in their dynamics by which they came to the more organized, less symmetric state they are in.

In a profound sense, complex systems that *develop* in this way, including both human organisms and ecosocial systems, are temporally extended entities. The system, as an individual entity, cannot be defined at one moment in time, because the dynamics which maintains it in being must occur over time. In each instant, it is dead; only over time is it alive. So much is true for any dissipative structure, but a truly *developing* system cannot be defined even over an interval of time limited to one stage in its developmental career, because its constitutive dynamics will be quite different in later stages. Only the system extended in time along its complete *developmental trajectory*, from formation to disintegration, from conception to decomposition, is a properly defined theoretical entity. We will refer hereafter to the developmental trajectory entity, meaning the system-over-its-lifetime, when necessary, to emphasize this new perspective. The caterpillar–pupa–butterfly is one individual developing system, as is the embryo–child–adult–elder. The notion of trajectory entities in this sense allows us to formulate new, genuinely dynamical definitions of ecosocial systems, cultural formations, language dialects, corporate institutions and even social individuals.

With the notion of developing systems we reach a new threshold in the specification hierarchy, but before we go beyond self-organizing dissipative structures, it is worth noting that all such systems exhibit a common thermodynamic outline to their trajectories of development (see Salthe 1989, 1993). Whether we are speaking of hurricanes, embryos, organisms or ecosystems, there is a common sequence of developmental stages. In the *ascendant* stage (or *phase*) the system is dissipating energy, producing heat and wastes (entropy), at a maximal rate in proportion to its total mass, and its internal organization and order are increasing at the maximum rate. This rate of generation of disorder (exported to the environment) and order (accumulated in the system itself) gradually slows as the system passes through its various developmental bifurcations, moving further from equilibrium, until some limit is reached, and a meta-stable state develops (*mature phase*) with minimum entropy production consistent with maintaining the mature organization of the system. Finally, there may be a *senescent phase* in which an overly self-regulated dynamics becomes vulnerable to external disturbances, eventually degrading and finally decaying back toward the path to equilibrium and death. (The most complex developing systems may be able to avoid terminal senescence, as we will see.)

The existence of such a generic developmental trajectory points the way to a new strategy for modeling complex systems. For any given system, it is not possible to anticipate bifurcations and predict dynamical futures beyond the current stage (or even whether there will be a new stage), but if the system is of a recognizable *type*, then there is a good chance that it will follow, at least up to a point, the typical developmental trajectory of its kind. Type-specific developmental change is predictable from a knowledge of the type. This is the basis of embryology, and of the prediction that most caterpillars, if they survive under more or less normal conditions, will eventually be butterflies. How does it happen, however, that developmental trajectories as specific to a set of ecological conditions as those leading to butterflies can become fixed and repeatable? This is the next order of complexity in dynamics, that of *epigenesis,* and defines the next more highly specific class of systems to which human communities belong.

An *epigenetic system* is a developing system that recapitulates the major stages along a developmental trajectory typical of its kind. It is a system that develops according to its kind, recapitulating a sequence of bifurcations in its dynamics that may have evolved over many generations of its predecessors. I hope it is clear that while we have for some time now been using the language of living systems, that at no point in the specification hierarchy that we have been defining (complex systems with irreversibility, dissipative structures, developing systems, epigenetic systems) is there a clear transition to life, as such. Hurricanes are alive in many significant ways; so is the planet as a whole. Organismic life as we know it is based on a very specific strategy (DNA-mediated epigenesis), but ecosystems are also alive and use a different strategy. What is special about the class of epigenetic systems is that the developmental trajectories of individuals recapitulate a prior evolution of the trajectory of their type.

The terms 'development' and 'evolution' are used loosely and often interchangeably outside biology. Because they are paradigms of different modes of change in the study of complex systems, however, it is important to separate them. Individuals develop; types evolve. Individual systems also individuate; that is, the developmental trajectory of an individual system recapitulates that of its type only in general. In many specific ways it is unique, reflecting its own individual history. In particular, an individual system may deviate from the type trajectory in a way that can be passed on and recapitulated by future developing systems; it may contribute to the evolution of the type. What evolves is the *developmental trajectory* of the type (and not, actually, the type as such). Evolution occurs when individuation leads to a new dynamical stage (through a new bifurcation, a phase change in the dynamics) which *can* be recapitulated, and when the new trajectory actually *is* recapitulated in the developmental trajectories of a significant number of successor systems.

How is recapitulation possible? Epigenesis further specifies the nature of development; epigenetic development is development guided by an environment that is approximately the same for different individual systems and that changes relatively slowly compared to the lifetime of these systems. The sequence of bifurcations, of development, cannot be left entirely to chance, to random fluctuations, if there is to be recapitulation. Random fluctuations must be harnessed and guided by an external source of information, regulation and control, and that can only reside in the environment of the developing system. An adequate analysis of a developing system must not only be extended in time, it must also extend beyond the system itself to examine system–environment interactions; it must extend to the immediate *supersystem* that contains both the system under focus and its immediate environment (cf. Lemke 1984 and the Postscript).

Dissipative structures and their environments must interact with each other. The sequence of bifurcations (i.e. the course of 'self-organization') will depend strongly on environmental conditions. If many individual systems develop under the same environmental conditions, the odds are that they will undergo similar sequences of bifurcations. Developing systems can and do also modify their environments (often for the worse, by exporting disorder into them), but they are dependent on these environments for energy, material resources and information–regulation–constraint.

In epigenetic systems, a new bifurcation in an individual leads to an effect on the environment that favors similar bifurcations in other individuals. A series of 'accidental' dust-devils in a narrow defile might erode landscape surfaces in a way that produces contours which favor the formation of other very similar dust-devils in that same place. Globules of organic polymers in a tidal pool, engaged in autocatalytic chemical reactions (i.e. proto-life), might modify the surrounding silicate clays (their external, proto-DNA) in ways that tend to favor recapitulation of their latest chemical innovations when future globules develop in the same pool. In each case, along with epigenesis comes a supersystem (dust-devils plus landscape, globules plus clays in tidal pool) and a hierarchical relation of system and supersystem. That hierarchical relation is one of *scale* (cf. Salthe 1985, 1989, 1993 who clearly distinguishes scale hierarchies from specification hierarchies), in which the supersystem is more stable, changes more slowly and exerts a regulatory influence on the dynamics of the now 'sub'-system. In the case of organismic lifeforms, the relatively stable 'environmental' molecules (RNA, DNA) were eventually internalized, incorporated into the supersystem which became the modern *cell*.

Epigenesis depends only on a system's being integrated into a supersystem which can in turn regulate the subsystem's development. It depends only on the possibility that innovations by individual subsystems can be recapitulated because information about them (or leading to them) is stored in the long term 'memory' of the supersystem environment. The DNA strategy of organismic life is only one specific way in which this can happen. Epigenesis is simply development under an environmental guidance that enables recapitulation of type trajectories in individual development.

This account of things (like many of the accounts of the origin of organismic life) is a bit backwards; there have always been supersystems, there have always been ecosystems, there has always been a planetary dynamical system. Particular self-organizing units always came into being in the context of supersystem environments. Life did not begin with micro-organisms that eventually got together to form ecosystems that eventually united into the living planetary system ('Gaia'). There was always Gaia, even before organic life, and there were always the chemical, atmospheric, oceanographic and geological precursors of biological ecosystems. What has happened in the history of the planet is that new *intermediate* levels of organization have emerged *between* the total Gaia system and her molecular subsystems. Ecosocial systems and the human cultures they sustain form one of those intermediate levels. These levels of organization, each on a different scale of physical size and mass, rates of change, energy transfer etc. is (partially) regulated by its integration into the larger ones that contain it, and in turn (partially) regulates the smaller scale ones that it contains.

All epigenetic systems belong to regulatory subsystem–supersystem hierarchies of this kind across a range of scales from the molecular to the planetary. At or near the human scale, organismic lifeforms are not the only epigenetic systems, there are also ecosystems. Considering them will lead us on to the final principles of complex dynamics needed for understanding cultural and social change.

Ecosystem Dynamics

Living forests, lakes and cities are also epigenetic systems, but they have evolved somewhat different strategies from those of organisms. Organisms and ecosystems are both larger scale supersystems constituted by and acting to integrate and regulate the smaller scale subsystems they contain. Organisms integrate the processes of organ systems, organs, tissues, cells and intra and extra-cellular body chemistry down to the molecular level. Ecosystems integrate the processes of interaction of organisms with each other (within and between species) and with the flows of matter, energy and information through the total system, including solar radiation and heat flows, water and nutrient flows, and hydrologic, atmospheric and geologic processes on local and larger scales.

Organisms show 'planned obsolescence'; they enter a developmental phase of terminal senescence and die. Most higher organisms seem to have a fairly definite maximum lifespan, after which they quickly return to the path to equilibrium. This is associated with their strategy of individual reproduction; organisms are like autocatalytic reactions, they multiply themselves to the limit of available resources or until they are regulated by the supersystem (e.g. by predator population increases). If such 'breeder' lifeforms did not die, they would soon overload the carry-capacity of any ecosystem to which they belonged. For ecosystems themselves, however, things are rather different (Odum 1983; Holling 1986; Schneider 1988).

Ecosystems do not seem to die of old age; neither do they directly reproduce new individual ecosystems. The relation between individuation, evolution and recapitulative development is different for this class of epigenetic system, but one exists nonetheless. Ecosystems do show a form of type specific recapitulative development, known as ecological succession. A newly opened area (a new volcanic island, a burned-out forest, abandoned farmland) is first colonized by one group of species that form an ascendant phase ecosystem with its own stage-specific dynamics. This ecosystem tends to spread rapidly, with fast-reproducing, short-lived species; it also alters the soil and local environment generally in a way that is favorable to its replacement (succession) by another group of species that forms a later phase of the ecosystem's developmental trajectory over time, and which can flourish in the conditions created by the first phase. This continues with a slowing in the rate of growth and the rate of dissipation and accumulation of structure; there are more complex couplings of species and nonbiotic elements, longer chains for the cycling of nutrients, more stored resources, etc., forming the now mature ecosystem.

Instead of heading on into terminal senescence, two things will have happened instead. The system may enter a stage of post-maturity in which it is not as resilient as it was previously and is more vulnerable to external disturbances, but at the same time it will have grown 'patchy' with a mosaic structure on many scales of small regions in which the dynamics are distinctively different. When a great oak or redwood finally dies, when a small fire burns out a part of the forest, when a storm damages part of a coral reef, when pollution degrades the environment in part of a lake, a mini-succession will begin again in that little 'patch', progressing faster or slower depending on proximity to other mature patches, on which species' propagules get there first, and on what the local soil, light and water conditions are. The natural topographical variations in soils, and for marine ecosystems the natural patchiness of nutrient flows and plankton populations, also ensures that ecosystems are everywhere 'patchy' mosaic aggregates. Stresses on patches may even cause a retrogression in the successional developmental sequence (Schneider 1988).

The result is that ecosystems are mixed-age aggregates. They consist of parts at different ages or stages of successional development. They consist more generally of little mini-ecosystems with slightly different mixes of species, or even different species in the same functional niches. Ecosystems do not, like organisms, reproduce new individuals with a distribution of variation in characteristics; they contain this diversity within themselves in simultaneous mosaic patches. Not only age, or successional stage, but every other characteristic of an ecosystem is present within it with a distribution of various values at various scales. Each patch is a mini-ecosystem which itself consists of a diverse mosaic of still smaller microsystem patches, etc. Ecosystems are mixed-age, mixed-character fractal mosaics.

Every ecosystem is an individual and, in a looser sense than for organisms, a member of a type. Its successional trajectory is not as rigid as that of an organism, but it has a recognizable outline. The succession of ecosystems is not under as tight a regulatory control as is the development of an organism, because the ecosystem is not itself part of as highly organized a supersystem as is a developing embryo. Ecosystem types are not as well-defined as organism species are; they are 'fuzzier' types. Ecosystem types certainly evolve (in our strict definition of evolution, it is actually their successional trajectories that evolve) and may do so very rapidly. The same set of species may form a different ecosystem if the dynamics of interaction in that system are different, and innovation (new couplings, interactions etc.) in a relatively young patch as it undergoes its partially unique succession can then spread in time through the territory of the total ecosystem, or at least be recapitulated in other patches, with evolution taking the statistical course of the most frequent pattern in future patches on each scale.

Ecosystems do not reproduce, but they do spread (and survive and 'dig in', becoming more resilient and stable occupants of their territory). The criteria of success, of 'fitness' for ecosystems cannot be posed in the same terms as for breeder lifeforms. For ecosystems the criteria of success include: persistence (meta-stability, resilience), adaptability, creation of a successful relation with an environmental supersystem (for resource inflow, waste outflow, buffering against disturbances), colonization potential and optimization of mosaic age and diversity distributions.

Ecosystems follow an epigenetic strategy that fosters the recapitulation of type (and microtype, i.e. 'patch') specific successional trajectories by both internal memory (the total ecosystem being a slowly changing, regulatory, environmental supersystem with respect to its patch subsystems) and external memory, such as modification of soils, water tables, local landforms, microclimate, etc. In this, in their lability to rapid local evolution, in their mosaic diversity, non-reproduction, and criteria for success, they seem to present a much more appropriate model for the dynamics of cities or human social communities than do organismic systems. This is because human social communities *are*, or more accurately, *are part of* ecosystems.

Ecosocial Dynamics and Semogenesis

We can now begin to link up our three basic arguments:

1   that human sociocultural systems are essentially systems of social practices linked in the historically and culturally specific semiotic formations from which they get their meanings;

2   that these practices are simultaneously material processes in a complex, hierarchically organized, developing and evolving ecosystem; and

3   that the interdependence between the semiotically and materially based couplings of these practices/processes is the basis of ecosocial dynamics.

Cultural dynamics is one aspect of the total dynamical complexity of what we are calling *ecosocial systems*. An ecosocial system is a human social community taken together with the material ecosystem that enables, supports and constrains it. An ecosocial system *is* an ecosystem, with all the characteristics and properties of ecosystems, but it is a more specified type of ecosystem: one that includes a community of organisms of our species and in which therefore the material interactions of its elements (people, other species, resources, material and energetic processes and flows) are biased, constrained and *organized*, in part in accordance with their cultural meanings and values.

The total ecosocial system includes not only human organisms and their interactions with one another, but all the material elements which act on, in and through humans and which humans act on, in and through. It includes all the other species with which we are co-dependent and with which we have co-evolved, including our food species, our diseases and parasites, our symbionts and co-dependent micro-organisms, and *their* webs of interdependent organisms, sources of materials and energy, and disposal routes for wastes, etc. An ecosocial system includes buildings and tools, cultivated fields and soil bacteria, generating stations and bread molds. It includes landforms and marine nutrient flows, atmospheric circulation and solar radiation levels. It includes manufacturing and waste production, education and intercourse, politics and warfare. It is a single, unitary system in which the dynamics of processes of human social interaction are not in principle or in practice separable from the dynamics of the rest of the ecosystem, except that cultural practices represent a second level of organization of material processes according to relations of social meaning. An ecosocial system is simultaneously a material and a social semiotic system.

Ecosocial systems show ecosystem organization in both the specifically culturally, semiotically mediated portions of, and in the rest of their material–ecophysical dynamics. They are foremost, in both respects, *not* systems of things (organisms, nutrients, persons, symbols) but systems of *processes* (gene exchange, predation, communication, symbolization). They are *systems* precisely in so far as these processes are *coupled*: linked, interconnected, interdependent. They are complex, open, dynamical, dissipative, self-organizing, developing, individuating, epigenetic systems, organized in a hierarchy of levels in which subsystem development and individuation is regulated by supersystem dynamics, and in which supersystem resilience and adaptability is ensured by subsystem variety and lability to change. Their hierarchical structure arises from the interpolation of new intermediate levels of dynamical organization. This happens when new patterns of process coupling (directly or through the coupling of social practices in cultural formations) lead to symmetry breaking and new dynamical states (*emergent structuration*). Ecosocial systems are mosaic aggregates of subsystems ('patches') of differing developmental age, composition and coupling patterns.

Within this general model of ecosocial dynamical systems, let us consider now in more detail the dynamics of social practices and formations, of cultural systems of meaning. Of all these, *language* has traditionally been regarded as the least materially coupled and has been most often offered as the paradigm case of autonomous semiotic dynamics. *Language-as-system* is an abstraction from *language-in-use*, however; that is, from the material social practices that we interpret as deploying the resources of such a meaning system. The materiality of speech and writing (in sound and ink, but also in brain, tongue and hand, and in pen, paper, keyboard, screen and associated hardware) is as critical to understanding their role in ecosocial dynamics as is their participation in social and cultural systems of meaning. If speech seems materially a matter of a breath and negligible energy, and writing of only the infinitesimal energy and entropy of inkstains on paper or magnetic domains in an electronic memory, the same could be said of the DNA genome that guides and channels the much larger energies of the chemistry of embryological development.

The genome, like language, has evolved to be what it is (and continues to evolve) exactly by serving this function, and thus precisely in and through its couplings to those larger material processes. It is just the same with language, through which we construe the meaning relations that tie together the social practices of every semiotic formation, so that we may learn to make sense of and with them. In what we *do* with language (and with every other semiotic resource system), strong couplings are made with the material processes through which we enact other social practices, many of which involve substantial shifts of matter and energy. Discourse formations construed in language guide the social practices of our architecture and our engineering, our agriculture and our industry, our warfare and our choices of foods and mates, allies and enemies.

The cultural dynamics of language cannot be independent of the uses to which language is put, but rather arises directly out of those uses. The cultural dynamics of language-as-system, the processes of language change, represent the effects on the overall semantic resources of a language of the new uses to which it is put, register by register, function by function, situation by situation. This 'putting to use' is always a putting to use in the material doings of an ecosocial system. If a language has an inertia, it is the inertia of its use by many organisms, a dynamical inertia grounded in neurological processes and social interactions (including, for the case of writing, material social practices of producing and interpreting stable, visible material images). If language has a momentum, it is the dynamic momentum of changes in the social practices of language use.

The notion of 'a language' is not only an abstraction from use, it is an abstraction from the empirical *diversity* of language-in-use. A language is a mosaic aggregate of its dialects and sociolects, on all scales of a hierarchy of loosely integrated subsystem 'patches' (cf. 'speech communities') from those of widely used dialects down to individual idiolects. This principle of mosaic diversity applies equally to registers and to discourse formations, and with respect to the latter, ecosocial *heteroglossia* encompasses the diversity of language use across different age-groups (cf. mixed-age mosaic ecosystems), genders, social classes, political persuasions, etc. Moreover, in every 'patch' of language use, in every functional 'niche' (situation type) for language use, the pattern of use is changing, developing, individuating.

We need look no further than the phenomena of creolization to observe recapitulative and individuating development of a language 'patch'. Just as extreme stress on an ecosystem, measured by the decoupling of processes and flows, by loss of differentiation and return toward greater symmetry and homogeneity, leads to a reversal of the stage sequence of succession (Schneider 1988), so the restriction of the use of a language to only a few situations and to speakers who can only learn the language in those situations ('pidginization') leads to a loss of functional and semantic differentiation (and so to phonological homogenization as well), a simplification of language not unlike the earlier stages of language learning by children or non-native speakers. A 'language patch' is cleared, or at least pushed back to a more primitive state of development, but it is still a patch in an ecosocial system; the diverse activities of the community are still being enacted, there is still a rich field of differentiated functions and contexts into which the 'pidgin' can spread. As it does so, its symmetries are broken, unitary forms become differentiated and multiply in meanings and uses, a 'full-service' language rapidly (in one generation) re-emerges. It is not identical to the original language, for it does not recapitulate a precise epigenetic trajectory like an organism (cf. a child learning the mother tongue), it is an individuated patch, where we will get a new dialect, enlarging a language family.

The stages of development of a creole dialect, which they may not recapitulate the history of the original language in detail (except in the presence of DNA-like environmental 'templates' which bias the development) will still proceed by a series of symmetry-breaking bifurcations, each the necessary predecessor of the next. Each later state of semantic and functional differentiation in language use patterns must be prepared for by prior developments that enable the meaning contexts to be created (and recognized) within which the dynamics can give rise to the subsequent ones. In this process, greatly accelerated in speed (cf. rates of succession or ontogenesis vs. those of evolution and phylogenesis), we see the same interdependence of social action patterns and semantic resource development that occurs in the normal course of language change.

The processes of symmetry-breaking common to all developing systems with complex non-linear, autocatalytic dynamics occur in developing ecosocial systems (as wholes and more obviously in each patch) and are reflected in the successive symmetry-breakings of normal linguistic change. Some of these have been documented for modern English by Halliday (1992), who has identified a process he calls *semogenesis*. In this process, a progressive semantic differentiation in the language system is built up by the context-dependent splitting of previously unitary semantic features and their subsequent independent recombination (see below). He also indicates how this same process, writ large, leads to the emergence of a true grammar as an intermediate level of semiotic organization between situations and utterances in children's language development.

The total 'semodynamic cycle' is far richer and more complex than the core semogenesis process itself. It is a cycle in which differences create (or enable the creation of) further differences, in which the frequency of occurrence of a feature proceeds from being equal across contexts to being unequal (symmetry-breaking), and in which the availability of new semantic features makes possible the differentiation of new contexts in which in turn further semogenesis can occur. An essential part of this cycle is the existence of pre-semiotic features of events or situations, material differences that do not yet have cultural significance, but which can enter the semiotic system as new features (cf. Lemke 1984 and the Postscript).

Bifurcations in the material dynamics of an ecosocial system generally lead to a breaking of the symmetries that existed in prior states of the system, so that new differences are potentially distinguishable; what was formerly one single context may now be separable into two somewhat different contexts. This difference of contexts may now be used to 'pry apart' a formerly unitary social practice, if distinguishable variations in the enactment of the practice begin to co-occur regularly with the difference in contexts (e.g. different pronunciations of the same word by members of two socially or physically different subgroups).

Every material instance of a form (e.g. pronouncing a word) exhibits both its *criterial features* (those needed to make it that word and not some other) and also *incidental features*, which do not matter as regards its semiotic identity. If some of these incidental features begin to co-occur in actual usage with different features of the context, and not just in isolated instances but regularly (owing either to material connections between them or to semiotically constructed ones) and recapitulably, then what was a single semiotic form, previously symmetrical as between these contexts, is now split into distinguishable variant forms, which can acquire different meanings as they come to be used differently across all contexts. The formerly incidental features are now criterial for these variants.

Material symmetry-breakings and couplings can lead to semiotic ones, and vice versa. Differentiations in material contexts can lead to differentiations of semiotic forms, and vice versa. When features uniformly co-occur (perfect redundancy) across all wider contexts, they are not semiotically separable as distinct features, but when they begin no longer to do so in *some* contexts, a semogenic process may begin in which they eventually become distinguishable in all contexts in which they occur. As their degree of redundancy (probability of co-occurrence) with some set of contexts of use falls from maximal toward zero, they become independent resources of the meaning system (see examples in Nesbitt and Plum 1988; Halliday 1991, 1992), increasing its information-carrying capacity.

When all possible actions are equally probable in all contexts, there is no culture. Redundancies and specific probabilities of co-occurrence define semiotic formations and increase the total organizational complexity of an ecosocial system. In the semodynamic cycle, as you might expect, there are also 'semolytic' processes by which previously distinguished features fuse, fall into disuse, or do not continue their distinctive associations with contexts. This completes the 'semodynamic cycle' in which new distinctions of meaning, new resources and new formations are continuously created and destroyed, all as part of the total material–semiotic dynamics of the ecosocial system.

The net result is that the meaning potential of the system of semiotic resources increases (as new features arc added, and become combinatorially independent, so that all possible combinations of features *can* occur), while at the same time the total organization of the semiotic behavior of the community also increases as the probabilities for particular combinations (e.g. of sounds forming words) become more and more associated with particular contexts of use.

It is perhaps easier to see this developmental dynamics at the level of semiotic formations rather than at that of the necessarily more abstract semiotic resource systems. Consider some system of technological practices, that is, some interlocking cultural formations of technology-using social practices in agriculture, manufacturing, warfare, etc. Now suppose that a nuclear holocaust destroyed the material base of the technologies, or caused a retrogression to a more primitive level of technology, but that the 'template' (say a discourse formation, the 'knowledge' of the technology) still existed. This is like the classic dilemma of a modern person in a stone-age society, the traveler back in time seeking to make use of advanced technological knowledge in the absence of its material base. Some shortcuts may be possible, but by and large the 'succession' in this 'patch' will have to recapitulate the historical (or at least the obligatory developmental) sequence of technological developments. Each development makes possible the next. In historical dynamics, each development makes possible newly emergent social practices, which may combine into new cultural activities and institutions, with new needs and interests, to spur new technologies to meet those needs, built on existing technologies which met earlier needs, and so on. Such sequences of emergent structuration are never inevitable, nor unique.

There is no inevitability to contemporary culture, technology or science, as there was no inevitability to the emergence of the the human species itself. How could evolution have turned out differently? Are there constraints on possible sequences of emergent species in ecosystems in evolution? We can know only by comparing different such sequences in different relatively isolated patches (e.g. Australian marsupial and Eurasian placental mammals and their ecosystems) or on other planets. Similarly we can judge the constraints, if they exist, on possible cultures, technologies and scientific beliefs only by comparing those relatively isolated from one another for long periods, or those developing in very distant periods of time. To me the diversity seems far more impressive than any commonalities, and the universal commonalities we can construct seem so abstract, vague and trivial as to constitute scarcely any evidence that our particular cultural practices (technologies, sciences, logics, mathematics) are driven by universal physical and biological constraints to take just the forms they do.

In processes of self-organization and emergent structuration the more universal a constraint is, the weaker it is. A constraint gains in influence over a specific set of possible futures proceeding from it precisely by being itself already the product of a very specific history: by being a very local and peculiar, not at all a universal constraint. Even for the least specified systems, like the elementary dynamical systems, where 'universal' constraints seem sufficient to describe all known systems, these constraints (interactional 'laws') are really just the ones of our particular post-Big Bang, post-Inflation universe, whose prior history, 'freezing in' just these laws gives them what power of specificity they have. It is precisely because they are *not* the laws of all possible universes that they apply to ours. How much more so as we move toward the center of the specification hierarchy, toward ecosocial systems, where the more local a generalization is, the better it describes a particular system, and where the more universal it is, the less useful it will be. The paradox, of course, is that even our models of elementary dynamical systems and their universe-specific laws are products of one very specific historical cultural system.

Ecosocial systems are hierarchically structured across many scales of organization. This does not mean that they are in any sense 'authority hierarchies' or that authoritarian social organizations are more natural than democratic ones. It means that each level of organization going 'up' the hierarchy is in fact a larger scale, more slowly changing supersystem coupling and integrating smaller scale, more rapidly changing subsystems at the next level 'down'. A nation is a supersystem of its cities and provinces; the global economy is a supersystem of national economies. In authoritarian social organizations, élites become smaller as one goes 'up' the hierarchy; in ecosocial systems, the higher levels are orders of magnitude *larger*.

Ecosocial systems, and each patch and subsystem within an ecosocial system, are also temporally extended, 'trajectory' entities; they are systems of coupled, interdependent processes, whose nature changes over the course of the system's developmental trajectory partly as a result of the effects on the system and its environment of the processes at each prior stage. Ecosocial systems generate their own futures; they create conditions that lead them to change, and they create at each developmental stage possibilities for the next stage that are not in principle predictable. Accidental, unique, historical configurations determine which of several possible 'branches' the developmental trajectory of the system will take.

At any given time the characteristic cultural patterns of action of a community must be enacted through material processes, by actual human organisms in interaction with each other and with other elements of the ecosystem. Each enactment of a ritual, each performance of a song, each making of a tool, each writing of a sonnet will be unique and different, but it will also re-enact criterial features common to a cultural formation. Other, initially incidental features, may in the course of cultural change become newly criterial ones for an evolved, future formation. Semiotic forms change because they must be instantiated as material processes, and in complex systems material processes are always unique, always show semiotically non-criterial features.

As an example, consider an actional semiotic formation, an 'action genre', 'activity type' or 'participation structure' as it variously has been called. For it to occur actors in various roles must perform various actions that couple the material processes of organisms and other ecosystem elements together in particular ways. The formation *defines* the roles and action types which constitute it in terms of criterial features of these material processes, and neglects incidental features. It is in terms of their cultural *meanings* that it prescribes the couplings of actions/processes, but each enactment of the event will still necessarily be different from any other. The organisms/social persons performing its key roles are themselves developing systems, with unique histories of participation in other actional formations of the culture; each is a unique constellation, with a slightly different view of the current role and how to perform it. Just as participants are changed by their participation in cultural events, the cultural events as types, as normative semiotic forms, may change as a result of their enactment by different, materially unique participants. Here we see the developmental process, the semodynamic process, at work. Each event, each participation, creates conditions that may lead to further change both in the individual organisms' or communities' histories and in the evolution of their kinds. Ecosocial systems are not stable; they create the conditions for their own change.

Prediction, Control and Responsibility

Type-specific, recapitulative development is both lawful and predictable (without, however, being the effect of any singular cause). Evolutionary change is lawful, but not predictable in detail beyond the short term in which environmental constraints set conditions for the spread or extinction of new patterns. Individuation is neither lawful nor predictable; it is the source of new variety in the history of the system, unique and accidental.

Recapitulative development of a system is only as faithful to the typical trajectory of its kind as accidental conditions and epigenetic regulation by the material supersystem allow. Actual system trajectories represent the combination of recapitulative development with unique individuation. The 'template' in ecosocial systems is not a stabilized internal DNA, but rather the persistence in the system's environment of the patterns of coupled processes that similarly shaped the developmental changes of others of its type. Recapitulative development is not causally driven; it does not have to happen as it does. It happens again each time as if for the first time, the result of a series of accidents that need not have happened, but which were more likely to happen under the prevailing (supersystem) conditions than the regularly available alternatives.

When an individual or a community 'learns' a new pattern of behavior (e.g. how to program a computer), there will be a certain recapitulation of the historical succession of skills that originally led to this activity type, guided and in part provoked by prevailing cultural discourses (texts, manuals) and other activity types (demonstrations, practice sessions), not unlike succession in a patch under the influence of propagules from the surrounding ecosystem. Each individual and community will nonetheless develop its own unique approach, however, and some of these approaches will spread and contribute to the evolution of this social practice (new styles of programming), while others will die out. At any given time there will be a mosaic of system 'patches', each with a variant approach, and the variants will most often arise in 'juvenile' patches (recent learners). The most significant differences will arise from deviations from the previous type trajectory *early* along its path (cf. *neoteny* in evolution, e.g. Gould 1977; Montagu 1981). This principle has some important educational implications, which we will discuss in the next chapter.

Evolutionary change is lawful in that at any given time it is possible to specify the conditions that favor or disfavor the persistence or spread of a particular innovation. The evolution of the type is determined, strictly speaking, by the changes in the frequency distribution of recapitulations of the various variants of the type. This short term predictability of evolutionary change depends on the fact that the relevant environmental conditions are relatively slowly changing, however, which is what we expect since the supersystem operates on a larger, and so normally slower scale. *Long term* evolutionary change is not in principle predictable because of the *development* of the supersystem (i.e. its individuation). The dynamics of the supersystem are also self-altering; it creates the possibility for its own change, for new couplings of its subsystems, for new couplings to exterior systems, for externally driven bifurcations to new states.

There is, however, one clear trend in what we may call the (non-recapitulative) development of an entire subsystem–supersystem hierarchy: progressive *hierarchical structuration*, that is, the emergence of new intermediate levels of organization. This accomplishes a tighter integration of the higher levels of the total system (through couplings among these intermediate level subsystems). The emergence of a tightly interdependent global economy, and of regional, multi-national economic federations are instances of this trend. At the same time, the ecological interdependence of all the subsystems of the living planet is growing greater as well, and these two trends will eventually combine to produce a bifurcation shift in ecosocial development: either a catastrophic retrogression in both, or a significant reorganization of both. In fact, it is often observed in ecosystem dynamics that a retrogression must precede a reorganization in order for the system to 'back up' to a branch-point from which the new organizational dynamics is accessible.

Closely linked to the question of predictability is the issue of control. We can and do make history, but certainly not just as we please. The situation is more complex however from the perspective of ecosocial dynamics. If social and cultural systems were relatively autonomous, then we might imagine that the cultural future at least was mainly up to us, but what must be controlled, if controlled it can be, is the whole of an ecosocial system, not culture or social organization alone.

There can be no question of long term social control from the present; the emergent properties of a developing evolving system preclude this absolutely. Only a continuing, adaptable, long term effort on the same time scale as the control sought could succeed, and clearly any such subsystem would quickly be entrained in the total ecosocial system, becoming a part of what it seeks to control. The same is true for short term control by any individual or group, which is necessarily already a subsystem of the ecosocial supersystem. Can a subsystem successfully regulate the supersystem of which is it a part? We do not speak here of accidental influence; the individuation of the supersystem is of course vulnerable to internal events. Regulation is more than impact, however, it is a governing, a systematic capacity to shift the far larger processes and energies of the supersystem by critical manipulations on a much smaller scale.

Such control-from-below is *not* in general possible in self-regulating, hierarchically organized systems because of the great differences in scale between levels (cf. Salthe 1985, 1993), and because such systems do not evolve with sensitive vulnerabilities to subsystem processes (ecosocial selection favors robustness and resilience, systems that proceed generally along their type trajectory irrespective of this or that peculiar happening at smaller scales inside of them). There are however certain special conditions under which a developing, self-organizing system becomes vulnerable to otherwise negligible influences. When the system is at a critical bifurcation point, when conditions are such that either of two (or occasionally more) dynamical configurations are newly possible for the system, its self-regulation is as it were suspended, and it becomes extremely sensitive to small fluctuations (cf. Prigogine 1980; Prigogine and Stengers 1984; or the discussion of the 'edge of chaos' in Kauffman 1993). Under these conditions, small perturbations from much smaller scales in the hierarchy may become greatly amplified, and coherent global effects can result, including the determination of which branch the system's further development takes. Effective control, however, does not extend in time beyond the critical juncture; it is only the unpredictable effects of that brief moment of control which may do so.

In a complex ecosocial system, it is possible that there are always numerous bifurcation possibilities 'available', especially at intermediate levels of organization. Coherent action by many subsystems, linked through communication, can affect supersystem behavior, especially near these critical branch-points, but also to a lesser degree away from them. The kind of action most likely to open up new dynamical pathways for the system is a reorganization of the coupling scheme, linking processes/practices not previously linked, or decoupling of those that formerly were. Such actions, semiotically, correspond to changes in what the community considers to be similar and different, allied or opposed. They include making semantic distinctions not previously made, combining thematic elements not previously combined, and thus making conceivable actions that link processes or subsystems not previously linked. It may be necessary to decouple and break some older linkages before recoupling processes in a new pattern, and it may be only in newer, younger, developing subsystems that the new dynamical patterns can first come into existence. (I will develop these themes in more specific political terms in Chapter 7.)

The meaning systems of a culture enable meanings to be made, and meaningful social activities to be enacted, but they also enjoin the making of other meanings, other actions. Where every possible action is equally likely in every situation or context, there is no meaning. So, where there are meanings enabled, there are necessarily also meanings disabled (cf. Lemke 1984 and the Postscript on 'disjunctions'). The panoply of meaning relations that define a culture is a figure against the ground of meaning non-relations, gaps that are not even seen as gaps. New coupling schemes of social practices (and so of material processes) that fill these gaps, that make meaning in the interstices of culture, in the dark places whose emptiness of meaning defines the boundaries (and so the potential growing edges) of what is meaningful, are especially likely to contribute to shifts in ecosocial organization at some level.

Mature ecosocial systems ward off terminal senility by incorporating a mixed-age mosaic of patches that serve as a reservoir of diversity. Some of these patches may even prevent the system's self-regulation from becoming overly rigid (and so unable to adapt to future environmental changes). In ecosystem dynamics it has been noted (Holling 1986) that some ecosystems never reach a quasi-stable 'stationary' state, because there are *no* stable values of the various population and other parameters which the system's dynamics will continue to regenerate (no 'fixed point'). It remains in a state of continual dynamic disequilibrium, with all its parameters fluctuating (sometimes in erratic cycles, sometimes chaotically), continually seeking a steady state it can never achieve. In such a system (and ecosocial systems are surely like this, at least in parts) no one species or dynamic coupling scheme ever 'wins'; all co-exist uneasily, in endless competition, with the result that the total diversity of the system remains higher than in any possible stable configuration.

In these terms we also serve, who obstruct stability, who contravene tradition, who say and do the forbidden. We do not know enough yet to identify the critical moments when our small influence might be amplified and guide the course of systems far larger and more complex than ourselves, but we can offer alternatives, even if only in small patches, and we can study the conditions of their survival potential relative to others. In the next and final chapter of this book, I want to examine some of the alternative intellectual and political agendas that might make sense in terms of the view of human communities as ecosocial systems that I have just presented. In order to pursue such agendas systematically we will need guiding theories far better developed than I have sketched here, but I believe that the theories we need will make use of many of these fundamental principles.

Chapter 7

Critical Praxis:
Education, Literacy, Politics

Social Control and Social Change

In this final chapter, we need to confront some uncomfortable issues. The theme of *textual politics* has led us to examine how our texts, our discourses, our ways of talking about and looking at the world shape the patterns of our society. Seeing a community as a system of interconnected *doings*, actions and behaviors that make sense for us, and that we use to make sense of others and of our world, has led us to see that these doings are always also material, physical processes that form a special sort of ecosystem. Our ecosystem is a place where people, tools, artifacts, landscapes and other species interact in complex self-organizing patterns. The flows of energy and matter that form these patterns depend in part on the meanings and values they have in the human culture that is also being enacted as part of the system.

An ecosocial system, including the human community and culture that form an integral part of it, changes constantly, driving itself toward new patterns of self-organization by its very efforts to maintain the old ones, opening new regimes of possibility that could not have existed before it had created earlier ones. Social dynamics is inseparable from ecosocial dynamics; social change is the normal, and largely unpredictable, course for an ecosocial system. Ecosocial systems seem subject to more rapid and radical changes than ecosystems that do not have the extra feedback loops provided by human cultural systems. Ecosocial systems are more complexly interdependent, more capable of amplifying small changes into large ones than are ecosystems where complex cultural meaning and value systems do not couple material processes to one another in new ways.

So how does it happen that many features of human social and cultural systems seem relatively stable from generation to generation? Despite rapid changes of many kinds, history seems to show long periods when the dominance of men over women, of older over younger, of rich over poor, of one cultural group over another has been maintained. The grammars of many languages have changed only relatively slowly. Many cultures have preserved their basic value systems over many generations. Sometimes social and cultural change is rapid and dramatic; the ecosocial system seems to reorganize itself spontaneously in a single generation or less. In other periods change is painfully, or comfortingly, slow.

We do not know, perhaps cannot know, from our limited perspective *within* an ecosocial system, just how close or how far the system may be at any given time from the threshold for major change and reorganization. We do not know which combinations of factors changing in which directions may push us over into a new dynamical phase. We can examine the processes by which change is resisted, however, the systematic social practices which tend to maintain, preserve and strengthen the social status quo. We can attempt to uncover how these processes work, how our discourses and other forms of activity, the beliefs and values that guide and shape our actions, play a role in minimizing the possibilities for fundamental social change.

This is a dangerous inquiry, because it is likely that many of our own fundamental beliefs and values prevent us from taking the very actions that might change society in directions we would like to see it go. Few of us believe that our society as it is today is as free from exploitation, coercion, oppression and injustice as its own values demand it should be. Many of us feel deeply the contradictions between social values and social practices. History records that the writers of many other times and places have felt as we do. Yet we still take our own values for granted. We blame social conditions, we create theories of human evil, we define categories of adversaries . . . we do everything except see the problem in ourselves, in the core beliefs and values that we have adopted from the cultural system around us.

Critical praxis is a shorthand way of saying that we need to examine ourselves, examine our own actions, beliefs and values to see how they connect up to the larger patterns and process of the system of which we are part, to understand how we are part of the problem in order to have any hope of becoming part of the solution. *Praxis* is a somewhat technical term for practice, for action that stands in a dialectical relation to theory; what we do should lead us to change our basic theories about our role in the world, and our theories should lead us to change the roles we play. (See the Postscript for further discussion of the theory–praxis relationship.)

Praxis is unstable and unpredictable; each step we take along this road makes new possibilities that were not there for us before. At every step, however, we are trying to be as aware as we can possibly be of the larger significances of what we are doing. *Critical praxis* practices the hermeneutic of suspicion (Ricoeur 1970); it assumes that we *are* part of the problem, that even our most basic beliefs and values should be suspect. Critical praxis should lead to changes in these beliefs and values as well as to changes in our actions.

This way of proceeding is uncomfortable. There is no solid ground on which to stand, no fixed and universal first principles from which to argue. There is no high ground from which to dominate those who do not agree with us. There is a near certainty that time and again we will come to see our own former beliefs, values and actions as having been part of the patterns of injustice that pain us.

We all participate in the processes of social control, the processes that work to inhibit fundamental social change. We participate in them through systems of beliefs and values, embodied in the discourses we speak, even to ourselves, and through all the other forms of social activity, of material physical action in the ecosocial world in which we engage. We do what we do, time and again, because of what we believe, what we value and how we make sense of issues and situations according to discourse patterns learned from our culture. We believe what we believe, value what we value and use the discourse patterns we do out of all those others also available in our culture because of what we have done, the life events in which we have participated – events in which we were caught up in the larger patterns of an ecosocial system. We are what we have done, what we have experienced. We are complex self-organizing subsystems of the greater ecosocial system, and like it we are composed of processes, including ways of doing that have meaning in our community. We participate in intermediate levels of organization within the larger system, as members of various subcultures, differently positioned in relation to each other and the whole.

How do we control the behavior of others? How do we participate in the processes of social control? I do not mean simply how we enable others to behave as they do, but how we stop others from behaving in ways that might change the patterns of society? We all influence and shape one another's behavior merely by being partners in the activity patterns and doings of our community. We are conversation partners and sex partners, collaborators at work and in play, making joint activity possible by playing our expected part in it. In the course of these activities, someone may behave differently, outside the expected patterns. We might simply ignore this and, by failing to respond to it in kind, leave this new social practice without an opportunity to have a wider influence on our behavior and the behavior of others. Very often we do more than this, however; we try to stop the behavior, perhaps first by relatively weak sanctions such as withdrawal of approval or active disagreement. These might cause mild discomfort. In other cases we may show anger, which always holds the threat of potential violence: that if they do not stop we will try to hurt them, to cause them pain. That pain may be emotional pain, none the less painful, or other and sometimes more severe kinds of physical, bodily pain.

Suppose the other person really wants to act as they do, suppose their beliefs and values are different from ours. Suppose they see their interests as requiring this action, and construct themselves as having the right or duty to perform it, to speak or act as they do. Their action then is part of an alternative pattern of belief, value and behavior that is in conflict with ours. It has the potential to spread in the community, to accomplish social and cultural change. We will not likely succeed in getting such people to stop just by withdrawing our cooperation or approval, nor by active disagreement, nor even by our anger and threats. The only way to ensure that our way remains dominant and theirs is contained or eliminated as a rival to it is to inflict pain on them, and in the extreme case to try to kill them.

Even withholding cooperation, withholding resources we control can be a direct cause of pain, or even death (withholding food, needed medicines). Death is an abstraction none of us have experienced. We fear it by proxy, by reputation only. Pain, on the other hand, we have all experienced. Pain and the threat of pain are powerful, direct, material, bodily modes of social control. Our bodies are vulnerable to pain, and the deliberate inflicting of pain on bodies is, I believe, the primary and fundamental mode of social control. Those of us who come from middle and upper-middle class subcultures, who identify with intellectual values, tend to resist thinking about socialization and social control in terms of bodies at all, and certainly in terms of pain. We would rather focus on verbal modes of control, on belief systems and value systems, on ideologies and discourses, on the purely textual politics of our society, but in an ecosocial system actions lead to change through linkages to other processes, linkages that are both semiotic and material. We do not, we cannot participate in processes of social control purely in terms of the meanings of our actions. Their physical effects must also function in the material ecosystem of the community.

To maintain and reproduce from generation to generation any patterns of social practices that can be seen by some participants in them as unjust or inequitable, even in particular individual instances, will require that some people impose these patterns on others by coercive, material force. Causing the deaths of those who resist the imposition of these patterns can be very disruptive to the social system, at least locally. Inflicting pain, with the threat of greater pain, is the normal basis of social control in Western society and in many others.

How much better of course if people do not resist, if they do not even realize that the pattern is unjust, that it exploits them for the benefit of others. The belief and value systems, the discourses that construct them, which we have called specifically ideological (Chapter 1, and see Postscript) tend to produce this less violent condition in a society. It is extremely difficult, however, to exploit people materially without some of them sensing in at least some situations that they are being expected to act in ways that do not benefit them, or that benefit others more, or that, at this moment, they simply do not want to go along with. The more common such events are, the more likely it is that they will lead to alternative beliefs and values that contradict the dominant ideology, that these alternative views will spread in the exploited segment of the community, and the more likely it is that the dominant group will resort to force and violence to oppose them.

Can there be any doubt of the pervasiveness of pain and the threat of greater pain as an instrument of social control in our own society? The domination of men over women in the activities of the family is widely enforced by physical abuse and the threat of physical violence, despite the cultural taboo on public violence by men against women. The domination of parents over children in the family is even more strongly grounded in the deliberate inflicting of bodily pain, emotional and otherwise. The domination of the owners and managers of property over the unemployed poor and the underpaid working classes is routinely maintained by police violence. The domination of some ethnic and racial groups over others is similarly maintained by police violence, by violence against prisoners, and by gang violence against the local Others.

Domestic violence, spouse abuse, marital rape, date rape, sexual abuse and harrassment; 'fag-bashing' of gays; 'nigger-bashing' of African-Americans; 'paki-bashing', etc. of Pakistanis, Indians, Asians; 'wilding' by black youths against whites; gang violence, bias crimes, child abuse, corporal punishment, elder abuse, police brutality and prison rape are all routine, common, frequent practices of social control. They help maintain the domination of some social categories of people over others in our social system. They are not rare, unusual or abnormal events with no structural social function. Some of them are only the most extreme forms of material social control, which also includes job and housing discrimination, unequal access to police protection, legal and judicial injustice and the normal operations of the penal system.

Wives submit to husbands, children submit to parental authority, gays and lesbians to the norms of the straight subculture, and oppressed groups generally to their oppressors largely out of fear of the pain of violence or extreme deprivation. The homeless, who are prey to every form of violence and exploitation, victims of countless pains, are disproportionately women, children, the elderly, the poor, people of color. Other examples include the openly gay teenager thrown out of his home and forced to turn to prostitution, the wife and young child running away from an abusive husband, people denied jobs, housing, credit, food and/or medical care. The threat of these pains hangs heavily over a very large segment of our society. It is a powerful tool for social control.

Historical examples, too, are not hard to find: the beatings, burnings and lynchings by which the Ku Klux Klan and its allies maintained a system of racial domination; the beatings, jailings and shootings by which owners, managers, hired strikebreakers, police and government troops maintained class domination against the early labor movement; the beatings, jailings and legal persecution by which conventional adult society sought to control and eliminate the hippies and counterculture movements of young people in the 1960s, the violence against peaceful protesters against the war in Vietnam by armed police and National Guard troops.

The level of violence in a society, private as well as public, state-sanctioned as well as state-criminalized, is a reasonable index of the level of injustice in that society, as defined by its own value systems. The incidence of deliberately inflicted pain might be a perfect index. The level of violence in the global ecosocial system, inflicted both by arms and by extreme deprivation, would equally be a reasonable measure of the injustice of international relations, for here too the domination of one group over others can normally be maintained only by coercive means.

The distribution of who suffers pain in a society is a reasonable index of which social groups and categories are unjustly oppressed, and the dominating groups may usually be identified by their use of power to prevent social, cultural and political deviation or change that they do not see as being in their interests.

With this less comfortable model of social control, which sees the effort to minimize social change as a result of both the textual politics of the beliefs, values and discourses in terms of which we see possible courses of action and the bodily politics of the use and threat of pain to control behavior and limit or eliminate rival social patterns, let's now take a closer look at our participation in just three arenas of social control: education, literacy and politics.

Education: Schooling, Curriculum and Social Control

In the broadest sense education is the process by which our participation in all social activity enables us to adapt more effectively and flexibly to the social environment. We learn through the activities and social interactions of the family and the peer culture, the mass media and the workplace – in every aspect of social life and all throughout our lives. In most human societies in most of human history, these are the only forms education takes. Education is so integral to the functioning of society that it is not generally recognized as a separate category of social activity. Specialized technical practices may be learned through more formal and recognized apprenticeships, and highly valued sacred and ritual practices may be explicitly taught in terms of rules and procedures for their correct performance.

There are certain kinds of human social practice that seem particularly difficult to learn through informal participation: those that operate in terms of an arbitrary code which can only with great difficulty be analyzed from its uses in context. Of such practices the most widespread, apart from the codes of esoteric symbolism and ritual, are the practices of literacy. I would assume that this category includes, in addition to the reading and writing of symbols that code language, the reading and writing of symbols that code other highly complex and variable phenomena (musical notations, mathematical systems, etc.). Of them all, literate symbologies can become the most difficult to decode from their use in activities (the least delicately co-varying with immediate situational context) because language can, to a very large extent, create its own contexts. Spoken language is learned through its intimate co-dependence with other features of the immediate situational context. Written language often functions in a culture in ways that preclude this, and so literate cultures tend to have 'schools'.

The basic function of schools is to teach the literacy code, but that code is generally taught in relation to specific, highly valued written texts (the Confucian classics, the Vedas, the Torah, the Qur'an, the Christian Bible) which embody dominant cultural values and socially useful knowledge and discourses. In this schools only extend the general program of education: the attempt to rear each next generation to embody the beliefs and values of the last. The difference is that schools are not representative of the full diversity of social beliefs, values, discourses and practices. They inculcate only those of the dominant group: the mandarins, the Brahmins, the Pharisees, the imams, the establishment élites. They do so not only through the texts they venerate and promulgate, but through the methods of teaching to which they require students to adapt. They are notoriously intolerant of deviations from orthodoxy, and famously prone to inflicting pain to maintain social control.

I need not repeat here the many analyses of how modern systems of schooling tend to reproduce social inequity from generation to generation (e.g. Bowles and Gintis 1976; Bourdieu and Passeron 1977; Willis 1981; Apple 1982). They do so most fundamentally by labeling students as more and less successful at tasks for which the children of the dominant groups are better prepared by their experiences before and outside of schools, especially their language socialization (cf. Heath 1983; Hasan 1986b; Hasan and Cloran 1990) and their comfort with the methods of instruction and general normative culture of the school. Students often resist the imposition of schools' beliefs and values, but this only makes it easier for them ultimately to be labeled unsuccessful. Other social agencies then turn school failure into limited opportunity for other kinds of social success, at least within the economic arrangements controlled by the dominant groups. Modern Western schools have only very recently and reluctantly abandoned corporal punishment as a mode of social control. The alternative modes, inflicting emotional pain and threatening the pain that follows economic failure in an ungenerous society, seem to work for only a much smaller fraction of the student population, those already more socialized toward dominant beliefs and values.

What I would like us to question here are some deeper and more fundamental assumptions that lie behind the practices of schooling even for the most privileged members of society. Schooling is not just an instance of social class domination and social control in the interests of the dominant class. It is not even simply an instance of gender domination, which operates in much the same way to the advantage of males, or of other forms of cultural domination, working to the advantage of European, and occasionally, and somewhat accidentally, also Asian cultural traditions and those reared in them. It is most fundamentally, and least visibly, an instance of age-group domination.

Inequity and injustice in the distribution of power, resources, legal and customary rights and protection from violence among culturally defined age-groups is only very recently becoming visible to our eyes as social analysts. Just as the ideological beliefs, values and discourses of earlier times made it seem perfectly natural that slaves, peasants, serfs, laborers, Africans, Asians, indigenous peoples and women could not participate equally in society with propertied European males, so today homologous ideologies assure us that neither can those younger or older than the presently dominant age-group.

In many societies the old exploit the young. Many social forms (marriage customs, esoteric rituals, economic arrangements) are best understood as contributing to means by which this becomes possible despite the greater physical strength and numbers among younger age-groups. By controlling wealth, rights of bestowal of women, and sacred knowledge, and by social arrangements that allow them to translate this power into sufficient control of some younger males to hold the others at bay, even the very oldest age-groups manage to maintain dominance in some societies (notably in many Asian cultures).

In our own modern, culturally European societies, the dominant power is held not by the oldest but by an age-group mainly in its fifties and sixties. This group (in alliance with their younger client age-groups) disempowers the eldest group by such devices as mandatory retirements. Ideologically functional beliefs about the feebleness and incompetence of the elderly buttress this dominance. The dominant group often manages to take over control of the management of the wealth and resources of their elders, and the phenomenon of the physical abuse of elders, often to obtain this control, is beginning to receive more public attention.

The dominant age-group controls younger adult age-groups through the authority hierarchies of the society, the accumulation of wealth and social influence, and in many, many other ways. It enforces this control through the police power of the state and rationalizes it by legislation. The ideology that supports this domination is one that lauds the value of experience, and even of seniority in and of itself, without regard for the actual distribution of specific competences.

The most disempowered age-groups, however, are the youngest ones. Non-industrial societies have traditionally conferred full customary and legal rights of adult status at the age of sexual maturity, traditionally about age 13, today a bit younger. In Western society citizens in the age-group from about 12–13 to 18–21 are denied most legal rights and are *de facto* wards and chattel in just the same ways, or worse, that women were before the twentieth century, and peasants, serfs and slaves before that. They are denied access to most gainful employment, do not have exclusive financial control of their own property, do not have the right to marry, to make their own medical decisions, to control their own education. They are officially forbidden to satisfy their most basic sexual needs. They are subject to socially accepted violence and customarily denied police protection against their masters. They have extremely limited civil rights, not including the right to vote or hold office, and rarely have recognized standing to sue in the courts for redress of grievances. In practice they have practically no independent rights of assembly or petition. Not only parents, but school officials frequently and traditionally deny them even rights of free speech and expression in entirely arbitrary ways. Their labor, where it has value, is normally exploited for the benefit of their parents. They are forced to attend schools in whose curricula they have no significant voice, and where, in some jurisdictions, they are even denied knowledge of how to protect themselves from fatal infectious diseases because of the prudery of older adults in their communities.

This outrageous denial of basic human rights generally passes without notice, or even with approval, in precisely the same way as did the similar oppression of women or the oppression of African-Americans only a very short time ago. It is sustained and legitimated by a precisely parallel ideology of the incompetence of young adults to manage their own affairs, perceive their own interests, or make their own decisions with the same advice older adults also need and receive. Fabulous fictions have been created about the effects of normal hormonal processes of maturation on their judgment, nearly identical to those told about women in an earlier era, and functionally parallel to the still earlier pseudo-scientific theories about the brains of African-Americans and other people of color. The fact that there are many millions of citizens in this age-group who show perfectly adult patterns of behavior, or deviate from them no more than do equal millions of older adults; the fact that in other societies that do not work so hard as ours does to infantilize young adults by denying them responsible social roles, people of the same age contribute meaningfully to their communities; these facts are not denied so much as ignored, explained away as somehow irrelevant.

It would be more apt to notice that economic and social arrangements whereby older adults, and most of all the dominant age-group, benefit are such that the competition for employment and resources by a free young adult population would work severely against their interests – again, exactly as was true with regard to previously disenfranchised groups.

Young adults are segregated from most of the normal opportunities enjoyed by older adults by being confined to schools. While their resistance has greatly eroded the effectiveness of the official requirements imposed on them, they have, according to the dominant age-group's paradoxical ideology, a right to a compulsory education. In the recent past, and possibly again in the near future, young adults may be physically forced to attend schools, on pain of punishments, and confined there just as in a prison. It does not matter that many older adults agree with them about the irrelevance and pedantry of the educations they suffer there. Their opinions regarding their own experiences, even when in agreement with those of many older adults, are counted as worth less than those of dominant older adults whose interests clearly bias their views.

Young adults have only a trivial choice in the directions and forms of their education in the schools. They are not even consulted in the construction of curriculum. Curriculum is constructed by people whose lives and interests are vastly different from the lived experience of most young adults. If we believe, as most critical educators today do, that traditional curricula are biased against the interests of women because they are made mostly by men, and biased against the interests of non-European Americans because they are mostly Eurocentric, then how can we not suspect that they are also biased against the interests of young adults because they are determined mainly by a dominant age-group which is patently oppressing them?

What would happen if young adults were free to direct the basic choices of their own educations according to their perceived needs and interests and their preferred methods of learning? Many of them would abandon schools that they believe are doing them no good at all. Many more would demand changes in the content of curricula and in methods of teaching. Many who initially left school would eventually return, better able to articulate their needs in relation to the realities of the larger social world of which they are kept ignorant in many crucial ways by older adults. There would be a shift of power. Schools would be forced to serve their constituencies instead of attempting to control them.

Young adults of the most privileged classes may very soon acquire this power. New information technologies will very soon make it possible for many young adults to pursue their educations partly or largely independent of schools and curricula. They will certainly be able to access information on any topic of their choice, and there will be large economic incentives to create easy and customizable ways of doing so, as well as tutorial programs that will remove many of the obstacles of cracking the codes of various specialized discourses and information sources in our society. There are also likely to be economic pressures to allow students to count electronic coursework and learning toward academic credentials (cf. Lemke 1994c). On a national scale, the scale on which these economic processes will operate, there will also necessarily arise a very great diversity of ways of satisfying the requirements. The power of specific curricula to dictate the precise content of a student's education will decline in proportion to this diversity. It is even possible, and in my opinion highly desirable, that we will move away from the overt domination of detailed uniform educational criteria of assessment and evaluation and toward the logical implications of the 'portfolio' model of educational assessment; each student's electronic portfolio of accomplishments will be subject to many different evaluations for many different purposes, and no specific certification credential will be required. (Cf. Lemke 1994d).

Most radically, such changes will mean that there will no longer be a single curriculum for all, even locally, to embody the interests of the dominant group. (Those interests of course will still make themselves felt in many other ways that will shape students' educations in the broadest sense.)

There are many members of our society younger than age 13. They too are counted only 'minor' citizens, lesser human beings without rights and protections, unable to discern their own interests or make decisions in accord with those interests. Many of these people could not effectively survive and maintain their independence under our present social arrangements if they were emancipated from adult control. For them, as for the young adults we have been discussing, what seems just is the maximum freedom and equality of rights and opportunities consistent with their actual ability to exercise such rights and avail themselves of such opportunities. The under-13 population is itself extremely heterogeneous by age-group. The very youngest members of our society clearly need constant support and assistance to survive and function in the dangerous world we have created for them. Our present trend toward guaranteeing them protection against abuse seems the most that can be done at present, but for those in the range of ages between perhaps four or five and 11 or 12, there is a gradually increasing capacity for independent discernment of interest and intelligent choice.

How far do our arguments concerning the rights of young adults to direct their own educations also apply to this intermediate group (whom I will call *juniors*)? This question raises an ancient and profound question of values, comparable to those concerning the proper relations of men and women, but perhaps even more critical in its consequences for social dynamics. Just as it has been a core belief of our dominant European cultural traditions, and of those of many other societies as well, that men have the right to control the lives of women, so it has been our view as well that parents have the right to control the lives of children. The Roman *paterfamilias* had the legal and customary right to kill his own children, a right challenged in many other societies only by the interests of the mother's clan in the future services of the child. While our present ideology claims that adults control the lives of children only for their own good (exactly the claim formerly made with regard to women, serfs and slaves), it is not clear just how far the interests of adults and children do converge, or to what extent adults really do sacrifice their interests on behalf of children, or whether in fact the interests of children do require that they come to believe what their parents believed and value what their parents valued.

By what right do parents impose religious beliefs on their children, or political beliefs, or social beliefs? They do so by ancient custom, but what is the ground of this custom, and what are its effects on the social system? The right adults claim to control the curriculum students learn in our schools, and the rights parents claim to veto this curriculum or substitute another more to their liking, even when the majority of society agree that the change may not be in the child's interest (as in the case of extreme religious groups, or parents opposed to education about vital health and safety concerns), are grounded in the fundamental belief that parents have the right to propagate not only their genes, but their beliefs and values as well.

If reproduction is a sort of immortality by proxy, as many parents seem to feel that it is, then the imposition of their beliefs and values, and in extreme cases, the effort to clone themselves in their children takes this myth to its logical conclusion. How many parents wish their children to be as different from themselves as possible? How many react with dismay or violence when they discover that the child has rejected their ideals or values? We call this 'natural', but it is clearly a condition of our cultural system.

In evolution, what evolves is the characteristic, statistically average trajectory of development of a type of organism from conception to senescence. The whole trajectory evolves and is adapted to the environment, not just the adult form. Children, despite their dependence on adults (a predictable part of their environments, to which they are accordingly adapted), are far more adaptable to changing biological (e.g. in their immune response) and social (in their rate of learning and plasticity of behavior) conditions than are adults. We do not need to impose our culture on them by coercive force for their own good; they are perfectly capable of adapting to the diversity of the world around them with only the help from us that they by and large seek out. They rapidly learn to adapt as they catch on to the basic principles needed to survive in any culture: the language system, the thresholds for violence, and the various other hazards, both natural and artificial in their environments, which they must face.

The social control of children's behavior, beliefs and values is the single most significant means of inhibiting fundamental social change. If the developmental trajectories of their beliefs and values were to diverge significantly from those of the previous generation at a relatively early age, then the ultimate degree of that divergence by adulthood could be very great indeed. No doubt many of us confidently believe that our culture's ways of looking at the world are so optimally adapted to the way it really is that a new generation, trying various alternatives, would eventually come around to our way of seeing things. We ignore the fact that most other human societies, civilizations and cultural traditions, some much older than our own, saw the world in very different terms than we do, and many of them got along very well for a very long time according to their own values. It is myopically arrogant to assume that our own culture sees the only true view of reality. If we did not impose our view on the next generation, they might conceivably diverge from us very quickly, and in entirely unpredictable ways.

Tradition, however, exercises its control in many ways. We have, after all, built a large part of the world to which the next generation must adapt. People do not acquire the whole of their education in either the family or the school. They may give us only a relatively small part of what we actually use to guide our adult lives. They do set us on certain paths rather than others, paths that foreclose many possible alternative trajectories of development in our patterns of beliefs, values and actions. Nevertheless, we educate ourselves by *all* our experiences in and with the world, and this broader education will necessarily draw us toward convergence with the earlier beliefs and values that shaped that world. Our educations in life, however, are far more likely to range over the full diversity of beliefs, values and social practices in the community, rather than just those sanctioned by the dominant groups and taught in schools. We will still be more likely to encounter the cultures of the particular ecosocial patches we live in, but most of us do not live only in our homes and neighborhoods; we regularly engage in the social practices of a significantly wider community.

Juniors, too, will soon have access through new information technologies to a much wider range of information, and perhaps eventually of points of view, than they now get through home life and school curricula. If they can exercise free choice to sample every cultural viewpoint that is offered to them, to pursue any interest and curiosity, this will be likely to increase the rate of cultural change. It will not suddenly free children from the culture of their parents – that culture is too pervasively written into every aspect of their environment – but it will certainly offer a potent rival to school curricula and to the authority of both teachers and parents (Hodas 1994; Lemke 1994d). I predict that adults will strive mightily to censor and control juniors' and even young adults' use of these technologies, and that they will inflict a lot of pain in the effort to do so. I hope they will fail, that the technologies will be designed in such a way that it will be nearly impossible to narrowly control access to points of view and types of information for anyone.

There are going to be great battles over these issues, among older adults and between us and those younger than us. Young adults are likely to win a greater measure of self-determination in the near future if only because our new technologies will also decrease the gap between their value to the dominant age-group and that of currently enfranchised adults. (In cyberspace nobody knows you're only 14.) Juniors will remain oppressed longer but perhaps they will be less effectively limited in their possibilities to create their own lives and cultures for the human future. I am afraid that in these struggles many of us will take what history will ultimately judge to have been the wrong side.

Literacy: Dialect, Genre and Social Diversity

I have been trying in this chapter to present beliefs, espouse values and articulate discourses that challenge or subvert a few key elements of the ideologies I believe sustain injustice in our society. The topics I have chosen are related to my own recent interests and those of the intellectual communities in which I participate. I certainly don't claim that they are the most important possible issues to be analyzed as part of a critical praxis; they are just some of the issues I have analyzed in reflecting on my own practice. I have looked at my own beliefs, values and social practices and asked how they have contributed to social control, how they have worked to inhibit the possibility of significant social change. I have been a lot more successful, I think, in changing my beliefs and values than in changing my practices, if only because most of those practices ultimately depend on social cooperation with others whose beliefs and values remain much as my own once were.

Neither do I claim that my new beliefs and values are the ones others ought to come to if they engage in a critical praxis of their own. Critical praxis must sometimes lead us in unpredictable directions, and different lives will lead to a diversity of new possibilities. It is this increasing diversity that I value, that I believe is good for the future adaptability of our society to the challenges it faces. My only aim is to dislodge us from complacency with accepted wisdom, because that 'wisdom' so often inhibits the kinds of changes that might redress inequities in our present social world.

Literacy is not just the mastery of an arbitrary code for writing the meanings we make with language. It is also a critical arena for cultural domination and social control. Dominant Western culture does not simply allow you to write whatever meanings you please in whatever manner you wish, at least not if you want to succeed in school, to find employment that pays well enough to live far from the risk of pain, to gain access to information on most specialized subjects, or to participate in ever so many domains of social activity. Now that discrimination against members of many oppressed groups in our society on the basis of race or ethnic and cultural background is officially illegal, a primary basis for discrimination against these same groups is the differences in the ways they use language, especially in writing.

Standardized written English (SWE) is a 'hyper-standardized' variety of the language (Milroy and Milroy 1985), in the sense that its canons of correctness are drastically more limiting of diversity (such as that found in the many spoken varieties of English) than is necessary for clear or even for minimally ambiguous communication. SWE is a modern creation, like all the standardized national languages created in the late eighteenth and nineteenth centuries as part of the process of nation-building. SWE is no more English than Parisian or literary French is French, Hochdeutsch is German, Florentine is Italian, or Mandarin is Chinese. Ask a Jamaican, a Provençal, a Bavarian, a Neapolitan or a Cantonese. The ideology of standard languages claims that their standardization is necessary for widescale communication, for specialized activities, and even for logical thinking. Of course there are good arguments that none of these claims should be taken seriously (see Lemke 1990c, 1990d and references therein).

Standard languages, like SWE, are the languages of the schools, and more critically of school examinations, civil service examinations, of the courts and the state bureaucracy, of corporate management and the mass media. They are the varieties of the language used by the agencies of power, they are based on the varieties used historically by the dominant groups, and their veneration and quasi-legal status legitimates ruthless discrimination against all other groups on the basis of their 'poor' English. Schools in fact refuse to teach people literacy in their home dialects, forcing them to master an alien dialect, the dialect very often of their oppressors, as the price of literacy itself. Schools will not accept or even tolerate writing in any dialect but the dominant one. Learning to write a different dialect, especially the social dialect of a subcommunity to which one does not belong, is extremely difficult, the more so because the semantic patterns favored by SWE are the product of dominant group values and styles of communication (cf. Halliday 1989; Hasan 1989b).

Not so long ago Native American children were beaten by white teachers in reservation schools for speaking their native languages in preference to English. Things are somewhat subtler today, but the price is still painfully high for maintaining loyalty to the dialect of your home community, the dialect that represents the semantic patterns of your own culture and in which a large part of your own identity is constructed. The price is paid not only by the members of dominated language minorities, but by society as a whole in the great reduction in diversity of semantic possibilities for meaning-making in written English. Discrimination on the basis of language variety should be just as illegal as discrimination on the basis of race, ethnicity or cultural heritage (for a fuller discussion of these issues, see Lemke 1990c, 1990d).

Different cultures and subcultures differ not just in their language varieties, but also in the ways they use language for particular social purposes. The forms of language used for narrative and for instruction differ widely from one group to another (cf. Heath 1983), despite the fact that each group considers its own way to be the only possible sensible way to tell a story or teach a point. It is the dominant groups, however, which are in a position to enforce their own certainty about how these things should be done. Schools actively support this form of arbitrary cultural discrimination and social control, working to limit and reduce the cultural and linguistic diversity in which we all have a stake.

There are some written genres that have arisen only in the dominant subculture because historically its members have monopolized access to the technical and professional activities in which these specialized ways of writing (e.g. scientific reports, legal documents, academic articles) are used. These are the 'genres of power' (Kress 1982; Martin 1989) and mastery of them is not only the entrance fee to these well-remunerated occupations but also the key to accessing the forms of power that are exercised through them. (Of course you cannot use this key if you are kept away from the door for other reasons.)

There has been a great debate in recent years over the importance of teaching students, especially students from dominated groups, to write the genres of power according to the dominant group's very strict and often rather subtle rules of how they must be written. Teachers whose models of good writing come from the humanities and literature oppose the teaching of genre rules as limiting students' creativity and free expression. Educators concerned about 'critical literacy' worry that the teaching of rules omits a critique of these rules and their covert social functions. Parents from the dominated groups who wish to see their children succeed in the present unjust social order often strongly favor the objectives of genre teaching. Educators who appreciate the power of informal participation and guided practice as a mode of learning are skeptical that explicit teaching of rules will actually lead students to master these genres, and point out that it does no good to master the rules of a written genre without a sense of the whole activity in which that genre is supposed to function. Some people even note that eminent practitioners of the professions break genre rules with impunity.

I think it is important in these debates to recognize that the genres of power both empower us and limit us. They are resources that we can some-times use for our own purposes, but access to them requires that we collude to some degree with the dominant cultural systems that have spawned them. Failure to master these genres provides the gatekeepers with an excuse to keep us out of places we may wish to go; these genres are conduits for the power of the dominant group to control our lives whether we master them or not. Of course we should critique them even as we teach them, and we should teach them on request and not by compulsion. We should point out the options and flexibility in genre forms and how their elements form a vocabulary that can become a potent resource for innovation. We should also point out, however, that one must already have power and credibility to get away with breaking their rules, and that to use their forms successfully as a resource we do indeed need to participate, critically, in the full activity in which they function.

Without a mastery of these genres the realms of science, mathematics, engineering, medicine, law, economics and numerous other important forms of social activity are closed to us, just as they are in fact closed to many of those critics who belittle their importance.

In addition to these genres (few of which are actually taught in the curriculum that is available, in principle, to all, being reserved for those in higher education who have already been screened by the gatekeepers), there are the more general rhetorical strategies of scientific, academic and exposi-tory writing of various kinds (cf. Bazerman 1988, 1994; Halliday 1989; Halliday and Martin 1993). These are often taught in the guise of 'school genres' such as lab reports and essays, where they have indeed been taken out of the contexts in which their distant professional cousins function, making it much harder to approach them critically. We shall have to wait and see if learning important semantic strategies in artificially simplified forms significantly helps students to learn more sophisticated genres later on, or whether anyone can offer any better way to do this. At the very least students have a right to get out of their school-prisons and see what the professional genres look like in their natural environments of use, and to do so from a very early age.

Just as the traditional writing curriculum gives all students practice at writing personal and fictional narratives, which count for few points later in the game of life, but little or no explicit instruction (except sometimes for the children of the dominant groups) in writing the genres of power, which will count for everything, so also the traditional curriculum when it does teach genres peddles the pervasive logocentrism of the dominant culture and ignores other literacies. Many of the genres of power are not exclusively verbal genres. Except perhaps for the law and a few areas of humanistic academic scholarship, technical, scientific, medical, economic and other professional genres rely heavily on visual literacies and mathematical and other symbolic literacies. These other literacies are not used as alternatives to verbal meaning-making, but in conjunction and close coordination with it, so that more diverse and precise meanings can be made with their combinations than could be made by any of them alone (Lemke 1993a). With the advent of computer-based multimedia and hypermedia, these even more complex multimodal literacies will increasingly form the basis for the genres of power in our future.

The children of privileged and dominant social groups have long been better prepared to pick up the necessary skills for reading and writing verbal–visual–symbolic genres, and they are now becoming better prepared, thanks only in very small part to school curricula, for the multimedia literacies of the near future. If members of other groups wish to pass these gates and obtain these forms of power, they will need far more help than they are now getting. Even if our goal is to critique and change these forms of power, that is far better done after having learned to understand them and how they work, and far easier accomplished politically if those who practice them are representative of the full diversity of our society rather than only of the sub-culture of the presently dominant groups.

Politics: Discourse, Democracy and Social Change

The most difficult discourses to analyze and critique are always those to which we have value commitments, but these are precisely the ones that may play the most crucial roles in inhibiting social change. Value commitments are of many kinds. In the semantics of English, and perhaps of many other languages, there appear to be a few specific dimensions along which we construct evaluations in our discourses (see Chapter 3 and Lemke 1992a, in preparation). Our commitments to the truth or probability of what we say and to its goodness or desirability seem to be the two fundamental dimensions of importance for contemporary value systems. I have tried to argue throughout this book that our modern separation of these two dimensions is highly artificial and culture-specific. We argue differently about truth and probability from how we argue about goodness and desirability; this disjunction is at the core of modernist ideology (see discussion of disjunctions in the Postscript).

We argue about the rights of older adults in moral and ethical terms, but we argue against the rights of young adults and juniors in terms of our beliefs about the facts of childhood, just as we once argued against the rights of women, of slaves of African ancestry, or of serfs in terms of our truths about them, rather than in terms of right and wrong. When we examine our treatment of these constructed categories of people *apart from* what we believe to be our factual knowledge about them, and solely in terms of our values, we find contradictions. Those contradictions are ordinarily hidden from us because we limit the domain of application of our values according to categories defined in terms of 'facts'. Some people are not allowed to vote, to control property, to choose for themselves because we assign them to a category of Others defined by our beliefs about the facts of their differences from us. Yet we moderns believe that matters of fact, or truth, *ought* to take precedence over matters of other, equally fundamental values, such as goodness or desirability.

Our discourses about the nature of younger people, of women, of other cultures are difficult to analyze because of our commitments to their truth value. Our discourses about politics are difficult to analyze because of our value commitments to their desirability. Where are the sustained analytical critiques today of such core political values as the commitment to democracy? How do our discourses about democracy limit us? How do they function to prevent social change toward other values: a more just society, a freer society, a society with a better quality of life for more people? There have been critiques of freedom as a social value, pointing out that if freedom is defined solely in terms of the individual, then some individuals will claim the freedom to hurt and exploit others. There have been critiques of 'quality of life' as a value, when it means only individual material comforts and is emotionally, socially and spiritually empty – when it is only consumerism writ large and does not count a sense of community or of higher purpose as essential to the quality of our lives.

There are no prevalent critiques of justice itself, arguments that society ought not be just, or ought to be less just than it is today. I myself cannot make sense of this possibility. For me, some notion of justice seems fundamental to the good society, the good life. In the discourse of democracy, justice is predicated on equality for individuals: equality of opportunity, equality in the distribution of goods, equality of legal and moral rights. Both the notions of equality as a social value and individuality as a cultural category can and should be subject to analytical critique, however. Our critical praxis demands no less.

The discourse of democratic political values is so dominant in our culture today that many people cannot analytically undo its conflations, its ways of mutually identifying core social values with one another; democracy means freedom, justice and equality; democracy provides the best political foundation for the highest quality of life. Does it?

Or is the discourse of democracy a particular historical product, enshrining the interests of a particular dominant caste? Does it function ideologically to limit our ability to envision and enact other social arrangements that might entail different notions about justice and quality of life? Does it function to prevent social change in directions many of us might, having envisioned or experienced them, consider preferable to the ideals of democracy? Is democratic discourse the last word on political values? Will there never come a time in all the future centuries and millennia of our species when people will look back on democracy as primitive? as transitional? as mistaken? as specific to one culture in one period of our history?

Are we to believe that the discourse of democracy is inherently universal in validity and application, despite the obvious historical facts that it arose in one cultural tradition and not in others, in one period of history and not in others? Can we even take seriously the manufactured pedigree and exaggerated historical continuity of the notion of democracy that we pretend for it? Would not the ancient Athenian democrats or Roman republicans have been horrified by our twentieth-century version of democracy? Would they even recognize it? Is not our democracy the very nightmare of the classical liberals of the eighteenth century? I am not speaking so much of our actual political arrangements, which are still fairly conservative, but of our acknowledged political ideals (e.g. universal suffrage, universal legal and social equality).

How can we understand the voices in other cultures who question whether democracy is as well suited to their values and traditions as it is to ours? How can we critique our policy of imposing democracy on other cultures because we know it is good for them, whether they want it or not? How can we understand the ways in which we ourselves are limited and controlled by our commitment to a particular discourse about political values?

Democracy, in its modern origins, was the product of the European struggle for power between an ancient landholding aristocracy and a new bourgeoisie. The aristocratic principle of the right to rule was that those with 'a landed interest in the kingdom', and so with the incentive to defend it against its external enemies, should hold the power, govern their domains individually and the kingdom collectively, and lead the defense. The feudal aristocracies began this way, yielded temporarily to a theory of the divine right of kings in order to control their own internecine warfare, and then reasserted their prerogatives. Their world was one of natural hierarchy, based on birth, sanctioned by religion. The rising economic power of the bourgeoisie led to a struggle for equality with the aristocrats, at least in matters that crucially affected economic interests. Freedom meant freedom to do business, to buy title to land, to marry into the aristocracy, to wear satin. Justice meant equal rights in the law between bourgeois and aristocrat, protection against aristocratic feudal power.

The notion of the political individual as a natural unit of the social order was created in opposition to the notion of the hierarchy of God, king, lord, vassal, peasant as the natural foundation of that order. As an individual, even the king could be 'under the law', and the law be made by negotiations between lords and commoners. As individuals, all were equal under the law; justice was justice for individuals without regard for rank. God never came under this system; His majesty was needed to legitimate the change from the feudal order to universal God-given rights, but the political order of the churches was subject to the same battle, against a hierarchical order dominated by the younger sons of the aristocracy (the bishops), and for a more democratic order organized according to individual congregations or other less hierarchical arrangements. The Christian God never quite became the President of Heaven; aristocratic hierarchical values never vanished, but their domains of application became ever more restricted.

The modern discourse of democracy clearly shows its ideological origins in this historic European struggle for power. Its notion of justice depends on the concepts of individuality and equality. To be an equal is to be the same as Us, those who had political power before you. To be admitted to the body politic as a full citizen, you must behave and think like the dominant caste: like a middle-aged male, like an upper-middle class northern European. You must share their values and their beliefs. You are admitted as an individual, stripped of your social identity as member of a community. You are equal as an individual, despite the inequality of power and status among communities and categories of persons. You are equal only in legal and economic rights, despite the inequality of your access to the power and resources necessary to exercise those rights. You are free, but only within the laws made by those with the power and resources to shape the law in their own interest. You have a right to justice, but only within those same laws, and only if you have the power and resources to secure justice. Your community has no political equality with other communities. The social categories to which you belong have no political equality with other categories, particularly not with the dominant categories.

The discourse of democracy is profoundly anti-communitarian. It dissolves the social order into a set of independent, autonomous, equal individuals without regard for the communities through which individuals construct their identities, learn their beliefs and values, or access power and resources through social networks. It conceals the unequal power and resources of the dominant subcommunity by denying the political relevance of communities as such. It shifts the debate from one about the real inequities between communities and categories of people to one about the equality and inequality of individuals. It can claim, in its own limiting terms, that legal equality of individuals is all that can realistically be expected, and that the manifold diversity of individuals leads inevitably to all other inequality. In this way it deflects discussion of the inequality between communities and between social categories (by gender, by age, by class, by culture) and of how that prior inequality arises and vitiates legal equality in practice.

The discourse of democracy is also profoundly anti-diversity. It rests on assumptions of the homogeneity of the community, its conformity to the norms, beliefs and values of the dominant caste. The very definition of community in the discourse of democracy rests on *shared* beliefs, *shared* values. In the actual politics of democracy, however, there is never a single community, and in so far as communities are defined as interest-groups, sharing common interests, communities are pitted against one another. For a community to protect its interests, when its power depends only on the number of individuals it can muster, that community must emphasize solidarity. The solidarity of the group, when it defines itself in terms of what is shared among all members, thereby also defines the group by exclusion and contributes to that divisiveness among the many weak which is decisive for the dominance of the strong few. The dominant group is solidly against all other groups.

The dominant group does not consider itself to be just another special interest group, however. As males do not think of themselves as gendered, as those neither too young nor too old are not socially defined by their age, as the middle class does not see itself as part of a class society, as European-Americans see their culture as simply American, so the dominant group paradoxically sees itself as 'the mainstream' when it is statistically only a tiny, highly unrepresentative fraction of the whole of society. It constructs itself as always in the majority, aligning different groups of Others with itself in different struggles, but only the dominant group is always part of the majority, whatever the issue, whatever the coalition.

In this dominant ideology, where communities and groups must define themselves by shared beliefs and values, that is by exclusion, it is abnormal and stigmatized to be a 'half-caste': a member of more than one group, with 'divided' loyalties. The division of groups from one another is a core strategy of domination. Groups themselves enforce solidarity/exclusion to protect themselves as best they can against the dominant group and its shifting coalition of allies, but the lived experience of many of us is that we are not 100 percent members of one and only one community, one and only one set of mutually exclusive social categories (cf. Lamphere 1992; Heath 1994). We can be both both masculine and feminine, both Eurocultural and Afrocultural, both youthful and mature, both conservative and radical, both American and Chinese, both working class and middle class, both man-loving and woman-loving, both Black and Latina, both Christian and Buddhist. These are not things we *are*, but things we *do*. All of us can, and many of us do in fact enact practices that are supposed to be mutually exclusive.

We participate in many communities in our lives. We have multiple grounds of affiliation to multiple communities. We construct multiplex personal identities which combine elements of our lived experience in these different communities, our different social practices. We enact the moments of our lives with resources from the whole combined repertory of practices we acquire through participation in diverse social groups and categories. Some of us participate, to one degree or another, in the dominant subcommunity or one or more of the dominant social categories. We also participate in dominated communities and as members of dominated categories.

Communities are not defined by unity, by solidarity, by shared beliefs and values. The system of social practices that constitutes a community is too complex and diverse to be known to or practiced by any individual. The set of social practices that defines a community is differentially distributed over individuals according to age, to gender, to class, to caste, to subculture. Any one individual enacts only a small fraction of the total system of practices that defines the community. What makes a community is the interdependence and interaction of these practices, both their functional integration and their systematic conflict. What makes a community is not homogeneity, but organized heterogeneity, not the sharing of practices but the systematic articulation of differences.

This is not the view on which the discourse of democratic political values is based. In this alternative view, individuals are not the natural unit of society; social practices are. Social practices form integrated, or at least articulated, self-organizing systems of practices which are distributed over individuals, and which intersect in individuals who participate in them. Individuals, accordingly, can participate in practices from different subcultures and subcommunities, and even from historically distinct cultural systems. We are permeable to cultures; we are not consistent, not all of one sort or all of another. We are all hybrids, mixtures, and not nearly as well integrated as we are supposed to pretend we are. Neither are cultures and communities the pure types they are supposed to be. In so far as multiplex individuals participate in them, cultural systems are also permeable to social practices, to beliefs, attitudes, values and norms that came historically from other cultures and communities.

The current discourse of multiculturalism recreates the discourse of democracy, with cultural groups as individuals writ large. Each culture is assumed to be homogeneous and separate from the others. Each social person is ideally assigned to one and only one of these cultures. Each culture is ideally taken to be the equal of each of the others. All this is assumed despite the fact that the notion of 'a culture' as a homogeneous grouping of similar individuals is itself a European construction, and despite the fact that few Americans, and few in any part of the world today, participate solely and entirely in cultural practices which formed a historically isolated system. (Probably there have never been such systems anywhere at any time.)

An alternative discourse of 'interculturalism', as we might call it, sees individuals and communities as permeable to the social practices of many historical ecosocial systems, always changing, always interacting with other ecosocial systems. It should speak in terms of 'intercommunities' in which many local communities on many scales of ecosocial organization interact, more strongly or more weakly (in terms of the exchange, transformation, and interdependence of their social practices) with one another. Our notions of even local communities should emphasize diversity at all scales and the interarticulation of divergent practices rather than the uniformity or conflict-free integration of shared practices. This applies to languages and techno-logies, to beliefs and values, to practices of education and social control.

A profound consequence of this shift in perspective is a glimpse of what might be post-democratic political ideals. If community does not depend on shared practices, then a community does not require a single uniform policy on all matters. It does not require institutions to determine and enforce that policy over wider and wider scales of social organization. What it requires instead are institutions to work out how to integrate, or at least interarticulate, divergent policies and practices at various scales of social organization. We need to understand better how to make 'peaceful coexistence' work, how to construct a viable *modus vivendi* for living with difference and diversity. Our species has a long history, not just of conflict, and not just of the effort to impose a single norm on everyone, but of living together, of negotiating differences, of getting along. Even conflict can be part of a *modus vivendi*, a continual renegotation of delicate balances.

The post-democratic political ideal is no longer a single ideal; it accommodates divergent political values. It does not need to be imposed on everyone; it accommodates even those who will seek to impose their views on everyone (but without yielding to those singular views). It does not assume that all views, all communities, people in all social categories have equal power; it recognizes inequalities and instead of trying to hide them, places them in the center of the process of articulation of differences. It does not require that all groups have equal power; its power lies in its ability to dissolve the unity of any group into the diversity of practices distributed among its individuals and shared with those distributed among the individuals of other groups. It does not depend on the notion of the individual as such, or the group. Starting from specific social practices, it works within individuals and across groups to find unique, local and doubtless temporary solutions to problems of social justice.

Beyond even the critique of democracy as the ideal solution to the problem of *human* justice is the more radical problem of whether human values in our own Western culture are proving themselves maladapted to the survival of our species and the health of larger ecosystems to which we belong. Centuries of humanism have put the interests and viewpoint of our species at the center of the value universe, where we once placed immortal, unhuman gods that stood for what is greater in our universe than ourselves. Today American culture is struggling toward a post-humanist system of values because we have begun to realize that we cannot rationally or morally place human interests above those of the ecosystems on which our survival depends, nor even on an equal level with them. Our cultural value systems must adapt themselves to the overall viability of the ecologies of the planet.

There will be serious human conflicts fought over competing humanist and post-humanist value systems. There will be great human pain resulting from the ecological disasters produced in part by existing value systems. As human actions guided by a desire for material aggrandizement begin to produce effects on larger and larger ecological scales, the world ecosocial system will act to reorganize itself across many scales toward some more viable pattern. Civilizations will fall, values will change; perhaps our species will survive, and perhaps not. These issues transcend humanity itself. Our values and our cultures, important as they are today for the organization of many ecosystems, are still only part of larger wholes. Our dominant culture promotes the illusion that we can control the complex, self-organizing systems of which we are only one part. That illusion benefits the interests of a small élite in the world community. We may all suffer terribly for their greed.

These mere glimpses of post-democratic and post-humanist arguments are as yet too undeveloped to compete rhetorically with centuries of democratic and humanist discourse. It is not at all clear yet how these new perspectives may change our values and definitions of social justice, nor how they might emerge from the present web of power relationships and the discourses and other practices through which these are legitimated and reproduced. My principal concern here is not with presenting alternatives to democratic or humanist discourse, but with opening up the possibility for analyzing and critiquing them. In politics, as in education, as in literacy, the issue of central concern is how our discourses, our texts, mediate the meanings that actions and events have for us, and so how we act. Discourses enable and they limit. They play a crucial role in processes of social control. They are critically linked to all the rest of our culturally meaningful, materially embodied social practices, especially those by which we exploit the vulnerability of human bodies to pain in order to control not only individual behavior, but the rate and direction of social change.

Although this is the last chapter of *Textual Politics*, I do not want to seem to have said the last word on any of the issues raised in this book. Someday those words will have been said, in a time when none of these issues will matter to people any more. Even today there are many people for whom these issues do not matter in their lived experience, in the discourses through which they make sense of their worlds. They matter for me, and perhaps for you, because of who we are and where and how we live in a particular social order and a particular moment of history. Even then, they matter only for some parts of our identities, in some aspects of our lives – but by that much they *do* matter. We do not need to construct any universal significance around them to make them seem to matter still more. We cannot afford such comforting illusions if we are to find new ways to understand these issues better, and new practices to help make our worlds more just, however differently we may see our visions of justice.

Textual Politics ends, not with this chapter, but with a long Retrospective Postscript. It presents substantial portions of the chain of earlier discourses that led me to what I have said here. These are the discourses in terms of which much of this book makes sense to me.

Retrospective Postscript:
Making Meaning, Making Trouble

Between 1976 and 1982 I wrote a series of exploratory essays in search of a theoretical framework for my studies of education and social dynamics (Lemke 1984). In 1976 I was writing as a physicist new to educational theory, trying to make sense of learning as a social process and as one aspect of human biological development. I saw learning as shaped by evolution and mediated by language and other semiotic systems.

My view of language was influenced by Roman Jakobson *et al.*'s (1965, 1971) discussions of the relations between paradigmatic alternatives and syntagmatic combinations, and by Noam Chomsky's (1957, 1965) distinctions between deep and surface structures. At that time I saw the communication of surface structures as a means to the unconscious learning of deep structures, not just in language, but in all areas of human behavior. (This was contrary to Chomsky's own conclusion that something innate in the brain was needed to get from surface structure experience to deep structure principles. To some degree this may be true regarding very general matters of syntactic structure, but in so far as meaning plays a role in such processes, the consistent patterns that connect utterances and events to their larger textual and situational contexts provide critical additional information not considered by Chomsky.)

I followed Jean Piaget (1970) and Claude Levi-Strauss (1963) in their structuralist view that all meaningful behavior was organized like language according to systems of abstract formal relations. I extended Piaget's (1971) concern with developmental biology to a general analysis of learning as an aspect of the self-organization of the 'instructional systems' (social interactions) in which we participate. In this I drew on the work of developmental and evolutionary biologists C.H. Waddington (1957) and Konrad Lorenz (1965) who were interested in complex behavior, physicists Ilya Prigogine (1961) and Erwin Schrodinger (1967) who had begun to ask how complex systems evade the law of entropy and become more organized with time rather than less, and early work in cybernetics and the theory of self-organization (von Bertalanffy 1950; Ashby 1956; Kauffman 1971; Thom 1975). I read Vygotsky (1963) and Luria (1959) for theories of the social mediation of intellectual development. In retrospect these perspectives seem only to have grown in significance since 1976.

By 1977 I had read Gregory Bateson's (1972) classic *Steps to an Ecology of Mind* and was trying to reconcile the then emerging (and thereafter long dominant) mentalist perspective on learning in cognitive science with what seemed to me to be much more powerful views of learning's social and cultural foundations. I also began to read the work of Michael Halliday (1975, 1976) and to add a functionalist view of language, that language is organized according to what it has evolved to do, to the formalist perspective of Chomsky's structuralism. Above all, however, it was Bateson's focus on meta-communication, and his proposal (1972: 132–3) that the notion of redundancy in cybernetics and information theory could be extended to include the role of context in meaning (meta-redundancy, see below), that enabled me to begin developing a general model for semiotics that was both formal and functional (Lemke 1984: 35–9) and fit with a dynamic model of social learning and development (Lemke 1984: 23–58).

Halliday's wonderful *Language as Social Semiotic* (1978) provided the tools for doing semiotic analysis of language and behavior without losing sight of the social contexts that provide the basis for both cultural meaning and individual development. By 1979 I had abandoned cognitive models of meaning for social and semiotic ones. I also began my research on communication of science in classrooms (Lemke 1983b, 1990a) and a long informal collaboration with Michael Halliday. I found myself traveling across the US and around the world trying to explain to people a new synthesis of ideas about social meaning and human development as aspects of the self-organization of complex social systems.

Many of the principles I was using were unfamiliar. Few educators or psychologists knew much about complex systems theory, linguistics or semiotics. Few people in linguistics in the US knew much about the alternatives to Chomskyan formalism that grew out of the East European and British traditions from which Halliday drew. I found sympathetic listeners among anthropologists interested in language and among biologists interested in system theory. I had an even more difficult time explaining what I was up to to my friends in the arts in New York. So I decided to write 'Making Trouble' (1982), which proved to be very popular and circulated in photocopies passed hand-to-hand even long after it was published as part of *Semiotics and Education* (Lemke 1984: 94–150). Even then, it was not widely available, and one or two offers to republish it as part of other volumes did not work out. When plans for this book were first being made, many friends and colleagues urged me to include it here.

'Making Trouble' was not written as a formal academic paper. It was never intended for publication and contained no footnotes or citations. It was partly an effort to write my way through to a fuller vision of the theoretical ideas I was working on, and partly an attempt to communicate those ideas as clearly as I could to a wide range of interested friends and colleagues. What follows are extended sections of 'Making Trouble', slightly edited, with some of the missing citations and an occasional comment added.

The original 'Making Trouble' began with an attempt to problematize the notion of objective truth. It proposed that *meaning* is a much more fundamental notion than *truth*, indeed more fundamental even than the notion of 'reality' itself. The basic argument was that claims about truth or reality are meanings made by people according to patterns that they have learned, and that trying to understand how and why people make the meanings they do is more useful than fighting over the truths of their claims. This leads naturally enough to the problem of whether a theory of social meaning-making is not itself just another claim about truth and reality. Confronting this paradox led me to reconceptualize the nature and role of theory itself, demoting it from its traditional status as the goal of inquiry to that of just a tool in social activity.

The Trap of Theory: Reflexivity and Praxis

Can any theory be a theory of itself? If I am building a theory of how people make meaning socially, can I build a theory of my own theory-building? If I can't, my theory can never be complete, and since my theory-building is just the sort of thing I want to make a theory of [i.e. social meaning-making], a theory that didn't cover *that* wouldn't be much of a theory at all. But if I do include my theory-building in the scope of the theory, I run into a different but no less serious problem.

Some time ago, Kurt Gödel (1931) tried to answer, within the limits of what other people would accept as a valid mathematical proof, the question of whether a formal system of mathematical or logical axioms, assumptions, proofs, theorems, etc. could prove theorems about itself. For example, could it show that within the system it was possible to prove all the theorems that followed from the axioms? or might some true theorems not be provable? His answer made a lot of people very unhappy. Gödel proved, to the satisfaction of other mathematicians and logicians, that no formal system with rigorous rules for what was a valid proof and what was a true theorem, even something as simple as the rules of arithmetic, much less anything as complicated as formal logic, could be proven to be *both* internally self-consistent (i.e. you couldn't prove the same theorem to be both true and false within the rules) *and* complete (in the sense that all the possibly true theorems could actually be proved true somehow within the rules).

Since neither Gödel nor anyone else he knew was interested in systems that were internally contradictory, his results showed that if the systems were free from internal inconsistencies, then they had to be incomplete; there had to be true theorems that could not be proven, or possible theorems for which one could not determine whether they were true or false. And the theorems that gave rise to this trouble were basically the theorems of self-reference, those that enabled the system to say things about itself, to contain itself in its own domain as a theory (see Kleene 1952; Hermes 1969; Hofstadter 1979). This means that the foundations of logic and mathematics, on which all of science and rational argument are based, cannot be proven both consistent and complete by their own criteria of truth and standards of proof. It also means that no formal theory can be built which includes itself in its own domain without inconsistencies. It means that no formal theory can explain or justify itself, not even logic itself. But this is exactly what a theory of social meaning has to do. It has to be reflexive, it has to account for the processes of making theories, of which it is itself one special case.

Do we really need formal theories? Could we be content with 'informal' ones that had no explicit assumptions, no strict procedures for deductions or criteria of logical consistency and truth? What do we need theory for at all? We need a theory because we always already have one. If we don't formulate explicitly our ways of making meaning in particular contexts, the meanings we make will be governed automatically, by default, by the limiting meaning systems of our narrow communities, even when we are not aware of this.

Making meaning is a practice, a process, an activity. It is not itself a formal system. All formal systems, all meaning relations, are immanent in and enacted by our actions, by what we do in using them. Our objective in inquiry is to add to and change the patterns of our actions in such a way that we can analyze and criticize the way things are done now and create new, different patterns in place of the automatic ones we are limited by. Our real goal then is not to make a theory of how things are, but to develop a *praxis*, a critical way of analyzing, doing, creating. Part of this praxis is going to be using theories, which are themselves just ways of talking and doing. Each of these will be partial and incomplete, but hopefully internally consistent. We may use different theories which are not inconsistent with one another because they are incommensurable, because they lead us to view the world, or a situation, in totally different terms. The practical consistency of theories does not depend on whether they generate statements about the world that are consistent in the sense that notions of a single truth about the world require. It depends only on how using these theories leads to the actions we take; it is their consistency within our praxis that matters.

We will use theories as tools in our praxis, not make them ends in themselves. We will not regard theories as goals in themselves, as pictures of the one true reality, but simply as tools we use in critical, creative, self-reflexive action. Our theories will not be directly self-reflexive; they will not contain themselves in their own domains. It is our praxis that must be self-reflexive; we must analyze and criticize our own processes of analysis and criticism, and all our newly created practices of every kind for getting inside of, and outside of, what we and other people do to make the kinds of meanings we make.

Praxis is the self-reflexive, self-critical, *unstable*, creative meta-practices of a community. If meta-theory means theory about what theories are and should be, then meta-practices are practices which practice on themselves, which are applied to themselves, like meta-criticism, the practice of criticizing your own ways of criticizing things. If we do this sort of thing, then our practices (and meta-practices) will be *unstable*, because at every turn we must turn back into and so out of that turn, making a next turn at which this must happen yet again. This is not so easy to do, or to live with.

Praxis is its own meta-praxis. Its practices *are* meta-practices. Praxis is also social; the practices are social activities in which we participate and over which none of us has sole control. The unstable character of praxis is an aspect of the dynamics of the social system of practices, its way of generating its own future by acting on itself and transacting with its environments.

For these same reasons, and contrary to many superficial arguments, Language as a formal semiotic system is not usefully regarded as being its own meta-language. It is only Language-in-use, language as part of material social practices (which can be recoded in the terms of *any* semiotic system), that can turn back on itself, represent itself, act upon itself. Only systems of material-semiotic social practices, regarded as action, as activity, can be reflexive. Mental processes as such cannot be, nor can formal linguistic or semiotic processes.

Part of good praxis is using theory. Not 'the theory' that claims to describe the way things *are*, but theories that are just ways of talking about something, ways that are useful for certain purposes, as part of certain activities. The tools we use in this sense are not just ways of 'talking'; they are never purely verbal, never consist solely of declarative propositions. They include many ways of doing: ways of writing, ways of moving, ways of making meaning with any action, practice or process at all. They can be ways of visualizing, ways of sequencing, arranging, juxtaposing, intercutting, branching, classifying, identifying, subordinating, superordinating, integrating, diversifying, and in general of bringing into and out of every possible kind of relationship we can make sense of. Visual artists, filmmakers, choreographers, architects, composers immensely enrich the ways of making meaning and the ways of sharing ways of making meaning beyond what talk alone can do.

Regarded as action, speech is never a purely linguistic phenomenon, and the meanings we make by speaking always also rely on other semiotic resources, such as gestures, facial expressions, movements, pauses, voice qualities, rhythms and tones, and a variety of non-verbal actions. Likewise writing always has its visual, typographic dimensions of meaning-making, and printed texts have long coevolved with the conventions of pictures, diagrams, maps, tables, graphs, etc. It is not the texts as objects, nor the speech as verbal text, that makes meaning, but our activity in interacting with these, producing and interpreting them, that makes meaning. Texts do not 'have' meaning; meanings are relations we make through practices in which we are never the sole participant, never the sole originator of the practice.

Communities as Dynamic Open Systems

Human communities *are* ecosystems. Ecosystems *are* biological, chemical and physical systems. The physics, chemistry and biology of complex self-organizing systems can tell us much that is useful about human communities: about the conditions necessary for the existence of human communities, about the properties human communities 'inherit' because they are special cases of more general kinds of systems, particularly ecosystems. Human individuals, as organisms and as socially constructed 'persons', are one level of organization in terms of which we can look at these complex systems of processes. Seeing how we are like more general kinds of natural systems also helps us to see how we are special, how the practices by which we make material objects and processes assume meaning in our communities lead us to interact materially with them in ways that would not occur in other kinds of systems, and lead to pathways of self-organization unique to human ecosocial systems. Human learning and development arise as aspects of our participation in these processes of self-organization, and so do social and cultural change.

Biology, when it is not trying to describe human communities in particular, but just telling us its ways of seeing all animal communities, and so ours among them, says such things as: Members of the community of different ages and sexes behave differently and treat one another differently, according to age and sex. Members of the community interact with one another in a very large number of different ways (showing off, sounding off, courting, mating, grooming, roughhousing, fighting, sharing food, mimicking one another, etc.) but have contacts with members of other communities in only very limited ways (usually fighting or scaring one another off). Individual differences between members may affect who mates with whom, or who fights whom and wins, but the patterns of behavior of the group will continue pretty much the same.

These patterns of behavior result from the interplay of our chemistries and our environments. The chemistry starts off at conception with the patterns of chemical reactions in a single cell. They depend on patterns from the mother's egg cell and the father's sperm cell chemistries, which are different in detail, but similar in broad qualitative outline for all members of the species. The environments for every chemical reaction, and for every system of interdependent chemical reactions, expand in larger and larger circles, from the neighboring molecular architecture to the large-scale cellular organelles, from the border chemistry of neighboring cells to the external flows of heat and nutrients around the developing embryo, from the internal chemistry and physiology of the mother to the external environment with which the mother–embryo system as a whole must transact to live.

From shortly after birth (and maybe for a time before), and all during the life of the organism, one of the most important environments in which the adaptive patterns of the species (our evolved, genetic patterns) become the actual behaviors of individuals is our *social* environment: the patterns of contacts with other members of our own species. We do not inherit behavior with our genes; we inherit only chemical possibilities. These possibilities become *us* through the direct and indirect interaction of our chemistries with their/our environments: with the food we eat, the climate we live in, the sunlight and other energies to which we are exposed, and a thousand other factors – but critically important among all of them is our interaction with other human beings.

Survival is not easy. Those strategies for making organisms that can survive and reproduce, which are 'economical' in their chemistry, have survived and prospered. One key survival strategy in our species and many others has been *not* to put all the information needed to make the behavior of the adult into the chemistry of egg and sperm, but to rely on the environment itself to supply much of this information. The chemistry of egg and sperm only provides a means of using environmental materials and information, a selective sensitivity to certain features of the environment. At each stage of development from embryo to elder, the processes of the previous stage, plus the input from the environment that that stage was 'waiting for', was selectively sensitive to and ready to use, makes a next stage which is now ready for something else. Not only does this *epigenetic* strategy save on the initial chemical investment in survival, but it can flexibly adapt, within limits, to changes in the environment, so that our course of development can change as new, 'current' information comes in.

This strategy can be risky in a highly unpredictable environment, so a back-up strategy has survived in the many species that are specifically *social*: the same lifelong chemistry-plus-environment strategy that results in children who are primed to learn also results in adults who are primed to teach. The selective sensitivity of the child gets tuned to a reliable source of information, reliable because that source – other people in its community – has similarly evolved to provide just that kind of information (e.g. about the local language in use in the community in that generation). The child sets off a teacher response in adults just as adults set off a learner response in children (this is stronger the younger the children are).

Have you ever felt a compulsion to make faces or noises at a baby? to talk to it, to try to make it smile, or react in a meaningful way? to interact with it in ways that are providing it with very useful information about and practice interacting with the kinds of sounds and facial patterns that can be significant in its community? Have you ever noticed that babies and young children have all sorts of things they do to trigger behaviors in you that will feed their need for information? Information on what language is spoken here, what the rules of behavior are, what is good and bad, what counts as meaningful and what doesn't, how to move your face muscles just the right way, how to make other people be good to you. The partnership of adults and infants/juveniles of the same species is a remarkably effective one because both can be guided by similar sequences, stage by stage, of building in environmental information.

This cooperative social strategy is not just for babies in interaction with adults. All of us, all the time, are meeting each others' needs for social information, helping and coercing each other into the behavior patterns of our community. We do not learn these once and for all at some particular time; we are reshaped into them again and again by the features, including behaviors of our fellow humans, of the specific situations to which they are adapted. What persists in us, for the most part, is just a disposition toward certain sorts of behaviors when in these situations. We do not need a complete model of how to behave; the situational environment will fill in the details for us, will remind us, will constrain us, keep us on track. This happens even when no other people are present. [This picture of development was based mainly on the models provided by Waddington (1969–71), Lorenz (1965) and Piaget (1971).]

In this sense all behavior, all development is learned, is a product of interaction with an environment that supplies essential information. Our own modern culture, however, has gone rather a long way toward the belief that behavior originates purely internally, either as the will of some mysterious Self which is not me because it is inside of, a mere part of the whole me (it used to be called the soul before psychology replaced theology), or as the causal result of some biochemical process that makes us be the way we 'are'.

So we are taught to say that babies are that way because of the *nature* of babies, and old people act as they do because that's what getting old does to you. It wouldn't do to say that kids are rebellious and troublesome because the way adults interact with them makes them that way, or that old people are crotchety and irritable and forgetful because that is how we make them be. No, we have to believe that it is all out of our hands, all a matter of hormones and oxygen levels in the brain. No matter that no one has ever established a direct link between these chemical conditions and complex patterns of meaningful social behavior – or that it is impossible in principle to do so because material causation and cultural patterns of meaning belong to two entirely incommensurable theories/discourses about the world. No matter either that we know that social interactions can lead to hormonal changes and differences in the level of oxygen in the brain. We are not taught to connect what we have not been taught to connect.

What does physics have to do with human communities? with learning and development in social systems? In the discourse of physics, a flame, a person, a community, and a city are examples of a particular kind of physical system: a dynamic open system. Such systems have a special kind of survival problem; they need to get from their environments the matter, energy and information that keeps them going, but in getting these and using them to live, they degrade the quality of the environment they depend on. The energy of fuels, food, sunlight is degraded into waste heat that is no longer useful for any other purpose of the system. That waste heat goes into the environment, and unless it dissipates away from the system, it can make the environment too hot for its survival. The matter in foods, fuels and raw materials of every sort is likewise degraded by the use we make of it into waste products that also must be carried away into the distant environment lest they poison us. And the information, the orderliness, on which not only meaning in general, but the special usefulness of energy and matter also depends is transformed by the processes of life into disorder, noise, randomness, a chaos that has no meaning in our system of meanings. That too can be deadly to us unless we can find ways to ensure that we will continue to have a physical and social environment with which we can interact to obtain the useful matter, energy and information we constantly need to survive.

A flame is a border zone between a fuel (wood, wax, gas, oil) and the oxygen that combines there with the fuel to make light, heat, smoke and all the waste products of burning. A flame is a dynamic open system. Or better to say: a flame can be usefully talked about in the discourse of dynamic open systems. It has a structure, often a visible shape or repeating pattern. It has currents of vaporized fuel and draughts of oxygen, bringing into the system from its environment what it needs to survive. The system must be *open* to its environment to survive; if we close off the flame from its source of fuel or oxygen, it dies. But in the system, through the system of processes we call a flame, those materials and the latent energy and order in them, react chemically. Latent chemical energy becomes 'used' energy in forcing the recombination of chemical atoms of fuel and oxygen, becomes heat that drives the currents that keep fuel and oxygen coming in and coming together, heat that drives the currents that carry away the smoke and waste products (including the heat itself) that would otherwise smother the system in its own byproducts (or disrupt it with its own heat). If these processes of burning, if its complex structure, were interrupted for even a moment, the flame would die.

Dynamic open systems are those which survive only by continuous interaction with their environments through processes that exchange matter, energy and information with those environments. In the exchange, the system survives at the expense of the environment, which is inevitably 'polluted', degraded, losing useful matter and energy and information, getting back waste heat and waste products and disorder. If the system is large and the environment small or limited, the system may exhaust the available resources of the environment, or it may use them up faster than the environment can make new supplies available, or it may produce so much heat or waste that it burns itself up or poisons itself because the environment cannot dissipate these rapidly enough. A system may create so much noise and disorder in its environment that its interactions with it become chaotic and the systematic pattern by which alone it can survive is disrupted, and it dies.

A delicately balanced ecosystem which internally recycles wastes is still only a larger scale example of a dynamic open system. The environmental paradox of life returns at a higher level of organization and complexity, as we will see.

[The discussions here of living, developing systems as dynamic open systems, or energy-dissipative thermodynamic structures, are based mainly on von Bertalanffy (1950), Prigogine (1961), and Schrodinger (1967).]

Babies are hot. Their bladders, bowels and bellies trickle, void and spit up erratically, fouling their environments. They crave the energy and matter of milk and food, and the information of social communication with others of their own species. As babies, and as children, in different ways, but always in *some* ways, they interact with their environments, physical and social, so that their own internal order and complexity increases as they grow and learn and develop, at the same time that they fill the environment, or would fill it if it were not for the community, with heat and wastes, with noise and trouble, with disorder of every sort. To be around one is to know firsthand what physicists call *entropy*, the property we can assign to anything to measure it on a scale from ordered, organized, useful and meaningful (low in entropy) to disordered, disorganized, useless and meaningless (high in entropy). A scale from language to noise, from food to waste, from the neatly piled toys to the chaotic aftermath of the play by which we grow, from the things that work to the same things broken and ruined by a use that is teaching a system of meaning even as it de-means [*sic*] what was used to teach.

Left to themselves, would babies survive? They are not built, we have not evolved, to develop alone. Our communities provide the information we need, the support system of information and organization which helps us maintain those interactions with the environment by which we live. Parents feed, change diapers, clean up after us. The community environment helps us get food and safely get rid of wastes. The parent, the community smiles at, talks to, give toys and removes dangers the child produces as byproducts of its development (all those broken bits). The community makes an environment filled with meaning, with information, with the patterns that have meaning in that community and to which, in the cycles of chemistry-plus-environmental-input (epigenesis) the child becomes selectively sensitive.

The child triggers off in us our side of the pattern's processes as we trigger off its in it. When the child makes noises that are not meaningful in our community's system of meanings, we talk at it, and to it, and with it in the orderly patterns of our language. And we do the same with hugs and smiles and gestures and foods, and with *when* we do *what*, and with what goes with what else, sharing and building with the child toward the shared patterns of the community. [These interactions also shape and change the adults who participate in them. Child-rearing is a powerful shaper of parental adult behavior, values, beliefs and practices.]

What would happen if the adult responded to the child only with non-sense talk? If we reflected back to the child the low levels of meaning, the 'noise' it is making, its only just-barely-patterned forms of vocalization? It would not come to share a language or a system of meaning with us. The community works diligently to ensure that the child's system of meaning and action comes close enough to common patterns to ensure the *community's* survival, for the community is also a dynamic open system that can die. Its structure lies in a pattern of human activities perpetuated through the pattern of meanings those activities enact. One of the raw materials that feeds it is the newborn, and one of the degraded waste products it must dispose of is the newly dead. Its patterns of meanings, its ways of doing things, can colonize other communities, or hybridize with them, forming joint communities with a hybrid meaning system and patterns of actions. And through its action systems and meaning systems it regulates the interactions of its members with each other and with their physical environment: our language, laws, attitudes, expectations, agriculture, transport, materials and energy supply, waste disposal, environmental conservation.

Dynamic open systems are peculiar among the kinds of systems physicists have traditionally studied. It was not until quite recently [i.e. the 1960s and 70s] that theories were made to describe them [notably Prigogine 1961, 1962, 1980]. Until the importance of our being *open* systems was recognized, that what we are and what we do depends as much on the state of our environments as on the state of whatever we choose to call 'us', it seemed that something happening *in* 'us' was the reverse of what happened in all other kinds of physical systems. Our entropy appears to go spontaneously *down*; we get less disordered, more organized, more complex and regular in our behavior as we mature – at least up to a point – and even after that point we still manage to hold our own against disorder until we begin to fail as a system, to die, to decompose, to dissipate back into the environment of which we were always an integral part, but in which we had maintained our identity as a system. All other kinds of physical systems are always spontaneously *increasing* their entropy; whatever they do, they go from a state of greater order and complexity to states of lesser organization, all the time. We have already described how dynamic open systems manage to grow and develop in complexity, at least while they last; they do it by processes that feed on the order of their environments. They are thus caught in a paradox of survival: to continue to live they must disturb and degrade the environments that sustain their lives.

This dilemma is partly overcome by the integration of dynamic open systems into larger *supersystems*. Neighbors help each other survive. Cells in a body are fed, and their waste products removed by the cooperative action of supersystems of cells: tissues, organs and the body itself. Bodies, organisms, people through communities do much the same thing. We act in ways that keep us all going – at the price of our submitting to the supersystem's overall patterns, which are simply the patterns of our interactions with each other and with our environments.

Note that the dilemma of life is also its motor of change; to live we must interact with and change our environments in ways that make our current ways of living less reliable for survival. We create the conditions which lead to change in our ways of being-through-interaction.

How do supersystems come to be, evolve and change? The theory of dynamic open systems is consistent with the possibility that, rather than simply having an individual system exist first, then interact, and eventually become dependent for its survival on participation in a supersystem, that instead an original larger scale system may become internally differentiated, different parts becoming more and more specialized, until eventually the original system is better seen as a supersystem with each of its parts functioning as a dynamic open subsystem. Then each of those subsystems can become internally differentiated and specialized, and so on. Either way we get a view of hierarchically related levels of organization in complex, dynamic open systems. For any particular level of interest, we can see it as being sustained both from below, by the actions of its subsystems, and from above by its participation in a still larger supersystem.

For a fuller discussion of hierarchical organization, see Salthe (1985, 1989, 1993). Internal differentiation of dynamic open systems is itself an aspect of general processes of self-organization; the evolution of the resulting subsystem interactions towards cooperative maintenance of the supersystem is simply a condition of their survival.

These complex systems still remain not only open, but dynamic. They must be able to change and respond to changes in the environments with which they have to interact to survive. They cannot afford to become perfectly internally self-regulating up and down their levels of supersystems and subsystems, because perfect regulation would make them rigid, inflexible, unable to respond – able only to go on and on in ways suited to prior environmental conditions. Too limited by its own policing of patterns of internal processes, the system would not be able to adapt and it would die. So successful systems, survivors, cannot be perfectly self-regulating. They must leave themselves room to maneuver; they build into their subsystem processes *contradictions*, processes that run *counter* to one another, and counter to self-regulation.

Dynamic open systems are never stable; at best they are meta-stable, temporarily stable in relation to some constant set of environmental conditions, but ready to change as their environments change – as the environments surely will do, if only because of the effects of the system on them.

Our communities and their patterns of action and meaning also reflect this fundamental strategic balance. There is self-regulation on one side, and on the other provision for necessary flexibility, for imperfect self-regulation, escape hatches, internal contradictions, and even counter-regulatory sub-systems (hopefully including our own unstable self-reflexive praxis) which enable the system to change.

Making Meaning: Contextualization and Meta-redundancy

We act, and, in acting, mean. We type, talk, move, eat . . . and make sense of every pattern of acting in relation to *other* actions: in relation to the possibil-ity of what we call 'doing nothing' and in relation to having done *this* rather than *that*.

Every act, including the acts we are taught to call perceiving or recog-nizing 'things' or 'events' has meaning for us as a *type* or kind of act, event, thing: a category or class. In our society we learn to see some acts as being of the same type as others, having certain kinds of similarities to other acts. We learn to construct particular sorts of relations of similarity or difference among acts. Any two acts have, in principle, an infinite number of *possible* similarities or differences, but only *some* of these are meaningful in a particu-lar community.

An act has as many possible meanings as there are relationships which the community can construct between it and other acts. Describing an act requires us to use terms of description that select or emphasize some of its possible meanings. What we call features of the act (or thing, or event) are really as much about what kinds of similarity and difference between acts matter in our community, as much about us, as they can be about the act 'itself'.

We say that when an act occurs it occurs in some *context*, and that 'its' meaning depends in part on what that context is. Better to say that we make the act meaningful *by* construing it in relation to some other acts, events, things (which we then call its contexts). The relations we construct to some (and not other possible) contexts select and emphasize some of the possible meanings of the act. In a particular community, only some acts–events–things are considered to be meaningful contexts for others; not every possible re-lationship is made, or regarded as meaningful; there are patterns and limits to meaning-making.

Meanings are normally made through the construction of two sorts of patterns at the same time: patterns of relations of an act to *other* acts that *might* have occurred (paradigmatic relations) and patterns of relations of an act to its contexts, that is to other acts that *did* occur (or events that are occurring). An act has meaning for us because it and not something else with a different meaning happened, and because both it and other acts happened that *together* have meaning. Both these sets of relations, the rela-tions of *alternatives* and the relations of *combinations*, are constructed differ-ently in different communities.

The two kinds of relations are not independent of each other either. Every act can be construed as belonging to many possible sets of alternatives; *which* set is relevant to its meaning at any time depends on the context, that is on other acts with which we see it as being in combination. Similarly, *what sort* of combination we recognize among a group of acts depends on the sets of alternatives to which we assign each act, on our guess as to the *kind* of act each is.

The key question is always: What goes with what? With what alternatives is an act in contrast? What are the relevant contexts in which the act has meaning? It is because there are patterns and limits to what is expected to go with what in a particular community, that meaning becomes *possible*. If there were no patterns and no limits, if every possible combination or set of alternatives were equally likely in every possible context, then there could be no meaning. Because there are patterns and limits, some meanings get made in a given community and others do not. And since the pattern of meanings made is enacted by the pattern of actions enacted, this also means that in a given community many possible things are simply never done – not just because they are forbidden or wrong, but because they are literally 'unthinkable', meaningless, invisible possibilities that never even occur to us. And yet sometimes we happen to do these things anyway.

Meaning consists in relations and systems of relations *of* relations. These relations are basically *contextualizing* relations; they tell us what the contexts are in relation to which an act or event has its meanings in our community. They specify what the *combinations* are that an event of a given type can belong to, *and* what the kinds of events are, the sets of alternative events or acts of the 'same' kinds, that can make up the various types of combinations.

In all cases, contextualizing relations are constructed or construed by meaning-making practices of the community. They cannot be deduced from inherent or intrinsic properties of acts, events, things, for these do not 'have' such properties. We attribute 'properties' to entities, but it is more useful to view their meanings in terms of relations. Entities – things, events, acts, as individuals rather than as types – are themselves complex constructions which we are taught to take as phenomenal givens, as first-order realities. What we are taught to understand as ourselves, as organisms and social identities, are complex meaning-constructions as well as aspects of the interactive processes of material systems; cf. Chapter 5.

The pattern of meaning relations constructed in a community can be called its Meaning System; it is enacted by the actions of people (with things) in that community. Those actions make meanings and they sustain the Meaning System of the community by not violating its limits, by conforming to its patterns. Sometimes we do things that cannot be made sense of in terms of the existing Meaning System. They may go unnoticed, even by us, because they lack all meaning; they are not meaningful acts, events. Or they may contribute to a change in the Meaning System, and, with it, the pattern of ways of doing things in the community. We will return to this issue when we consider how the relations between the community as a system of meaning-making practices and the community as a self-organizing dynamic open system of material interaction processes tend to both keep the community stable and keep it changing.

How can we describe the meaning system of a community? It is first necessary to appreciate the nature of its complexity. It is not just that it includes all the cultural practices by which we make things, acts and events of different kinds meaningful. It is not even just complex because this system of practices constructs many different kinds of contextualizing relations among all these different things, acts and events. It is fundamentally complex because it also necessarily constructs such contextualizing relations among the contextualizing practices themselves. It is a system of relations of relations, of contextualizations of contextualizations, of combinations of combinations, of alternative sets of alternative sets.

Does this recursive complexity make the task of describing the meaning system hopeless? Gödel's paradox certainly applies here; the complete description of the Meaning System would have to include itself as part of the description, and that act of self-description would inevitably change the system being described, etc. But we do not need complete descriptions for our praxis. What is needed is a way of keeping straight the complex architecture of a meaning system while we explore any part of it far enough to expose how its limits hide themselves from us through our own actions.

[In fact, it is pointless to concern ourselves with the notion of 'the whole meaning system' as if there could be a unitary, global self-consistent system there. The meaning system is everywhere local; it is a vast number of bits and pieces, specific ways of making meaning in specific contexts, and while it is possible to construct useful relations among these different bits and pieces, there is no need to assume that all the bits and pieces could ever be fit together in any one grand consistent scheme. We should stop assuming that such a totalizing scheme exists despite the fact that it is impossible to describe it. There are local meaning-making practices. There are interesting relations we can construct between these. But there is no global meaning system. What we mean in using the term is really 'the meaning system way of looking at things' in each local domain, or across various such domains (but never all at once). A better way to think of the global architecture of the meaning system is as a fractal mosaic of patches, as in the discussion of ecosocial systems in Chapter 6.]

The contextualizing relations of a meaning system can be described as a hierarchy of *meta-redundancy relations*. Redundancy is a formal way of describing what goes with what else. [The negative connotations of 'redundant' as the word is used informally come from a puritan culture of efficiency that sees anything that is not necessary as wasteful. In both ordinary usage and the more specialized uses of the word in information theory, cybernetics and semiotics, two things are 'redundant' when they go together in a predictable way; if you see one, you can be pretty sure the other is somewhere around too. In communcation, redundant information repeats information already available in another part of the same signal or transmission. It is useful for double-checking the accuracy of a message. Whether redundancy is necessary or not depends on how likely it is that messages get partly scrambled in transmission. In semiotics, however, redundancy is always necessary for the construction of meaning. Since events, including spoken or written words, do not have intrinsic meanings, but only the meanings we make for them by fitting them into various contexts, regular or predictable ways of combining events and contexts are necessary. If all possible combinations occured with equal likelihood in all situations, we couldn't make or communicate meanings at all.]

Meta-redundancy is just a way of describing how the redundancy, the predictable relation or connection of two things, can itself be redundant (i.e. have a predictable connection) with something else. This is redundancy of redundancy, or meta-redundancy. [The basic notion was introduced by Grègory Bateson (1972: 132–3) and is closely related to his views on meta-communication (messages about messages) and meta-learning (learning how to learn); cf. also meta-mathematics (the mathematical theory of mathematical theories).] If there can be meta-redundancy, then why not meta-meta-redundancy? As we will see there is a whole hierarchy of levels of meta-meta-meta- . . . redundancies which provide a formal description of the relations and patterns that make up the meaning system of a culture. The human brain seems to rebel against thinking about more than one meta-step at a time, so let's take these ideas slowly and carefully to see what they really mean.

Think of any two sets of alternatives, say a set of different words and a set of different facial expressions. We can say that a redundancy relation exists between these two sets whenever not all possible combinations of words and facial expressions are equally likely, or tend to occur equally often. When this relationship exists, then if we already know the word, we can make a better than random guess as to which facial expression it will go with, and if we already see the expression, we can similarly predict the word. The visual information and the verbal information are redundant with each other. If for every word you could say in our culture there was just one possible facial expression that had to go with it, and vice versa, then the sets of words and expressions would be *totally* redundant and no meaning would be added by having combinations of words and expressions above and beyond the meaning that could be made with either one alone.

The last statement here is not quite correct. No *information* would be added in this case, but there would be additional *meaning* because language and the visual semiotics of facial expressions are not commensurable, they do not create the same *kind* of information, do not make meaning in relation to the same sets of alternatives, combinations, contexts, etc. The additional meaning, however, would be simply the 'sum' of the separate meanings, there would be no possibility of 'multiplying' the meanings, that is, having flexible possibilities of combining them in different ways to index different situations or further contexts. The increase in 'information-carrying capacity' of the system would be the minimum possible.

But the actual relationship between these two sets in our culture, in our meaning system, is much more complicated. You *can* of course say almost anything with almost any facial expression, but most of the possible combinations would not make sense to anybody, and they don't happen very often. Some combinations are usual, and others are comic, perverse, bizarre, crazy or just meaningless. Still, there are many possible words that can go with a particular facial expression, and many possible facial expressions that can go with most words, so we can in fact make more meaning with combinations of facial expressions and words than we can make with either form of communication alone.

In information theory, the combined information-carrying capacity of two sets of events or signs, two codes, used simultaneously is reduced as they become more redundant. The information, or 'surprise' value of any particular combination depends on the probability or frequency with which each of the possible combinations occurs. In semiotics, on the other hand, the meaning value of a combination only depends on the existence of other possible combinations, and its meaning relationships to them, and not on their frequency of occurrence. This leads to some of the differences in perspective between semiotics and information theory, even though they are perfectly consistent with one another. Information theory is concerned with information to the extent that all information is alike; semiotics is concerned with information in the sense that all information is different. Information theory looks for the common denominator in all forms of information and quantifies information in common units (e.g. bits, bytes); semiotics identifies the significant ways in which units that carry information differ from one another. Semiotics seeks to explain how the combinations of units that occur depend on their distinctive differences from one another; information theory is concerned only with the overall frequencies of combinations that result. Determining the amount of information that a text could contain is very different from determining the possible meanings that a text could have in a community.

Which facial expressions we combine with *which* words depends on the situation, on the context. If you smile when you say 'I hate you', maybe you're crazy, but more likely there is something special about the situation. In fact, even if we knew nothing else about the event than that this combination had happened, we would *expect* something to be different about the situation. In different contexts, the pattern of what goes with what is different, and has different meaning, even in the same culture, the same meaning system. Change the situation, change the context, and we might expect different facial expressions to accompany particular words. Part of how we know what the situation is is by paying attention to which patterns of combinations seem to be in use. These patterns are part of what defines the situation, what makes the situation what it is (joking, sarcasm, fear, insanity, etc.). So there is a partly predictable relation between situational contexts and the pattern of combinations of words and facial expressions. That is, there is a redundancy between the set of contexts and the set of redundancy relations between words and expressions.

In the way we behave meaningfully in our culture, the appropriate patterns of combination of words and facial expressions depend in part on the situation, and the situation is defined, in part, by which pattern of combinations people normally use in that type of situation. What is the set of situations redundant with? Not the sets of words by itself, nor the set of facial expressions by itself. It is redundant with the pattern of combinations of words and expressions, with the redundancy relations between the words and expressions. Situations are redundant with the redundancy between words and expressions. The words and expressions stand in a relation of first-order redundancy to each other, and the situations stand in a relation of second-order, or meta-redundancy to the redundancy of the words and expressions.

Redundancy is a formal relation, and formally relations of relations are of a different 'logical type' than the first-order relations. See Bateson (1972) or Russell and Whitehead (1913) or any discussion of meta-mathematics and logical theory (e.g. Kleene 1952; Hermes 1969). Meta-redundancy is a three-term or ternary relation that is not reducible to any combination of two-term or binary relations all at the same level, that is, of the same logical type. C.S. Peirce (e.g. 1955) long ago argued that semiotic relations had to be irreducible ternary relations because *something* (an Interpretant) had to determine in what relation a sign (or Representamen) stands to what it stands for (its Object). Peirce's semiotic model is certainly more flexible than Bateson's, but precisely because it is a model of pure logical relations that apply in all domains, it can be more difficult to see exactly how to apply it to specific meaning-making practices. Bateson's model has the advantage, for my purposes, that it takes human social communication and learning as its paradigm instances of semiotic behavior.

The pattern of redundancy between the set of words and the set of facial expressions can be presented symbolically as:

[Words/Expressions]

This is a pattern we create by how we use these words and expressions.

Formally, this symbolism represents the joint conditional probabilities of the sets of words and expressions:

$C(i, j)$ [Word(i), Expression(j)]

So far, though, this is not yet a meta-redundancy relation. It is not a *contextualizing relation*. It does not tell us anything about how this pattern of combinations helps to define a context, or how it might be different in different contexts. The meaning that a particular combination of a word and facial expression has for us depends on the situational context; without a context there are many possible meanings for each combination (each perhaps corresponding to a different context, a different set of assumptions for interpreting the meaning of the combination), the combinations, like the isolated words and expressions themselves, only has a *meaning potential* [cf. Halliday 1977, 1978].

The contextualizing relation is represented by the larger meta-redundancy pattern we have been describing, symbolically:

[(Words/Expressions)//Situations]

or more simply:

[Words/Expressions//Situations].

The first slash-mark stands for the basic redundancy relation (first-order redundancy); the double slash-mark indicates the meta-redundancy (second-order redundancy, of higher logical type). Perhaps it is even better to think of the whole formula as representing the meta-redundancy relation among the three sets: words, expressions, and situations. In mathematical terms this could be represented by the joint conditional probability distribution:

$$C(i,j;k) [Word(i), Expression(j); Situation(k)]$$

which tells us, for each situation-type (k), what the probabilities are that various possible probability distributions $C(i,j)$ will be found in that situation type. If there were total redundancy between situations and use-patterns for words and facial expressions, only one pattern would be possible in each type of situation, but in general human cultural behavior is more complex than this; some patterns are simply more likely in some situations, but there are always other, less likely patterns possible. In a particular event, we might see only one pattern, but even then the meaning of that pattern depends in part on the fact that other patterns could have occurred, other patterns which do show up sometimes in other, similar events of generally the same situation type.

For the same sorts of reasons, we have to recognize that this whole meta-redundancy system of relationships among situations, words and facial expressions could also be different under some circumstances. Are the connections we make between situations and word–facial expression combinations the same if we are watching a play, perhaps an avant-garde one, as they are for ordinary events of daily life? Couldn't a playwright (or a novelist) create a fictional world where we learned to take as normal very different connections between situations and word–facial expression combinations?

Couldn't we create a stage-world where when people smiled and said nasty things the situation was normal, but if someone said something nasty and scowled we'd suspect an unusual situation? There could be many such drama worlds, each with their own conventions about such things. If we tuned in in the middle of a televised drama, and discerned a pattern in the relations of [Words/Expressions//Situations], couldn't we then make a better than random guess about which playwright's world we were probably viewing? There would now be a new, still higher level meta-meta-redundancy between the set of such worlds and the meta-redundancy relations of [Words/Expressions] and Situations:

[Words/Expressions//Situations///Worlds].

Of course, worlds are not just created on the stage. There are communities very different from ours, different cultures, different societies, different periods of history. They might have, within them, special worlds, such as those of drama, or myth, or rituals, or worlds where only men or only women participate. In each of these worlds, there might be different patterns of [Words/Expressions//Situations], redundant with the set of alternative worlds. Even beyond all this, these different communities, these different overall meaning systems that contextualize the different worlds the community recognizes will have different particular patterns of [Words/Expressions//Situations /// Worlds], and so these patterns would then be redundant at some very high level with the set of alternative meaning systems human communities have enacted in different times and places. Symbolically:

[Words/Expressions//Situations///Worlds////Meaning Systems].

Building a contextualization hierarchy of meta-redundancy relations starting from words and facial expressions was just for purposes of providing an example. We could have started from any two sets of types of meaningful events that are redundant in our community, that is, that are not equally likely to combine in all possible ways, but are more likely to make certain combinations. We would then generally find that which combinations were more likely and which combinations less likely would depend on some sorts of contexts. Alternatively we could say that these combinations are part of our basis for recognizing (construing) and for enacting (constructing) these contexts. What is a context? It can be *anything*, at any level of complexity, with which some pattern of combination of other things is redundant. What matters is *when* and *for what* it is a context, when and for what it is relevant to constructing/construing the meaning. Contextualization relations *are* meaning relations; they are the relations we construe/construct to make something meaningful. They tell us what to relate it to, and in what way, and under what circumstances. All meaning is relational. Nothing has meaning in and of itself. Something has meaning only in terms of how we relate it to other things, how we contextualize it. A description of how and when these contextualizing relations are made in a community is a complete description of its meaning system. [For more ways of using meta-redundancy relations to interpret contextualizing practices in a community, that is, its ways of making meaning, see Lemke 1984: 33–58.]

It is important to notice that at every level of the meta-redundancy hierarchy, redundancy relations are *symmetrical*. If A is redundant with B, then B is redundant with A. In this way, while the higher levels in a hierarchy contextualize the lower ones, the relations among the lower ones constitute or contribute to the patterns that define the higher ones. The context is itself as much defined by the patterns of what is going on in it as it defines the frame of reference for interpreting the meanings of those patterns. Symmetrical hierarchies are very different from the control hierarchies we usually think about; in the command relations of generals to captains, and captains to sergeants, and sergeants to privates there is no symmetry. Of course, as social semiotic relations, there is still an important symmetry even in control hierarchies; chiefs and indians are both constituted by their relations to one another. [For a discussion of different kinds of hierarchies, see Salthe 1993.]

We have already talked about still another kind of hierarchy, the constituency hierarchy of supersystems and subsystems of a complex dynamic open system. Here also the higher level supersystems are constituted by the material, interactional processes among the lower-level subsystems which they in turn limit and regulate. Since these two hierarchies, the supersystem hierarchy and the contextualization (meta-redundancy) hierarchy seem to be enough to describe everything that is meaningful within our meaning system, what we really want to know is how to use both at once.

The meaning system consists of contextualizing relations for making meaningful connections among things, for making them mean for us. These relations describe our meaning-making practices, what we do with language and other forms of action and interaction. These doings are themselves meaningful cultural *practices*. But they are always also material *processes* of the dynamic open systems we call human communities in their (physical, ecological) environments. When we describe these systems we use a variety of different discourses or ways of talking that emphasize different kinds of relationships among the processes/practices. The discourses of the natural sciences discuss the kinds of meaningful relationships among processes that are spoken of in terms of relations of exchange of matter, energy and information/entropy. The discourses of the semiotic sciences discuss the kinds of meaningful relationships that are spoken of in terms of similarity and difference, classification and categorization, evaluation, orientation and contextualization. The natural sciences *are* semiotic sciences, with specialized interests. They can only describe systems of material processes by using systems of semiotic practices. But equally, every semiotic practice can be described by the discourses of the natural sciences as a material process. Human communities can be adequately modeled only when we combine both these viewpoints: when we examine how the semiotic cultural values of material processes play a part in the material self-organization of ecosocial systems, and when we understand the role of material self-organization in producing the regularities (redundancies) that are meaning systems.

Consider the system of interactions that constitutes the community as a dynamic open system. Those interactions include human actions recognized as meaningful by the community, but they also include processes which occur in the environment which are part of the total dynamic open system, even if they are *not* recognized as meaningful in that community. The totality of processes of this interaction system enacts, constitutes, or grounds all the possible meaning systems of the community. The actions and processes recognized as meaningful in the community represent its actual meaning system, and it is only in terms of this meaning system that the processes of the interaction system are meaningful.

One can imagine that there must be 'invisible' processes, meaningless and not even recognized *as* processes in our present meaning system. But meaning systems change; processes that were not processes for us *become* recognized as new kinds of meanings, constructed in the new meaning system. The meaning-making practices by which we recognize them are now also new material processes of the interaction system of the community. We can say that the interaction system materially constitutes the meaning system, that the meaning system is *immanent* in, is a pattern of meaning-making practices we construct with the processes of the interaction system. Yet we cannot see, analyze or talk about the interaction system except through our current meaning system, the one we are enacting now through the patterns of our actions. Nevertheless, that meaning system has limits and gaps, however invisible these are for us most of the time. There *can* be meanings outside the limits of the current meaning system; the system can change.

Every meaning system *seems* complete, but, by the now familiar argument of Gödel, no such system can ever *be* complete. Every such system is constituted by an Interaction System that cannot be stable and drives the meaning system to reveal its incompleteness by changing.

Do not confuse the Interaction System with a 'material world out there' existing independently of the meaning system. The two systems are simply two different, intimately interrelated aspects of the same material, semiotic system [the ecosocial system of Chapter 6]. These two systems are two different viewpoints or perspectives on one system; as discourses, they are themselves tools for making meaning. Neither has precedence, neither has greater claim to truth or reality, each is as essentially incomplete as any coherent, consistent view must necessarily be. The possibility of 'slippage' between these two ways of making sense of human cultures and communities can help us to talk about system change.

Making Trouble: Disjunctions, Slippage and System Change

Regarded as interaction systems, as dynamic open material ecosystems, human communities develop in ways that preserve their ability to respond to changing environments. They do not develop so as to be perfectly self-regulating, since this would lead them to follow the same patterns regardless of what was happening in their environments. It is in the nature of dynamic open systems that they themselves tend to change their environments by interacting with them, and the results can sometimes be unpredictable. So such systems ensure that they have something in reserve, a repertory of possible behaviors, ways of interacting, that gives them some flexibility, some plasticity of response. Some of their internal interactions work counter to perfect self-regulation; these systems embody contradictions to enlarge their range of behaviors, enhance their resilience (cf. Holling 1986).

The meaning system of a community participates in this general strategy. Not only do meaning systems operate so as to limit change, to narrow the range of behaviors that people might meaningfully imagine doing, they must also incorporate gaps and contradictions, incomplete sets of alternatives, counterfunctional subsystems that tend to destabilize the meaning system and prevent its complete closure, the perfect homeostasis that would keep the community from changing how it makes meaning to enable it to adapt to inevitable changes in its material environments.

How do meaning systems limit our vision? How do they contain the reserve alternatives necessary for adaptation, while managing to withhold these from view, or limit their range of operation? And how and when does self-regulation break down and radical system change take over?

How do meaning systems hide their limits from us? One way seems to be through the *absence* of certain contextualizations. There are certain combinations of things, certain connections, it never occurs to us to make. There are gaps in the system of contextualizing relations that do not seem to be there because all those that *are* in use form a pattern that leads us 'around' the absent ones. In order for a gap to remain unnoticed, there must not be any possible combination of meaning-making practices that could lead us into it. I believe that these gaps exist *everywhere* in the meaning system; they must, because meaning-making is only possible so long as not all combinations, not all connections are equally likely to be made in all situations. And since, at least locally [that is, patch-by-patch across the many scales of a fractal mosaic system], the connections which *are* made from a system, that is, are complexly interdependent on one another, the effect of the gaps pervades the system. One function of every meaning-making practice in a culture is to participate in a meaning system which avoids leading us into its own gaps. One could say that there is, in this sense, a global [really 'mosaic'] *system of disjunctions*, that is a system of meaning-making practices that 'avoids' the gaps.

A meaning system without a system of disjunctions would have to be either too unstable or too stable for survival as a dynamic open system. If the practices of the meaning system allowed us to make *any* connection, then many of these would be incompatible with the operations of the community and could eventually lead to disintegration of the intimately interdependent network of cultural practices. The same system of disjunctions also prevents excessive stability. By preserving a reservoir of unrealized possibilities, some of which *are* compatible with a future, expanded or revised, successor of the meaning system, the system of disjunctions preserves the adaptability of the community, the space of incompleteness where change can work. The same system of disjunctions that resists change thus makes change possible. The gaps are points of tension, of contradiction and of potential change within the system.

It is, for example, quite common for people's politics to be democratic, while their religion remains 'monarchical'. Historically, both would have been monarchical, but one changed without the other seeming to require a corresponding change because there was a disjunction in the meaning system between the discourses and practices of the political domain and those of the religious domain. Historians might quite possibly show us some of the semiotic work that was done in the relevant periods to create or maintain this disjunction, to repair it when breached. Social semiotics ought to be able to show us how the disjunction continues to operate in people's lives, in their ways of talking about and thinking about these domains. Some of us can now see the presence of this disjunction because we operate with a meaning system in which these connections have been made.

Consider again how we have historically used exactly the same arguments to justify the denial of equal legal and political rights to serfs and peasants, to the propertyless, to members of non-white races and non-European cultures, to women and to children. When each of these arguments fell, the others remained largely unaffected, because there were disjunctions in the meaning system rendering them all fundamentally 'different' despite their (now) obvious similarities. The similarities had to be *constructed* by contextualizing practices, by making the connections. In earlier versions of the dominant meaning system in our cultural tradition, the practices for doing this simply did not exist. [Arguments of this general kind are also made by Foucault; cf. the general program of his *The Archeology of Knowledge* (1969) and examples in *The Order of Things* (1966).] Even today, most people do not make this connection in the case of oppression of younger humans by older ones [see discussion in Chapter 7]. The system of disjunctions preserves for us the possibility of further change, at the same time it prevents us from doubting all our beliefs each time we change one of them. In a meaning system, however, because it is a system, every belief, every meaning-making practice is interdependent with every other – in ways we are not supposed to be able to see. [Note that the pathways of such interdependencies may lead outside what is currently recognized as/by the meaning system, through connections of material processes in the ecosocial system.]

Still another powerful example of the system of disjunctions is the separation of the prestige discourses of our community into three general domains, each of which resists any synthesis with the other two: science, art and politics. (Religion used to be a separate domain, and belonged to an older and somewhat different system of disjunctions.) Science speaks the language of truth, art the language of beauty, and politics the language of good. More generally, the discourses of science are those that are concerned with the truth of propositions about how the world, including the human world, 'is' in some objective sense. They include the discourses of philosophy and the social sciences, and even of history and literary criticism, all the academic discourses, all the technical discourses of our community. They are the discourses we are meant to assent to; their power is the power to compel belief in the truth of what they say. The discourses of art, on the other hand, are not mainly concerned with truth, but rather with honesty, authenticity, the feel of things, their emotional effect upon us when we interact with them. Their power is the power to make us feel, to engage us more totally, more bodily, than the discourses of science. This is the language of poetry and literature, of music and visual art, drama, film and performance ['language' in the sense of a semiotic system of resources and patterns of using them; a system of practices, not necessarily only verbal language itself].

Finally, there is the language of action, of politics and rhetoric, which moves us to act in the name of the good. It concerns itself with values and action, with what ought to be done in the material and social world. Its power is that it can move us to act.

A discourse, a way of speaking, is considered less scientific, or even rendered 'unscientific' exactly to the extent that it includes elements either of the language of feeling or of the language of action and values. Use the linguistic and stylistic resources of the poet or artist for scientific communication, and you will not have standing as being scientific. Argue from values or the implications of propositions for action and social consequences, and again you are considered outside the bounds of science. Suggest that science is really art masquerading as objective truth, that it is stories we tell about the world, narratives and fictions that are useful for certain social purposes, and the defenders of the disjunctions will (paradoxically) rail against your views as if science really were a matter of core values and the good. Argue that human social values shape every aspect of science, that science is inherently political, that science is and should be subordinate to and subject to political analysis and control, and the disjunctions will become starkly visible. These disjunctions operate successfully mainly in so far as they are tacitly accepted. Once you begin to look for the aesthetic dimension in science or its dependence on specific cultural and historical values, the connections are easily made. The disjunctions themselves are recent and local products of one particular historical, cultural tradition.

Art also repels both the scientific and the political in our dominant cultural tradition. Art which limits itself to the scientifically true is considered narrow and unimaginative, or overly 'technical'. Art which incorporates political values and a call for social action is considered tendentious and propagandistic. Art is not supposed to concern itself significantly with either truth or politics.

Political rhetoric, in the broad sense of argument for social action based on appeals to social values, is also supposed to remain 'rational' and not ground itself in the powerful emotional appeals of art, lest it be called 'demagoguery'. It is also supposed to maintain a clear distinction between 'facts' (matters of science) and 'values', or else it will be accused either of 'interfering' with the freedom of science to pursue truth objectively, or of 'misusing' facts to support policy.

It should be very clear that this system of disjunctions strongly stabilizes our cultural system by forbidding to science and politics the language of love, which would make us trust them; forbidding politics and poetry the language of objectivity, which would make us uncritical of them; and forbidding poetry and science the language of justice, which could move us to act. At the same time, these disjunctions also preserve powerful possibilities for meaning in reserve.

It should be clear that those disjunctions that favor the interests of social castes who have the power to 'police' violations of them, and who work to keep them from spreading or undermining other disjunctions or meaning-making practices from which they benefit, are more likely to persist for longer periods of time. These are the specifically ideological disjunctions embodied in the meaning system of a community; cf. Chapter 1.

[I omit here a discussion that traces the pattern of mutual reinforcement among these disjunctions in order to identify the most fundamental or core beliefs that they protect from effective challenge. The result of this analysis essentially converges with the postmodernist critique of the notions of objective truth and objective reality as sketched in Chapter 1.]

Breaking through the limits of our meaning system, breaching its disjunctions or making a connection, enacting a practice, that lies outside it, does not in itself necessarily change the meaning system. We often do things, make meanings that go outside the usual patterns of the system, but they tend to go unrecognized and unrepeated. They are counted as 'slips' or 'accidents' and 'errors' by the terms of the prevailing meaning system. Connections which are not recognized by the system are labeled as accidental or 'coincidences', as meaningless. These non-events, these almost-were meanings, lie at the borders of the meaning system, usually well policed by our acceptance of the system of disjunctions. The disjunctions here work to keep these 'slips' isolated, unconnected to anything and so no threat to the rest of the meaning system. Only when the limits are broken in a way that *does* make systematic connections, that creates a *rival* set of meanings, is there a real possibility of system change. [It is in these cases that power relations come into play and policing becomes a conscious activity, a value-based opposition, even though neither side may have a good sense of just what larger aspects of the meaning system, and of the interaction system, are at stake.]

Contradictions do not exist just within the meaning system (gaps or disjunctions); they necessarily also exist between the meaning system and the interaction system. This is another fundamental source of potential system change.

The meaning system perspective and the interaction system perspective are not just two different ways of looking at a human community as a dynamic open system of processes/practices. They are also radically incommensurable perspectives. There is no possible one-to-one relationship between the two descriptions in any domain.

This point has often been made in many different ways. Bateson (1972) talks about the distinction between 'digital' (discrete, typological, categorial, 'lumped') aspects of meaning and 'analogue' (continuous, topological, 'distributed') aspects. Pike (1982) uses a similar notion to distinguish 'particle' aspects (discrete, typological) from 'wave' and 'field' (continuous, topological) aspects. Verbal-semantic meaning systems (especially word-relations) are predominantly typological; visual-motor meaning systems are predominantly topological. Much of the mathematics of classical science seems to represent a bridge from the verbal-typological to the continuous-topological, just as its visual representation schemes, such as graphs, attempt to bridge this difference from the other side. Some aspects of verbal meaning are more topological in character, as with the gradable semantics of evaluations, but most of the topological meaning in speech is considered 'paralinguistic'.

A phenomenon that has a topological description, that is, a phenomenon which we construct *as* a phenomenon by using meaning-making practices that make connections of the topological kind (e.g. the acoustic soundstream of speech as recorded by an oscilloscope or sonograph), can never be completely and exhaustively described by a digital or typological code (e.g. the categorical system of phonemes, tonemes, etc. in formal linguistics). It always 'overflows' our attempts to 'capture' it in our category systems. It can be endlessly reclassified according to infinitely many different systems of classification, each of which construes it as having a different set of relevant features (cf. *distinctive features* in linguistic phonology).

The creative process in art often leads to the making of new meanings through the 'slippage' between the meaning system and the interaction system. Imagine a choreographer making a new dance. He is a fluent speaker of the dance idiom, usually a dancer or former dancer himself. He is involved in creating a polysemiotic construction: the meaning-making practices of music, of narrative, and of dance movement are being combined according to a meaning system that specifies which combinations of rhythms and movements and sequences are meaningful and valued in his culture. He envisions, and perhaps feels in his own body, the next possible sequence of movements he would like his dancers to perform. He comes into the studio, the musical phrases for these movements begin, and the dancers start to enact his instructions. Those instructions, and much of his plan for the dance, are couched in terms of the verbal language and the visual image language of choreography; they represent meaningful movements and combinations of movements, movement *types*. These movement types are categories or ideals of movement. Real human movements are construed, are seen (by the dancer himself, felt) as instances of these categories to the extent that certain criterial features of the movement, defined by the category system, look 'right'.

But this dancer and that dancer never do the 'same' movement (as defined by the movement-type category) exactly the same way. Even the same dancer will never (*can* never, from the interaction system perspective) do it the same way twice. But most of these differences do not 'matter'; the movement still counts as 'right', as of the same type, so long as it meets the criteria that *do* matter. Bateson defined information (or in our terms, meaning) as: 'a difference that makes a difference'. Here we are considering the differences that do *not* make a difference. So far as the categorial meaning of the movement goes, it is the 'same' movement. Overlaid on this basic system of categories there will be other meaningful differences: a bold version of the movement, a strong version, a light version; a style to the movement associated with this school of dance training or that school. These are finer subdivisions or cross-categorizations. At some point there may be just the identifiable style of a particular dancer, and maybe of that dancer at a particular period of her or his career. [These are 'indexical' meanings, meanings that index a context. The feature combinations that define them are redundant with this or that style, this or that dancer's manner, training, etc.]

Finally there are the differences, the variations, that simply don't count, that don't mean anything at all. They may be very small differences, a fraction of a degree in an angle, a fraction of a second difference in timing. Or they may be bigger differences, but not ones that matter for any of the meaningful kinds of difference in the culture of dance. [They index nothing.]

But these subcriterial, infra-semiotic differences, while they are redundant with nothing in the meaning system, lead to no meaningful similarities or differences of category or type or meaning, may still enter into relationships in the interaction system that sometimes cannot be ignored.

The dancers follow the choreographer's instructions, perform what was semiotically conceived as a sequence, but somehow something goes wrong. A new combination or sequence doesn't feel right, or doesn't look as right on the dancers' bodies as it did in the choreographer's imagination. Real bodies do not perform ideal movements, they perform real movements which always have additional features besides the criterial ones they need to have to count as dance movements of the right types. Sometimes when these real movements are juxtaposed, or when two dancers have to coordinate their separate movements, something that seemed workable when viewed solely in terms of ideal movement types is not physically, anatomically possible or comfortable on the real bodies of the dancers.

The choreographer now sees what is happening in terms of both the semiotic categories of dance and in terms of the deviations, the 'slippage' between real, material movements, and ideal movement types defined by only some of the infinity of features that any real movement can be construed as having. The simplest solution is to have the dancers execute the 'same' movements in a slightly different way, but maybe that doesn't work. One could try asking other dancers to try it, but that is rarely practical. In fact, choreographers tend to improvise in such situations. What they see on the dancers is not exactly what they envisioned in terms of the idiom of dance. More is always happening than that idiom takes into account or cares about. And that *more* can lead the choreographer to see the movement possibilities differently than before, to imagine a possibility he could not have imagined if he had never seen this 'slippage'. The interaction system is at work; material interactional processes are producing possibilities of self-organization that may never have existed until that particular configuration came into being. The choreographer may begin to create a meaning for the slippage; differences that were not significant before can become visible, become significant. A new plan for the movement may emerge from this. Perhaps a new sense of movement possibilities. Perhaps even a new movement style, a new movement type, which, if taken over by others, if seen by others and danced by others, could represent ultimately a change in the meaning system of dance.

In every semiotic system we find this same slippage. In language, the interaction system view enables us to describe the patterns of sound energy continuously varying in time and as a function of the range of frequencies in the sound. But most of that continuous variation is not relevant to whether we hear a 'b' or a 'p', a 'b' or a 'v'. Only a very few general, average, outline features of the acoustic soundstream are criterial for which phoneme we hear, whether we hear 'bear' or 'pear'. You and I can both make soundstreams that others will hear as having these criterially different features, but the details of our soundstreams will be different. I cannot even say exactly the same speech sound in exactly the same way twice. Again, most of the differences do not matter. The meaning system is concerned only with which phoneme we utter, but we cannot in fact, in terms of the interaction system perspective, utter a pure phoneme. We have to utter a 'phone', a real sound that has many acoustic features other than the ones that matter, the ones that distinguish one linguistically meaningful sound from another, the ones that are redundant with differences in words, in meanings.

Some of the differences in the ways I might say 'bear' will not index different words, but might index whether I sound fresh or tired, excited or frightened. Other differences might simply index that it is I who am speaking, or my 'accent' as a member of some group. And an infinite number of other differences will index nothing at all, signify nothing at all. But someone who has an oscilloscope that creates potentially visually meaningful patterns from otherwise meaningless sound features might learn to shape their speech in new ways, and recognize that shape, and teach this to others, so that it might in time become a recognized index of something and enter the meaning system. The oscilloscope was built according to prescriptions of some other part of the meaning system, one disconnected from that having to do with the interpretation of speech sounds. But the interaction system relations between the physical machine and the physical acoustical sounds can create the possibility of new meanings, changes in the meaning system.

When a new meaning gets made, either through the opportunities afforded by slippage or by breaching a disjunction, it is usually not even recognized as a meaning, or as an event. If it is recognized at all, the system of disjunctions will label it 'just a slip' or non-sense, 'that doesn't make sense'. Sometimes the new connection is recognized and not isolated but seen as part of a whole new possible system of meanings, as implying a more general new way of making meaning that could apply also in other contexts. It may spread and be used in some new subcommunity indexed by its use. Most often this new little piece of a meaning system gets added on to the existing system in such a way that it stays quarantined to its little subcommunity, and after a time other subcommunities that interact with it find a way to accommodate it (cf. the possibilities for heteroglossic relations among divergent discourses, as in Chapter 3). They may label it a peculiarity of another group, and they will most likely also consider it unimportant or inferior to their own practices.

But sometimes a new system of meaning-making practices, new ways of doing things, new ways of talking about something, can form a genuinely rival alternative system which competes for the hearts and minds of members of a community. It represents an alternative mode of self-organization of the processes/practices of the community. Perhaps it is one that could only come into existence once the previous system had developed in a certain way. Or perhaps it originated in a separate, alien culture.

When a rival meaning system gets made within a community, rather than being encountered from outside, there is a key difference; it is more likely to 'fit' with the gaps in the existing majority system, to be compatible with the interaction system of the community, and so to be a serious rival contender. It can appeal to members of the community despite its violation of disjunctions precisely because it is in some sense (in relation to the interaction system) still a part of the community. It is more likely to know where the family skeletons are buried, that is, to expose and threaten specific parts of the local system of disjunctions. But it is also more easily coopted, more easily out-maneuvered by the rest of that system. It is, after all, just this sort of rival that the system of disjunctions had historically evolved to prevent, or defeat. A completely alien system, on the other hand, is more likely to take it by surprise, unprepared. But then an alien system is also less likely to catch on, less likely to prove adapted to the interaction system of the community. It is not as easily coopted, but it is more easily isolated.

Radical systemic changes in the culture of a community, occurring over

short periods of time, must generally involve major changes in the interaction system as well as in the meaning system. These are major reorganiza-
tions of the material processes of the community, major by the criteria of the
interaction system: major shifts in the distributions and flows of energy and
matter in the system. Such shifts can be triggered by relatively minor (by
matter-energy criteria) changes in the meaning-making practices of the
community, but such changes (e.g. in its value system or beliefs) would then
have to be counted as major by the criteria of the meaning system.

Leaving aside encounters with external meaning systems, we can imagine two modes of internal subversion of a meaning system. Because the
totality of meanings, that is the background realm of no-meaning [recall that
where all meanings are equally likely, there is no meaning; the *pleroma* or
totality is also the no-meaning realm], is also the ground against which all
specific meanings are figured, and grounds every material act, 'alien' meanings will also be made within the community itself. These include not just the
'accidental' slippages we have already discussed, but also 'playful' meanings.
Play happens wherever the system of disjunctions fails to get us to police
ourselves, wherever Chaos is a welcome friend, embraced in laughter and
not shut out in terror of no-meaning. Play is the complement and antithesis
of praxis, of the systematic, reflexive explication of the system of disjunctions
as it operates in our own practice. Play is the unspeakable source of the
possibility of praxis because it creates the possibility of a meaning-space outside
the meaning system, beyond the limits set by the system of disjunctions, from
which that system can become visible to us in its effects on our practice.

[The metaphors of war between rival meaning systems are masculinist
figures of speech; they create a mood of seriousness, responsibility, danger.
They call for the virtues of courage and strength. They are allies of the
system of disjunctions, moving us closer to the center which that system
protects: the perspective of the dominant caste who have shaped our meaning system. The sign of *play* escapes this system, or at least shifts us toward
its periphery, towards the elements it marginalizes. To be playful is to be not-
serious, to drop responsibilities, to laugh at rivalries, to get free of the Ought
and the Is. Play has no goals, it makes itself unpredictably. Play makes trouble
for every system. Play makes possible every system, and no-system.]

Make trouble.

[Play!]

References

ALTHUSSER, L. (1971) 'Ideology and Ideological State Apparatuses', in *Lenin and Philosophy and Other Essays*, New York: Monthly Review Press, pp. 127–86.

APPLE, M. (1982) *Education and Power*, Boston, MA: Routledge.

ASHBY, W.R. (1956) *Introduction to Cybernetics*, New York: Wiley.

BAKHTIN, M. (1935/1981) 'Discourse in the novel', in M. HOLQUIST (Ed.) *The Dialogic Imagination*, Austin, TX: University of Texas Press.

BAKHTIN, M. (1953/1986) *Speech Genres and Other Late Essays*, Austin, TX: University of Texas Press.

BATESON, G. (1972) *Steps to an Ecology of Mind*, New York: Ballantine.

BAZERMAN, C. (1988) *Shaping Written Knowledge*, Madison, WI: University of Wisconsin Press.

BAZERMAN, C. (1994) 'Systems of Genres and the Enactment of Social Intentions', in A. FREEDMAN and P. MEDWAY (Eds) *Rethinking Genre*, London: Falmer Press.

BERGE, P., POMEAU, Y. and VIDAL, C. (1984) *Order Within Chaos*, New York: Wiley.

BERNSTEIN, B. (1971) *Class, Codes, and Control*, Volume 1, London: Routledge.

BERNSTEIN, B. (1975) *Class, Codes, and Control*, Volume 2, London: Routledge.

BERNSTEIN, B. (1981) 'Codes, modalities, and the process of cultural reproduction', *Language in Society*, **10**(3), pp. 327–64.

BERNSTEIN, B. (1987) 'Social class, codes, and communication', in U. AMMON, N. DITTMAR and K.J. MATTHIER (Eds) *Sociolinguistics: An International Handbook of the Science of Society*, Berlin: de Gruyter.

BOURDIEU, P. (1972) *Outline of a Theory of Practice*, Cambridge: Cambridge University Press.

BOURDIEU, P. (1979/1984) *Distinction: A Social Critique of the Judgement of Taste*, Cambridge, MA: Harvard University Press.

BOURDIEU, P. (1990a) *Homo Academicus*, Stanford, CA: Stanford University Press.

BOURDIEU, P. (1990b) *The Logic of Practice*, Stanford, CA: Stanford University Press.

BOURDIEU, P. (1991) *Language and Symbolic Power*, Cambridge, MA: Harvard University Press.

BOURDIEU, P. and PASSERON, J.C. (1977) *Reproduction in Education, Society, and Culture*, Beverly Hills, CA: Sage.

BOURDIEU, P. and WACQUANT, L.J.D. (1992) *An Invitation to Reflexive Sociology*, Chicago, IL: University of Chicago Press.

BOWLES, S. and GINTIS, H. (1976) *Schooling in Capitalist America*, New York: Basic Books.

BRUNER, J.S. (1983) *In Search of Mind*, New York: Harper & Row.

BRUNER, J.S. (1991) 'The Invention of Self: Autobiography and Its Forms', in D.R. OLSON and N. TORRANCE (Eds) *Literacy and Orality*, Cambridge: Cambridge University Press.

BRUNER, J.S. and WEISSER, S. (1992) *Autobiography and the Construction of Self*, Cambridge, MA: Harvard University Press.

CHOMSKY, N. (1957) *Syntactic Structures*, The Hague: Mouton.

CHOMSKY, N. (1965) *Aspects of the Theory of Syntax*, Cambridge, MA: MIT Press.

COLE, M., GAY, J., GLICK, J. and SHARP, D. (1971) *The Cultural Context of Learning and Thinking*, New York: Basic Books.

ECO, U. (1976) *A Theory of Semiotics*, Bloomington, IN: Indiana University.

EDELMAN, G. (1992) *Bright Air, Brilliant Fire*, New York: Basic Books.

FAIRCLOUGH, N. (1989) *Language and Power*, New York: Longman.

FAUSTO-STERLING, A. (1993) 'The Five Sexes', *The Sciences*, **33**(2), pp. 20–5.

FAWCETT, R. (1980) *Cognitive Linguistics and Social Interaction*, Heidelberg: Julius Gross Verlag.

FOUCAULT, M. (1966) *The Order of Things*, New York: Random House.

FOUCAULT, M. (1969) *The Archeology of Knowledge*, New York: Random House.

FOUCAULT, M. (1980) *The History of Sexuality*, Volume 1, New York: Random House.

GEE, J.P. (1990) *Social Linguistics and Literacies*, London: Falmer Press.

GEERTZ, C. (1973) *The Interpretation of Cultures*, New York: Basic Books.

GEERTZ, C. (1983) *Local Knowledge*, New York: Basic Books.

GIDDENS, A. (1984) *The Constitution of Society: Outline of the Theory of Structuration*, Berkeley, CA: University of California Press.

GLEICK, J. (1987) *Chaos: The Making of a New Science*, New York: Viking.

GÖDEL, K. (1931/1962) *On Formally Undecidable Propositions*, New York: Basic Books.

GOULD, S.J. (1977) *Ontogeny and Phylogeny*, Cambridge, MA: Harvard University Press.

GRAMSCI, A. (1935/1971) *Prison Notebooks: 1929–1935*, New York: International Publishers.

GRAUE, M.E., WEINSTEIN, T. and WALBERG, H.J. (1983) 'School-based Home Instruction and Learning: A Quantitative Synthesis', *Journal of Educational Research*, **76**, pp. 351–60.

GREGORY, M. (1967) 'Aspects of Varieties Differentiation', *Journal of Linguistics*, **3**, pp. 177–98.

GREGORY, M. and MALCOLM, K. (1981) 'Generic situation and discourse phase', Toronto: Glendon College, Applied Linguistics Research Working Group Papers.

GREIMAS, A. and COURTES, J. (1983) *Semiotic and Language: An Analytical Dictionary*, Bloomington, IN: Indiana University Press.

HABERMAS, J. (1983) *The Theory of Communicative Action*, Boston, MA: Beacon Press.

HALLIDAY, M.A.K. (1967) *Grammar, Society, and the Noun*, London: H.K. Lewis for University College London.

HALLIDAY, M.A.K. (1975) *Learning How to Mean*, London: Edward Arnold.

HALLIDAY, M.A.K. (1976) in G. KRESS (Ed.) *Halliday: System and Function in Language* (Edited by KRESS, G.), London: Oxford University Press.

HALLIDAY, M.A.K. (1977) 'Text as Semantic Choice in Social Context', in T.A. VAN DYCK and J. PETÖFI (Eds) *Grammars and Descriptions*, Berlin: de Gruyter.

HALLIDAY, M.A.K. (1978) *Language as Social Semiotic*, London: Edward Arnold.

HALLIDAY, M.A.K. (1982) 'The De-automatization of Grammar', in J. ANDERSON (Ed.) *Language Form and Linguistic Variation*, Amsterdam: John Benjamins, pp. 129–59.

HALLIDAY, M.A.K. (1985) *An Introduction to Functional Grammar*, London: Edward Arnold.

HALLIDAY, M.A.K. (1988) 'On the Language of Physical Science', in M. GHADESSY (Ed.) *Registers of Written English*, London: Pinter Publishers.

HALLIDAY, M.A.K. (1989) *Spoken and Written Language*, Oxford: Oxford University Press.

HALLIDAY, M.A.K. (1990) 'New ways of meaning', in S. EFSTATHIADIS (Ed.) *Selected Papers from the Ninth World Congress of Applied Linguistics*, special issue of *Journal of Applied Linguistics*, **6**, Thessaloniki: Applied Linguistics Association of Greece.

HALLIDAY, M.A.K. (1991) 'Towards Probabilistic Interpretations', in E. VENTOLA (Ed.) *Recent Systemic and Other Functional Views on Language*, Berlin-New York: Mouton/deGruyter, pp. 39–62.

HALLIDAY, M.A.K. (1992) 'How do you mean?' in M. DAVIES and L. RAVELLI (Eds) *Advances in Systemic Linguistics: Recent Theory and Practice*, London: Pinter, pp. 20–36.

HALLIDAY, M.A.K. (1993) 'Towards a language-based theory of learning', *Linguistics and Education*, **5**(2), pp. 93–116.

HALLIDAY, M.A.K. and HASAN, R. (1976) *Cohesion in English*, London: Longman.

HALLIDAY, M.A.K. and HASAN, R. (1989) *Language, Context, and Text*, London: Oxford University Press.

HALLIDAY, M.A.K. and MARTIN, J.R. (1993) *Writing Science*, Pittsburgh, PA: University of Pittsburgh Press.

HARAWAY, D. (1989) *Primate Visions*, New York: Routledge.

HARAWAY, D. (1991) *Simians, Cyborgs, and Women*, New York: Routledge.

HARDING, S. (1986) *The Science Question in Feminism*, Ithaca, NY: Cornell University Press.

HARRISON, L. (1982) 'An Overview of Kinetic Theory in Developmental Modeling', in S. SUBTELNY and P. GREEN (Eds) *Developmental Order: Its Origin and Regulation*, New York: Alan R. Liss.

HASAN, R. (1984a) 'Coherence and Cohesive Harmony', in J. FLOOD (Ed.) *Understanding Reading Comprehension*, Newark, DE: International Reading Association.

HASAN, R. (1984b) 'The Structure of the Nursery Tale', in L. COVERI (Ed.) *Linguistica Testuale*, Rome: Bulzoni.

HASAN, R. (1985) 'Lending and Borrowing: From Grammar to Lexis', in J. CLARK (Ed.) *The Cultivated Australian (Beitrage zur Phonetik und Linguistik, 48)*, Hambrug: Helmut Buske Verlag, pp. 55–67.

HASAN, R. (1986a) 'The Grammarian's Dream: Lexis as Most Delicate Grammar', in M.A.K. HALLIDAY and R. FAWCETT (Eds) *New Developments in Systemic Linguistics*, London: Frances Pinter.

HASAN, R. (1986b) 'The Ontogenesis of Ideology', in T. THREADGOLD, E.A. GROSZ, G. KRESS and M.A.K. HALLIDAY (Eds) *Semiotics, Ideology, Language*, Sydney: Sydney Association for Studies in Society and Culture.

HASAN, R. (1988) 'The Analysis of One Poem', in L.M. O'TOOLE and D. BIRCH (Eds) *Functions of Style*, London: Pinter.

HASAN, R. (1989a) 'The Structure of a Text', in M.A.K. HALLIDAY and R. HASAN (Eds) *Language, Context, and Text*, London: Oxford University Press.

HASAN, R. (1989b) 'Semantic Variation and Sociolinguistics', *Australian Journal of Linguistics*, **9**, pp. 221–76.

HASAN, R. (1994) 'The Conception of Context in Text', in M. GREGORY and P. FRIES (Eds) *Discourse in Society: Functional Perspectives*, Norwood, NJ: Ablex Publishing.

HASAN, R. and CLORAN, C. (1990) 'A Sociolinguistic Interpretation of Everyday Talk between Mothers and Children', in M.A.K. HALLIDAY, J. GIBBONS and H. NICHOLAS (Eds) *Learning, Keeping, and Using Language*, Amsterdam: John Benjamins.

HEATH, S.B. (1983) *Ways with Words*, London: Cambridge University Press.

HEATH, S.B. (1994) 'Cracks in the Mirror: Class, Gender, and Ethnicity in Multicultural Education', paper presented at the Annual Meeting of the American Educational Research Association, New Orleans, April.

HERMES, H. (1969) *Enumerability, Decidability, Computability*, Berlin: Springer Verlag.

HODAS, S. (1994) 'Technology Refusal and the Organizational Culture of Schools', in *Cyberspace Superhighways: Access, Ethics, and Control*, proceedings of the Fourth Conference on Computers, Freedom, and Privacy, Chicago, IL: John Marshall Law School, pp. 54–75.

HODGE, R. and KRESS, G. (1988) *Social Semiotics*, Ithaca, NY: Cornell University Press.

HOFSTADTER, D.R. (1979) *Gödel, Escher, Bach*, New York: Basic Books.

HOLLING, C.S. (1986) 'The resilience of terrestrial ecosystems', in W.C. CLARK and R.E. Munn (Eds) *Sustainable Development of the Biosphere*, Cambridge: Cambridge University Press.

Huddleston, R.D., Hudson, R.A., Winter, E.O. and Henrici, A. (1968) *Sentence and Clause in Scientific English*, London: University College London, Communication Research Centre.

Jackson, E.A. (1989) *Perspectives of Non-Linear Development*, Cambridge: Cambridge University Press.

Jakobson, R., Fant, C.G.M. and Halle, M. (1965) *Preliminaries to Speech Analysis*, Cambridge, MA: MIT Press.

Jakobson, R. and Halle, M. (1971) *Fundamentals of Language*, 2nd Edn, The Hague: Mouton.

Jameson, F. (1991) *Postmodernism, or, The Cultural Logic of Late Capitalism*, Durham, NC: Duke University Press.

Johnson, T. (1984) 'Gay as Religion: Free Thought in a Free Society', *The Advocate*, 27 November, pp. 26–8.

Johnston, M. (1983) *Gays Under Grace*, Nashville, TN: Winston-Derek.

Kauffman, S.A. (1971) 'Behavior of Randomly Constructed Boolean Nets', in C.H. Waddington (Ed.) *Towards a Theoretical Biology*, Volume 3, Chicago, IL: Aldine Publishing.

Kauffman, S.A. (1993) *The Origins of Order: Self-Organization and Selection in Evolution*, New York: Oxford University Press.

Kleene, S. (1952) *Introduction to Metamathematics*, New York: van Nostrand.

Kress, G. (1982) *Learning to Write*, London: Routledge.

Kristeva, J. (1980) *Desire in Language*, New York: Columbia University Press.

Lamphere, L. (1992) *Structuring Diversity*, Chicago, IL: University of Chicago Press.

Latour, B. (1987) *Science in Action*, Cambridge, MA: Harvard University Press.

Latour, B. (1988) *The Pasteurization of France*, Cambridge, MA: Harvard University Press.

Lemke, J.L. (1983a) 'Thematic Analysis: Systems, Structures, and Strategies', *Semiotic Inquiry*, **3**(2), pp. 159–87.

Lemke, J.L. (1983b) *Classroom Communication of Science*, Final Report to the US National Science Foundation, Arlington, VA: ERIC Documents Service (ED 222 346).

Lemke, J.L. (1984) *Semiotics and Education*, Toronto: Victoria College/Toronto Semiotic Circle Monographs.

Lemke, J.L. (1985) 'Ideology, Intertextuality, and the Notion of Register', in J.D. Benson and W.S. Greaves (Eds) *Systemic Perspectives on Discourse*, Norwood, NJ: Ablex.

Lemke, J.L. (1987) 'Strategic Deployment of Speech and Action: A Sociosemiotic Analysis', in J. Evans and J. Deely (Eds) *Semiotics 1983: Proceedings of the Semiotic Society of America*, New York: University Press of America.

Lemke, J.L. (1988a) 'Text structure and text semantics', in R. Veltman and

E. STEINER (Eds) *Pragmatics, Discourse, and Text: Systemic Approaches*, London: Pinter.

LEMKE, J.L. (1988b) 'Towards a Social Semiotics of the Material Subject', in *SASSC Working Papers*, **2**(1), pp. 1–17, Sydney: Sydney Association for Studies in Society and Culture.

LEMKE, J.L. (1988c) 'Discourses in Conflict: Heteroglossia and text semantics', in J.D. BENSON and W.S. GREAVES (Eds) *Functional Perspectives on Discourse*, Norwood, NJ: Ablex Publishing.

LEMKE, J.L. (1989a) *Using Language in the Classroom*, London: Oxford University Press.

LEMKE, J.L. (1989b) 'Social Semiotics: A New Model for Literacy Education', in D. BLOOME (Ed.) *Classrooms and Literacy*, Norwood, NJ: Ablex Publishing, pp. 289–309.

LEMKE, J.L. (1989c) 'Semantics and social values', *WORD*, **40**(1–2), pp. 37–50.

LEMKE, J.L. (1990a) *Talking Science: Language, Learning, and Values*, Norwood, NJ: Ablex Publishing.

LEMKE, J.L. (1990b) 'Technical Discourse and Technocratic Ideology', in M.A.K. HALLIDAY, J. GIBBONS and H. NICHOLAS (Eds) *Learning, Keeping, and Using Language: Selected Papers from the 8th AILA World Congress of Applied Linguistics*, Volume II, Amsterdam: John Benjamins, pp. 435–60.

LEMKE, J.L. (1990c) 'Language Diversity and Literacy Education', *Australian Journal of Reading*, **13**(4), pp. 320–5.

LEMKE, J.L. (1990d) 'Literacy and Diversity', in R. GIBLETT and J. O'CARROLL (Eds) *Discipline, Dialogue, Difference*, Murdoch University (Australia): Duration Publications, pp. 147–69.

LEMKE, J.L. (1992a) 'Interpersonal Meaning in Discourse: Value Orientations', in M. DAVIES and L. RAVELLI (Eds) *Advances in Systemic Linguistics: Recent Theory and Practice*, London: Pinter, pp. 82–104.

LEMKE, J.L. (1992b) 'Notes on Violence, Pain, and the Material-textual Body', unpublished manuscript.

LEMKE, J.L. (1993a) 'Multiplying Meaning: Literacy in a Multi-media World', paper presented at the National Reading Conference, Charleston, SC, December.

LEMKE, J.L. (1993b) 'Semiotics, Subjectivity, and Science', paper presented at the Developmental Psychology Seminar, City University of New York Graduate School and University Center, New York, NY, October.

LEMKE, J.L. (1993c) '"Practice, Politique, Postmodernism", A review of Pierre Bourdieu and Lois J.D. Wacquant's *An Invitation to Reflexive Sociology*', *Postmodern Culture* [PMC-LIST on Listserv@listserv.ncsu.edu. Get PMC-LIST REVIEW-4.993].

LEMKE, J.L. (1993d) 'Intertextuality and Educational Research', *Linguistics and Education*, **4**(3–4), pp. 257–68.

LEMKE, J.L. (1994a) 'Discourse, Dynamics, and Social Change', *Cultural Dynamics*, **6**(1), pp. 243–75.

LEMKE, J.L. (1994b) 'Intertextuality and Text Semantics', in M. GREGORY and

P. Fries (Eds) *Discourse in Society: Functional Perspectives*, Norwood, NJ: Ablex Publishing, pp. 85–114.

Lemke, J.L. (1994c) 'Hypermedia and Higher Education', in T.M. Harrison and T.D. Stephen (Eds) *Computer Networking and Scholarship in the 21st Century University*, Albany: SUNY Press.

Lemke, J.L. (1994d) 'The Coming Paradigm Wars in Education: Curriculum vs. Information Access', in *Cyberspace Superhighways: Access, Ethics, and Control*, Proceedings of the Fourth Conference on Computers, Freedom, and Privacy, Chicago, IL: John Marshall Law School, pp. 76–85.

Lemke, J.L. (in preparation) 'Resources for Attitudinal Meaning: Facts, Projections, and Epithets'.

Leontiev, A.N. (1978) *Activity, Consciousness, and Personality*, Englewood Cliffs, NJ: Prentice-Hall.

Levi-Strauss, C. (1963) *Structural Anthropology*, New York: Basic Books.

Liberty Home Bible Institute (n.d.) 'Homosexuality' (occasional publication, tract) Lynchburg, VA: Liberty Home Bible Institute.

Lorenz, K. (1965) *Evolution and Modification of Behavior*, Chicago, IL: University of Chicago Press.

Lovelock, J. (1989) *The Ages of Gaia: A Biography of Our Living Earth*, Oxford: Oxford University Press.

Luria, A.R. (1959) *Speech and the Development of Mental Processes in the Child*, London: Staples Press.

Lyotard, J.-F. (1984) *The Postmodern Condition*, Minneapolis, MN: University of Minnesota Press.

Mansfield, A. (1987) 'A Cartography of Resistance: The British State and Derry Republicanism', PhD dissertation, University College of North Wales, Bangor, Wales.

Markus, G. (1987) 'Why Is There No Hermeneutics of Natural Science?' *Science in Context*, **1**(1), pp. 5–51.

Martin, J.R. (1989) *Factual Writing: Exploring and Challenging Social Reality*, London: Oxford University Press.

Martin, J.R. (1992) *English Text*, Philadelphia, PA: John Benjamins.

Marx, K. and Engels, F. (1970) *The German Ideology*, in Arthur, C.J., London: Lawrence & Wishart.

Milroy, J. and Milroy, L. (1985) *Authority in Language: Investigating Language Prescription and Language Standardization*, London: Routledge.

Mitchell, T.F. (1975) 'The Language of Buying and Selling in Cyrenaica', in Mitchell, T.F. (Ed.) *Principles of Firthian Linguistics*, London: Longman.

Montagu, A. (1981) *Growing Young*, New York: McGraw-Hill.

Nesbitt, C. and Plum, G. (1988) 'Probabilities in a Systemic Grammar: The Clause Complex in English', in R.P. Fawcett and D.J. Young (Eds) *New Developments in Systemic Linguistics*, Volume 2, London: Pinter.

Odum, H.T. (1983) *Systems Ecology*, New York: John Wiley.

Peirce, C.S. (1955) 'Logic as Semiotic: The Theory of Signs', in J. Buchler (Ed.) *Philosophical Writings of Peirce*, New York: Dover.

PIAGET, J. (1970) *Structuralism*, New York: Basic Books.

PIAGET, J. (1971) *Biology and Knowledge*, Chicago: University of Chicago Press.

PIKE, K. (1982) *Linguistic Concepts*, Lincoln, NB: University of Nebraska Press.

PRIGOGINE, I. (1961) *Introduction to the Thermodynamics of Irreversible Processes*, New York: Interscience.

PRIGOGINE, I. (1962) *Non-equilibrium Statistical Mechanics*, New York: Wiley.

PRIGOGINE, I. (1980) *From Being to Becoming: Time and Complexity in the Physical Sciences*, New York: W.H. Freeman.

PRIGOGINE, I. and STENGERS, I. (1984) *Order out of Chaos*, New York: Bantam.

PROPP, V. (1928/1968) *The Morphology of the Folktale*, Austin, TX: University of Texas Press.

RICOEUR, P. (1970) *Freud and Philosophy*, New Haven, CT: Yale University Press.

ROSEN, R. (1985) *Anticipatory Systems*, Oxford: Pergamon Press.

RUSSELL, B. and WHITEHEAD, A.N. (1913) *Principia Mathematica*, 2nd edn, Cambridge: Cambridge University Press.

SALTHE, S. (1985) *Evolving Hierarchical Systems*, New York: Columbia University Press.

SALTHE, S. (1989) 'Self-organization in Hierarchically Structured systems', *Systems Research*, **6**(3), pp. 199–208.

SALTHE, S. (1993) *Development and Evolution*, Cambridge, MA: MIT Press.

SAUSSURE, F. DE (1959) *Course in General Linguistics*, New York: McGraw-Hill.

SCHNEIDER, E. (1988) 'Thermodynamics, Ecological Succession, and Natural Selection', in B.H. WEBER, D.J. DEPEW and J.D. SMITH (Eds) *Entropy, Information, and Evolution*, Cambridge, MA: MIT Press.

SCHRODINGER, E. (1967) *What is Life?* Cambridge: Cambridge University Press.

THIBAULT, P. (1986) *Text, Discourse, and Context: A Social Semiotic Perspective*, Toronto, Victoria University: Toronto Semiotic Circle Monographs.

THIBAULT, P. (1989a) 'Semantic Variation, Social Heteroglossia, Intertextuality, *Critical Studies*, **1**(2), pp. 181–209.

THIBAULT, P. (1989b) 'Genres, Social Action, and Pedagogy: A Critical Social Semiotic Account', *Southern Review* (Australia) **22**(3), pp. 338–62.

THIBAULT, P. (1991) *Social Semiotics as Praxis*, Minneapolis, MN: University of Minnesota Press.

THOM, R. (1975) *Structural Stability and Morphogenesis*, Reading, MA: W.A. Benjamin.

THREADGOLD, T. (1986) 'Semiotics-Ideology-Language', in T. THREADGOLD, E.A. GROSZ, G. KRESS and M.A.K. HALLIDAY (Eds) *Semiotics, Ideology, Language*, Sydney: Sydney Association for Studies in Society and Culture.

THREADGOLD, T. (1989) 'Paradigms of Culture and Semiosis', in W.A. KOCH (Ed.) *Evolution of Culture*, Bochum: Studienverlag Brockmeyer.

THREADGOLD, T. and KRESS, G. (1988) 'Towards a Social Theory of Genre, *Southern Review*, **21**, pp. 215–43.

URE, J. and ELLIS, J. (1974) 'Register in Descriptive Linguistics and Linguistic Sociology', in O. URIBE-VILLEGAS (Ed.) *Issues in Sociolinguistics*, The Hague: Mouton.

US DEPARTMENT OF EDUCATION (1986) *What Works: Research About Teaching and Learning*, Washington DC: US Government Printing Office.

VENTOLA, E. (1987) *The Structure of Social Interaction: A Systemic Approach to the Semiotics of Service Encounters*, London: Frances Pinter.

VENTOLA, E. (1991) *Recent Systemic and Other Functional Views on Language*, Berlin: Mouton/deGruyter.

VOLOSHINOV, V.N. (1929, 1986) *Marxism and the Philosophy of Language*, Cambridge, MA: Harvard University Press. (1986 edition).

VON BERTALANFFY, L. (1950) 'Theory of Open Systems in Physics and Biology', *Science*, **111**, pp. 23–9.

VYGOTSKY, L. (1963) *Thought and Language*, Cambridge, MA: MIT Press.

WADDINGTON, C.H. (1957) *The Strategy of the Genes*, London: Allen & Unwin.

WADDINGTON, C.H. (Ed.) (1969–71) *Towards a Theoretical Biology*, 4 volumes, Chicago: Aldine Publishing.

WALBERG, H.J. (1985) 'Improving the Productivity of America's Schools', *Educational Leadership*, **41**(8), pp. 19–27.

WALLACE, A.F.C. (1970) *Culture and Personality*, 2nd edn, New York: Random House.

WEBER, B.H., DEPEW, D.J. and SMITH, J.D. (Eds) (1988) *Entropy, Information, and Evolution*, Cambridge, MA: MIT Press.

WERTSCH, J. (1991) *Voices of the Mind*, Cambridge, MA: Harvard University Press.

WILLIS, P. (1981) *Learning to Labor*, New York: Columbia University Press.

Subject Index